SNAKES OF
THE AMERICAN WEST

SNAKES OF THE

AMERICAN WEST

Charles E. Shaw and
Sheldon Campbell

 New York   Alfred A. Knopf   1974

THIS IS A BORZOI BOOK
PUBLISHED BY ALFRED A. KNOPF, INC.

Library of Congress Cataloging in Publication Data

Shaw, Charles E   Snakes of the American West.

Bibliography: p.
1. Snakes — The West. 2. Reptiles — The West.
I. Campbell. Sheldon, joint author. II. Title.
QL665.S5   598.1'2'0978   73–7304
ISBN 0–394–48882–2

Manufactured in the United States of America
First Edition

*In deepest gratitude
this book is dedicated to the memory
of two great herpetologists
of the American West:*

*C. B. "Si" Perkins,
curator of reptiles,
San Diego Zoo*

*Laurence M. Klauber,
industrialist,
zoo trustee, and scientist*

CONTENTS

» » » » » »

We ought not childishly neglect the study of the meaner animals because there is something wonderful in all of nature. We ought to investigate all sorts of animals because all of them will reveal something of nature and something of beauty.

–ARISTOTLE

PREFACE

》》》》》

In writing *Snakes of the American West* we kept in mind a varied popular audience. In our thoughts were always two "ghosts"—two young teen-aged males interested in natural science and encountering for the first time the wonders of snakes, just as we had encountered these wonders years ago when we first read and shared with one another Raymond L. Ditmars's *Snakes of the World.*

But we also knew there was a bigger audience interested in snakes. People may grimace, pretend to be sickened, or shudder in mock or actual fright, but the fact remains that a reptile house full of snakes in all their variety is one of the most frequented places at any zoo. Take a preference poll and you will find snake exhibits at the bottom of any list, but count the visitors and the reptile house will lead in popularity. People are both fascinated and repelled by snakes, and when they are given the opportunity to view snakes behind glass where they cannot "slither" at anyone, fascination wins.

So there is a general audience of interested people. In that audience are many more people interested in the outdoors than ever before—backpackers, dune buggy riders, vagabonds in campers, trailers, and mobil homes. Consequently, encounters between men and snakes in the remaining wilderness are likely to become more frequent—unfortunately for the snakes. We hope that this group of "outdoors" people will find this book useful as well as entertaining. Through understanding snakes and their ways the reader—whether in camper, trailer, or mobil home—may be less inclined to kill them willy-nilly.

A word about the organization of this book. First, we arbitrarily decided that the American West would include those states from the Rocky Mountains westward. Of course, the snakes themselves have not been so arbitrary: many species found west of the Rockies are the same as those found to the east, with perhaps some subspecific variation. Still, the Rocky Mountains are a natural barrier that makes sense in establishing an arbitrary geographical entity. In scientific terms the Rockies are certainly a more sensible border than the hypothetical lines that separate the United States from Canada and from Mexico.

We next decided that we would present the western snakes in order of their evolution, starting with the most primitive and ending with the most highly evolved snakes. The extremes are fairly easy; anyone can see at a glance that a rattlesnake is a more complex organism than a slender blind snake. In between the extremes, however, determination is not quite so easy. It is more difficult to determine the relative evolutionary standings of kingsnakes and garter snakes, for example.

Since the use of venom to subdue prey took hundreds of thousands of years to develop, the venomous snakes represent an advanced stage in snakedom. For this reason and for one other they are dealt with last. The other reason is simple: venomous snakes are the only ones that pose any threat to man. All other snakes are harmless and should be protected. The reader of this book therefore can go immediately to the last four chapters if he has any difficulty deciding whether or not a particular snake he has seen is harmless or venomous. (If it were not for the fact that some harmless snakes vibrate their tails as rattlers do, the camper or hiker in the American West could tell venomous from harmless by this very simple test. Only the rattlesnakes can cause death—and then remarkably seldom. The western coral snake has never in recorded history killed a human being.)

Finally, in writing this book, we tried to bring to each reader some sense of the marvelous in snakes. They are like most creatures—the more one understands about their complexity, about their varied habits, the more one marvels at them and at nature that produced them. To emphasize this sense of the marvelous, much recent research, never before published in book form, has been included. But since we did not want to bog the reader down in thickets of footnotes, we have included the names of the appropriate scientific journals and books in the bibliography rather than in the text. For the reader who wants to dig deeper, the titles of the works will relate them, in most instances, to particular sections of this book. Moreover, we have not discussed every subspecies of the nearly seventy separate species of snakes in the American West, although some subspecies are included because of their importance or unique status. Appendix II takes care of all subspecies, their scale counts, and other facts important to herpetologists but perhaps not to the lay reader who simply wants to read about snakes.

Charles E. Shaw died before this book was finished. He was keenly interested in the book and its purpose and had spent many of his final hours assembling materials, typing up notes, writing roughs on some chapters. His coauthor was fortunate in having available Chuck's papers and his written observations, combined with nearly forty years of association that involved many collecting trips in the West and conversations about western snakes. Moreover, Chuck left several devoted friends, all of whom were eager to assist in finishing the book.

Very particular thanks go to Dr. Findlay E. Russell, of the Laboratory of Neurological Research, Los Angeles County Hospital, who was kind enough to read chapter 14, "Encountering Venomous Snakes," and offer invaluable suggestions. And above all we offer gratitude to Charles M. Bogert, former chairman and curator, Department of Amphibians and Reptiles, American Museum of Natural History, who took the time to read and criticize the entire book in manuscript form. Much of Charles Bogert is in this book.

Many others helped—in particular, Mrs. Hope Warren Shaw, Chuck's widow, who brought together notes, assembled photos, and spoke needed words of encouragement. She was aided greatly by

Kirstie Shaw and Thomas D. Shaw. Marjorie Betts Shaw, librarian of the San Diego Zoo, was of inestimable help. Others on the zoo staff who should be singled out are Charles R. Schroeder, Frederick Childress, Ron Garrison, Edna Heublein, Edalee Harwell, and Jerry H. Staedeli.

John Tashjian selflessly contributed material and photographs he had assembled for his own book. Susan Wallen contributed much research at a critical period; her father, Stanley de Treville helped with illustrations. Ralph Hodges gave a needed hand.

Many scientists, naturalists, and herpetologists contributed their ideas, suggestions, or assistance in obtaining photographs; they include Robert L. Brown, Dr. Howard Campbell, Dr. Nathan W. Cohen, Joseph T. Collins, Dr. Roger Conant, Robert Craig, Dr. Frederick R. Gehlbach, Jan Jones, Carl Kauffeld, Merritt S. Keasey, Mervin W. Larsen, Dr. Richard B. Loomis, Charles R. Peterson, Dr. Joseph M. Pylka, Dr. Douglas A. Rossman, Dr. Vincent Roth, Dr. Hobart M. Smith, Tim Walker, and Kenneth L. Williams.

Finally, let me note that writers need both sustenance and the application of psychological Band-Aids. Both Louise Copp and Florence Campbell contributed their culinary skill for needed "book conferences," and Florence not only aided a succession of secretaries, including Willie Clifford, at the typewriter, but also spent much time applying those Band-Aids when they were required.

A book is much more than its authors.

SHELDON CAMPBELL

San Diego, California
March, 1974

PART ONE

» » » » » »

SNAKES OF
THE AMERICAN WEST

Chapter 1

» » » » »

OF SNAKES
AND MEN

In writing this book, we wanted to bring to the reader a sense of the marvelous in snakes. The more one understands them in all their complexity, the more one marvels at the evolutionary processes that produced them.

The western United States is rich in its variety of snakes. Of the some 2,700 species of snakes in the world, approximately seventy species, some with many subspecies,* are found in the states west of the Rocky Mountains. Many of these are true natives, having their ranges entirely within the boundaries of the United States. Others, more truly native to Mexico, range northward across the border, for snakes, like most other animals, established their ranges long before borders were drawn by man.

Five of the thirteen snake families are represented in the western states. Those represented are the Leptotyphlopidae, or blind snakes (there is some dispute as to whether they are in fact snakes); the Boidae, or boas; the Colubridae, the largest family which con-

*We have not discussed every subspecies; some subspecies are described because of their importance or unique status. Appendix II lists all the subspecies and their characteristics.

tains most of the nonpoisonous (or in some instances mildly poisonous) snakes found in the world; the Elapidae, or cobras and their American relatives, the coral snakes; and the Crotalidae, or pit vipers.

Perhaps in the festooned swamps of the South, like the great Okefenokee and the Everglades, there are greater numbers of snakes, for many species of water snakes abound there, and water snakes are prolific. But the West boasts plentiful species, and in the western deserts particularly are found some of the most beautiful snakes in the world.

All snakes are predators; that is, they survive by killing other animals for food, without malice. In the American West the objects of snake predation range from the tiny termites eaten by blind snakes to the cottontail rabbits that may be struck by red diamond rattlesnakes. Mice, lizards, birds, and other snakes may be preyed upon; kingsnakes, for example, eat all of these.

Any predator—snake, bird, mammal, fish, or insect—in its search for food unknowingly advances the evolution of the animals it preys upon. From their numbers the predator weeds the lame, the dim-witted, and the weak, leaving the strong to survive and perpetuate the race. Not consciously does the rattlesnake pick out the slower rabbit: the rattlesnake gets the rabbit because it is slow. The faster rabbits survive, and thus the race of rabbits may be made faster.

Snakes as predators provide direct benefits to man. As farmers increasingly have come to realize, snakes that feed principally on rodents help provide effective rodent control. The experienced farmer treats his local bullsnake or gopher snake as a blessing, for the snake will eat many a field mouse that otherwise would be consuming the farmer's grain. In one year a six-foot bullsnake can eat hundreds of mice and rats.

Snakes, of course, have always been prey as well as predators. Several species of birds and mammals include snakes as a regular portion of their diet. In wild country it is not unusual to see a red-tailed hawk flying over with a snake dangling from its claws. Even rattlers are not excluded as prey, for kingsnakes, which prey even on their own species, are immune to rattlesnake venom and will readily kill and eat a rattler.

But the loss of snakes that become prey in the normal course of natural events does not contribute to a sharp decline in total snake numbers. Sudden, sharp reductions in any animal population come most often at the hands of man. They come because man, consciously or unconsciously, preempts earth, water, and air to his own uses and in doing so alters them so that other living creatures cannot survive. So it is with snakes.

Snakes, like most animals, are territorial; that is to say, an individual snake establishes an area within which it largely remains. This area, the territory, meets the requirements of the snake's habitat, that combination of elements, dryness or wetness, shade and light, flora and fauna, that forms the necessary and often delicately balanced life-support system for the species. The habitat, in turn, is within the range, the total number of square miles covered by the species to the outer limits of the territory of the widest ranging members. Not all parts of the range provide a suitable habitat for the species. Thus the range of the common garter snake and all of its many subspecies covers much of the United States, but very little of that range provides suitable habitat, which for this snake is marshy areas, ponds, or streams with frog and fish populations to provide food.

From the Cretaceous period of the Mesozoic era, when snakes first developed, until the present, snakes have gone about their business—seeking prey, sleeping, mating, denning up or otherwise hibernating during cold periods. But in the twentieth century a series of developments wrought by man has altered forever the ancient habits of many animals. Snakes are fast disappearing from the face of the earth, declining in numbers as human populations build. As human population increases in the western states, so do snakes disappear, killed off by man or their ranges usurped by man. Only a few species like the ringneck snake are unobtrusive enough in size, habitat, and eating habits to permit their continued survival in close proximity to man.

Man has destroyed snakes in several ways: directly by killing them, sometimes in self defense, most often maliciously; indirectly by destroying their habitats or through poisons administered for other reasons to the land. Man seems to have an innate aversion to snakes and often kills them without real reason. When the snake is a rattler, found in the immediate vicinity of houses, this predilection to kill is understandable—it is basically defensive. But there is little need to destroy a rattler found in wilderness areas far from homes or well-traveled trails. Many people can't tell venomous from nonvenomous snakes and therefore treat all snakes the same. In his ignorance a man may slay harmless snakes, even those varieties that are beneficial to humans. Or, sadly, the killer may be one who has no respect for other forms of life and with simple indifference—and sometimes pleasure—moves to stamp them out.

Some investigators believe that man's tendency to fear snakes stems from a deeply rooted instinct, the same kind of instinct that prompts a house cat to hunt even though it is well fed. Proponents of this idea believe that fear of snakes originated in the experiences of man's remote ancestors, for whom the bite of a venomous snake meant almost certain death. Constantly repeated techniques of avoiding snakes or killing them would tend to create over time an automatic response through an evolutionary process we have only begun to understand.

Environmentalists, on the other hand, believe that fear of snakes is "learned" behavior. They point to the fact that babies show no fear of reptiles and that young children often keep pet snakes, which they capture without apparent fear. The proponents of learned behavior say that people fear snakes because they were taught to do so while young. This teaching may have been direct: "Be careful of snakes, dear; they're filthy, loathsome, poisonous creatures—if they bite you you'll die!" Or the teaching may have been indirect: "Keep that awful snake away from me!"

Whatever the cause, an unreasoning fear leads many people to kill snakes with no questions asked. And as human populations have increased, so many snake populations have been decimated.

No one knows for certain the effect on snakes of pesticides or poisons used in rodent control. In those areas where pesticides are heavily sprayed on crops, snakes are killed just as other animals are if they receive a concentration of poison beyond the level they can safely tolerate. In agricultural areas where pesticides are sprayed by airplane, at best an inexact method, wind or other weather conditions may cause one area to receive a heavier dose of poison than another, and animals living in that area may die.

Chemical pesticides of the DDT family—chlorinated hydro-carbons—may have a further effect on snake populations. It is now established that these chemicals, when taken in the food of birds such as the California brown pelican, react with the birds' internal chemistry and cause them to produce thin-shelled eggs that break in the nest before the young have fully developed. The oviparous, or egg-laying, snakes may be affected the same way. In one study of DDT residues in the fat of aquatic animals, the northern water snake *(Natrix sipedon)* had the greatest amount, one specimen showing 36.4 parts per million (Meeks, 1968).

It is probable that snakes occasionally become the accidental victims of poisons intended for the rodents upon which they feed. If a bullsnake, for example, were to capture and eat two or three rats that had fed on poisoned grain but had not yet died, the bullsnake might well be killed by the dose.

Destruction of habitat is the result of the inexorable march of the bulldozer—scraping off chaparral, shoving boulders aside, pushing dirt into marshes, reshaping the land. And for every acre of chaparral cleared, for every boulder shoved aside, for every marsh filled, untold numbers of animals, including snakes, lose their homes, and often their lives. Some animals are less vulnerable than others to destruction of habitat. Birds find new trees or adjust to new surroundings, so that a businessman in a downtown office building may observe sparrow hawks using a TV antenna on a neighboring skyscraper as their base of operations. But snakes are exceedingly vulnerable to destruction of habitat. Often, as we have indicated, their habitat is a small, restricted part of their range, surrounded by inhospitable land. When the habitat is destroyed, they have nowhere to go. During the thirties the western aquatic garter snake, which has a high reproductive rate, was one of the most common snakes in San Diego County, California. Today the snake is seldom seen, simply because the marshy streams and ponds that it requires have mostly disappeared in the wake of dam builders and subdividers.

The increased desire for bizarre pets, deplored by conservationists, has become another cause of declining snake populations; for when a snake is kept alone in a cage, it no longer contributes to the preservation of the race. Yet, nonscientific snake hunters—really no more than bounty hunters—collect snakes that can be sold to pet dealers, themselves businessmen whose interests are commercial and whose regard for the exotic pets to be sold seldom extends further than their dollar value. The pity is that many of the snakes collected do not make good pets under any circumstances. Few snakes eat well in captivity, either because the food offered is not part of their normal diet or because captivity does not allow them to behave normally—to hunt, to burrow, to climb, to swim, to move around—and they grow morose. So most pet snakes die within a year after they are captured. Fortunately, in this day of ecological awareness, communities are beginning to pass laws that protect snakes from professional collectors. In San Diego County, for example, in 1971 the Board of Supervisors passed a law limiting the number of snakes that any one person could capture. Arizona has placed all snakes under protection.

By all odds the most destructive force affecting snake populations is the automobile. Every road built cuts through some snake's territory or habitat; therefore, sooner or later, the snake may cross that road during his normal search for prey or mate. Moreover, the highway holds the sun's heat into evening and early night, thus providing attractive warmth to snakes during the time they are most active. Crossing a single-track dirt road does not greatly endanger a snake. Even a two-lane cement or asphalt road, depending on how well-traveled it is, gives the snake a chance to cross it unscathed. But a heavily traveled four-lane highway presents a nearly impassable barrier to the ranging snake. Almost every inch of the snake's body (excluding only his tail aft of the cloaca) is vulnerable to the crushing impact of an automobile tire, and in crossing the highway the snake presents a fully stretched out target; the longer it is the greater the chance it will be hit. Moreover, a snake probably does not perceive (as, for example, a coyote would), the danger the highway represents. Innocently, the snake treats the highway as it would any other stretch of land and unwittingly moves forward to its own destruction.

Motorcycles, dune buggies, and other off-the-road vehicles endanger snake populations even in remaining wilderness. Fortunately for snakes, off-the-road enthusiasts don't generally cross the land in early morning or late evening, the times most snakes are active during spring and summer.

But for the person who realizes that snakes are an important part of the natural environment all is not lost. Even in the well-traveled, heavily populated eastern United States snakes still hold their own, and there remains in the West much wild country where in relative peace the smaller wild creatures carry on as they did before white men trod upon the land.

Perhaps the reader of this book, as he learns about the various species and gains the knowledge that most snakes are of economic benefit to man, will curb his prejudice. And perhaps he will influence others to refrain from thoughtless slaughter of snakes—to kill only if a person is genuinely threatened by a rattlesnake, the only venomous snake that poses any real threat in the western United States. No other snake, with the single possible exception of an extraordinarily large coral snake, can significantly harm man. On the contrary, most snakes benefit man in their beauty and their predatory ways.

Of the eleven states considered in this book—Arizona, California, Colorado, Idaho, Montana, Nevada, New Mexico, Oregon, Utah, Washington, and Wyoming—the one with the greatest number of species of snakes is Arizona. In fact, the Southwest, embracing Arizona, New Mexico, and southern California, presents a more favorable climate to snakes than colder areas do and consequently the majority of species discussed in this book are found in the Southwest. Arizona, for example, has eleven species of rattlesnakes, whereas in Oregon and Washington there is only one.

The western snakes are presented in order of their evolutionary standing. Starting with the most primitive, we move through the book to the most highly evolved snakes. The extremes are fairly easy to determine; one can see at a glance that a rattlesnake is a more complex organism than a slender blind snake. But between the extremes determination of evolutionary standing is not simple. In general, however, we have kept to our plan of first treating the most simple and then moving to the more complex.

Venomous snakes are discussed last since they represent an advanced stage in snakedom. (The use of venom to subdue prey took hundreds of thousands of years to develop.) The reader should remember that venomous snakes are the only snakes that pose any threat to man; all others are harmless and should be protected.

Of Snakes and Men

Chapter 2

»»»»»

GENERAL CHARACTERISTICS

The student of animal classification—called a taxonomist—places the snakes in the phylum Chordata, which includes all animals with a spinal cord; in the class Reptilia, which includes all reptiles; in the order Squamata, which includes both snakes and lizards; and finally, in the suborder Serpentes. In the development of life on earth, the reptiles evolved between the earlier amphibians and the later birds. The Squamata are relative newcomers among the reptiles, having evolved around 160 million years after the first reptiles appeared. And among the Squamata, snakes first appeared on earth some 125 million years ago. Most herpetologists agree that snakes evolved from earlier lizard forms in a divergence that saw some lizards remain terrestrial, while others moved underground and became primarily burrowers. As the centuries passed, some of these subterrestrial forms discarded such impediments to effective burrowing as eyelids, external ears, and external limbs. Many of the burrowers, in fact, became blind: living in darkness, they had no need of eyes. Others, however, began to spend time above ground and regained use of their eyes, though they had lost their external ears and limbs.

Most modern snakes live as surface creatures, though most often in the cover of grass, brush, or under stones and logs. Some snakes— the shovel-nosed snake, for example—are part-time burrowers in sand or loose dirt. Others, the blind snakes particularly, spend almost all their lives as burrowers or dwellers in crevices and cracks.

Snakes differ from lizards in several ways not so apparent as their lack of movable eyelids or limbs. (A few lizards are legless—the so-called glass snakes, for example.) Lizards have rigid jaws with a bone hinge, similar to that of humans. Snakes have flexible jaws. Instead of a bone hinge at the juncture of the upper and lower jaw, the snake's jaws are connected by what is called the quadrate bone that allows maximum "gape," or opening of the mouth. An elastic ligament allows separation and flexibility between the two halves of the lower jaw at the chin. Therefore, snakes can swallow prey far larger in proportion to their body size than lizards can. It means also that snakes can go longer without food than lizards can, since snakes ingest relatively more food at one feeding. Nor can snakes take bites out of food as some lizards can. The snake's meal is always swallowed whole.

In a snake's skull the brain is well protected, being completely boxed in by the bony braincase. This protection is particularly valuable during the engulfing process, when the brain tissues could be damaged through the palate by sharp edges of the prey. The complete brain box of snakes contrasts with the open front of a lizard's braincase, which exposes the brain.

Most modern snake species have no vestige of limbs whatsoever, no shoulder or hip girdles, no remnants of legs. A few exceptions exist—that is, snakes with vestigial limbs, some of which actually protrude from the body as tiny spurs.

Even in scale patterns snakes and lizards differ. Lizards have the same basic scale pattern on the belly and on the back. Snakes, on the other hand, generally have a single row of highly developed ventral (belly) scales, or scutes. The scutes serve to flatten the snake's underside and provide it with a better means of gripping the surface in moving over the ground—a problem that the ordinary lizard with its four well-developed legs does not have.

Differences Between Snakes and Lizards

QUADRATE BONE

The quadrate bone loosely connects the lower jaw to the snake's skull and acts as an expanding hinge.

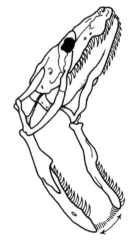

An elastic muscle allows the two halves of a snake's lower jaw to separate enabling it to swallow objects larger than the snake itself.

QUADRATE BONE AND ELASTIC MUSCLE

SNAKE SCALE
NOMENCLATURE

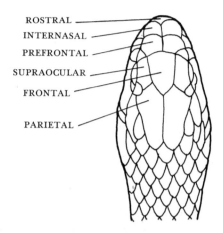

ROSTRAL
INTERNASAL
PREFRONTAL
SUPRAOCULAR
FRONTAL
PARIETAL

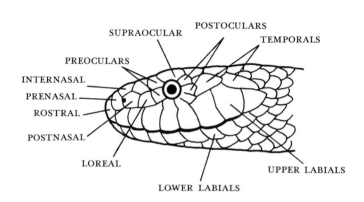

SUPRAOCULAR
POSTOCULARS
TEMPORALS
PREOCULARS
INTERNASAL
PRENASAL
ROSTRAL
POSTNASAL
LOREAL
LOWER LABIALS
UPPER LABIALS

Skin

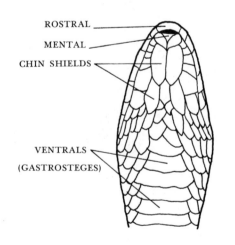

ROSTRAL
MENTAL
CHIN SHIELDS
VENTRALS
(GASTROSTEGES)

A snake's skin has the same three layers characteristic of other vertebrates, but it has been modified to serve the snake's specialized form of locomotion. The innermost layer of soft, fibrous material is extremely pliable. Between this and the outer layer lies the dermis, which contains all the pigments and cells that make up the snake's distinguishing pattern and color. The epidermis, or outer layer, is formed of a substance called keratin, the same basic material that forms nails, claws, and hair in mammals. This epidermis of keratin provides the snake with the extraordinarily tough covering that it needs to protect its internal organs and to reduce friction as it moves over rough stones, through gritty sand, across splintery logs, or over the stubble of grass. Parts of this keratin covering, thicker than others, are folded back to make the snake's scales, the rear and less restricted portion of each scale overlapping the front of the scale behind it. Between scales lies folded-back connecting material, also of keratin, also part of the epidermis. This connecting skin stretches as the snake undulates in its movement or swallows food that is larger than the usual circumference of the snake's body.

People have always been fascinated by the fact that snakes grow

12

SNAKES OF THE AMERICAN WEST

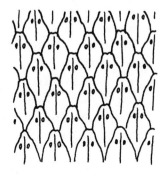

KEELED SCALES WITH APICAL PITS

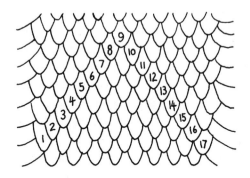

METHOD OF COUNTING DORSAL SCALE ROWS

new skin and discard old in a process known as shedding or molting. In fact, the shed skin of snakes—like foxes' ears and lizards' tails— has been used in legendary witches' brews (and probably also in many folk remedies).

Many people believe that snakes shed but once a year, and then in late summer. Not so. Snakes may shed four or five times a year, depending on weather conditions, food supply, the age of the snake, and other factors. The process of shedding is quite simple. The snake grows a new layer of epidermis underneath the old. When the new layer is complete, the snake secretes a fluid between the new layer and the old. This fluid causes the snake's old skin to have a bluish white cast and the snake's eyes appear milky and opaque—largely because "spectacles," the scales that protect the snake's lidless eyes, are part of the epidermis and are about to be shed with the rest of the old skin. After a few days, during which the snake is largely or totally blind, the old skin is ready to be cast off. The snake works its head against rocks or logs or anything rough until the old skin cracks and the snake, like a butterfly emerging from the chrysalis, can begin to work itself out of it. Almost as though it were reborn,

ANAL PLATES

VENTRALS   SUBCAUDALS

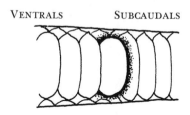

ANAL SINGLE

VENTRALS   SUBCAUDALS

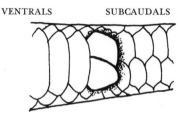

ANAL DIVIDED

General Characteristics

13

the snake emerges more brilliantly colored, clear of eye, scale surfaces bright, undulled by contact with bruising, scratching earth and brush.

Internal Organs

For the most part the internal organs of a snake resemble those of any vertebrate animal but are more drawn out. Heart, lungs, liver, stomach, intestine, and all the other organs are shaped to fit into the long, narrow body cavity of the snake. But there are some unique features about a snake's innards, the most notable of which is that most snakes have only one lung. Here, too, snakes differ from lizards, which have two lungs. The organs in snakes that have remained paired—kidneys, for example—are generally arranged in tandem rather than side by side, and one, usually the one on the right, is better developed than the other.

In some ways the snake with its attenuated arrangement of organs achieves greater efficiency than other animals. The lung, for example, is normally drawn out to more than half the snake's body length, with the part closest to the head and the windpipe serving as the oxygen-intake organ, while the lower half is used as an air reservoir. The esophagus-stomach-intestine arrangement is a straight line from mouth to cloaca, that chamber into which the intestinal, urinary, and reproductive tracts open. The cloaca in turn opens to the exterior through the anus, or vent.

The heart and circulatory system are basically like those of any other vertebrate. A snake's heart has three chambers, however, whereas in more advanced animals, including crocodiles among the reptiles, there are four. Snakes do not have any internal means of regulating the temperature of their blood. They lack the "thermostat" possessed by warm-blooded birds and mammals. Called cold-blooded, snakes actually have blood that is responsive to the varying temperature of the immediate environment. Consequently snakes can regulate blood temperature to some degree by moving around. Blood can be warmed by staying in a sunny spot for a few moments; it can be cooled by movement into shade. What the snake must avoid are the two extremes. If it stays too long in the direct sunlight (and too long may be four to seven minutes on a hot day), the snake will die horribly, its blood heated beyond tolerance. Left in ice or snow, the snake will freeze to death. Consequently, in temperate zones with pronounced seasonal changes, snakes have adapted to winter's onslaught by denning together, coiling in caves or crevices beneath the earth in a kind of hibernation that provides life-sustaining warmth.

This responsiveness to the temperature of the immediate environment has been in the past (and, alas, may still be) the key to the handling of large snakes by snake charmers in carnivals and circuses. By keeping the snakes cold in icebox or refrigerator, but not so cold as to kill them, the handlers make them sluggish and unable to strike or bite efficiently.

Snakes have most of the skeletal characteristics of other vertebrates, but their skeletal system has some unusual modifications. The head, with its loosely articulated jaws and complete bony brain box is specialized for engulfing large prey. Having no limbs, a snake has no need for adaptations of the vertebrae to accommodate a pelvis. In those snakes with rudimentary pelvic girdles, the girdle is not attached to the backbone. Nearly every individual vertebra along the snake's spinal column bears a set of ribs, including some near the tail that actually are fused to the vertebra itself. A snake has from 175 to more than 400 vertebrae in its backbone, depending on whether the snake is a relatively stubby viper or a seven-foot bullsnake. Vertebrae are locked to one another by two means: (1) by a ball-and-socket joint consisting of a round part of the rear of each vertebra that fits into a smooth hollow at the front of the vertebra behind it; and (2) by zygapophyses, which are arrowhead-shaped prongs of bone that thrust forward from each vertebra to touch rear-pointing projections from the vertebra ahead of it.

The combination of the many vertebrae, the zygapophyses, and the intervertebral ball-and-socket joints results in an extremely strong backbone that has great side-to-side flexibility, up to twenty-five degrees at each joint. Up-and-down flexibility, however, is narrowly restricted; each joint will allow only a few degrees (one notes here that the cobra, using a vertical stance for its striking or biting activities, cannot obtain the efficiency or accuracy of a rattlesnake, which uses the horizontally thrown S curve with only a few degrees of upward movement when it straightens out the S in striking). Snakes require great flexibility to facilitate their limbless

Skeletal Modifications and Locomotion

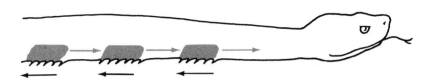

BELLY SCALE CRAWL—Some snakes such as large rattlesnakes or constrictors often crawl in a straight line by undulating the broad flat belly scales to provide the necessary traction.

SERPENTINE CRAWL—In this, the most common method of crawling, the snake uses rocks and other objects to gain leverage to push its body along the ground.

movement. Of the four main methods of snake locomotion, only one—the rectilinear or caterpillar crawl—could be used without a flexible backbone. Rectilinear locomotion is generally used by large snakes that have proportionately great bulk to move over the ground. The movement consists of sliding on the skin, the body inside supported by stationary ribs. The snake inches forward along the ground in a straight-line manner. The ventral scales (scutes) are used as feet. A muscular ripple moves from head to tail, along the belly, each scute being moved forward slightly and pressed firmly against the earth. The scute then appears to move back as the snake's bulk moves ahead over it. This caterpillar approach is slow, and snakes that relied wholly upon it in searching for prey would frequently find themselves going hungry.

More familiar as a means of locomotion in snakes is the serpentine movement, in which the snake moves forward in a series of side-to-side undulations as in a string of S's. This most common method of snake movement requires a surface that is irregular—a rock here, a stick there, a ridge of earth another place—because the snake presses its sides against these irregularities to push itself

16

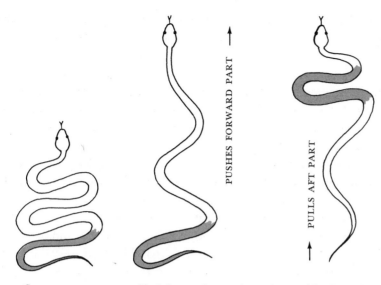

PUSHES FORWARD PART

PULLS AFT PART

CONCERTINA CRAWL—Shaded areas show anchor points used by the snake to push and pull itself forward, contracting and expanding its body like a concertina.

SIDEWINDING
Shaded areas show tracks made by a side-winder rattlesnake in soft sand.

This part of body is raised clear of sand leaving no tracks.

Hook mark made by forepart of sidewinder's body.

forward. On a sheet of glass the serpentine movement gets the snake nowhere; it thrashes helplessly, bending its flexible body but finding nothing to press its sides against. The longer and thinner the snake, the more efficient is its serpentine movement, for it can create more body loops.

A third type of snake locomotion is the concertina movement. The snake acts like an accordion. The greater part of its length is compressed into flattened, ground-hugging loops from which the snake's head and upper third of the body are thrust forward. The ventral scutes then grip the ground as the body is compressed again for a new thrust forward. It is as though a spring were alternately compressed and released. Once again, the snake requires a rough surface with something to thrust back against when it springs forward.

In the deserts of the world, covered by immense dunes of shifting sands, fluid and insubstantial rather than solid and enduring, none of the above means of snake locomotion work with great efficiency. Rectilinear creeping in shifting sands makes progress difficult. In neither the serpentine nor concertina methods does the

General Characteristics

17

snake find the solid surface it requires to thrust itself forward. But in these deserts there has developed a unique adaptation to the environment, the sidewinding method of snake locomotion. Sidewinding is used only by a few of the desert-dwelling snakes, most notably the sidewinder rattlesnake of the American West and a few quite similar vipers in the deserts of Africa. These instances of sidewinding provide an interesting example of parallel evolution in two widely separated places.

The sidewinder moves forward by throwing a loop of its body forward and then pulling itself up on it. The snake gets leverage by pressing head and neck down against the sand as the body loop is thrown forward. Then, straightening out and pressing body against the ground, the snake throws head and neck forward and sideways to start the next thrust. The head-neck combination and the body loop are in effect the two feet upon which the snake walks.

In the sidewinding movement the snake's body is roughly perpendicular to the direction in which it is going. Consequently, the observer may be bewildered, since his preconception leads him to associate snake movement with a head that leads and a body that follows. But it appears that the sidewinder is going sideways, its head pointed east, say, while its body moves north. The head is the clue. It points where the sidewinder is going—precisely where it wants to go, and very effectively, too. Behind it, the sidewinder leaves a trail like a series of fishhooks laid side by side.

Individual species of snakes are not confined to a single method of locomotion. A snake tends to use the method best suited to the terrain over which it has to travel. Even nonsidewinding snakes may use an awkward sidewinding motion when they find themselves in sand. Snakes can move backward, although they don't normally do so unless they are retreating from an enemy.

When snakes swim—and snakes are good swimmers—they use the serpentine method, in this case pushing their sides back against the water to obtain forward thrust.

Snakes appear deficient in some of the senses found in other animals. On most snakes the lidless eyes, protected only by the "spectacles" of the outer skin, lack the fovea, that special region of the retina just in front of the optic nerve that allows the eye to see sharp images. Only a few snakes, mostly tree snakes, have a fovea. Moreover, snakes' eyes are located on either side of the head, which means that they cannot judge distances in the manner of animals that have eyes pointed forward to obtain three-dimensional vision. Some snakes, the racers and whipsnakes for example, may compensate for lack of three-dimensional vision through triangulation by moving the head from side to side as they focus on an object. Moreover, it has been hypothesized that some animals, including some snakes, have grooves or lines from eye to nostril that allow accurate sighting on fast-moving prey.

Most books on snakes have stated that snakes cannot hear airborne sounds. This theory was based on the fact that snakes lack external eardrums and middle ears, although they do have inner ears. But through recent experiments involving the implanting of electrodes in the midbrain of snakes, Howard W. Campbell and Peter H. Hartline (1969) proved beyond all doubt that airborne sound frequencies are received in a snake's brain.

In other words, all previous theory has been upset—snakes *can* hear. They have two separate and wholly independent systems that receive both airborne and earthborne sound frequencies. One of these systems, the somatic, involves transmission of frequencies through ventral skin receptors via the spinal cord. The other system, the auditory, involves skin-received vibrations that are transmitted mechanically through the snake's attenuated lung to the eighth cranial nerve and the inner ear. A snake's sensitivity to vibration is extremely high, on the order of one angstrom, which means that in a quiet room a snake can hear a person speaking with a soft voice at a distance of about ten feet.

The role of the snake's lung as a conductor of sound is particularly fascinating. Hartline (1971) proved this role beyond all doubt by a simple but ingenious experiment. He implanted an electrode at the anterior end of the attenuated lung and then set up sound frequencies at the posterior end. Apparently traveling through the air in the lung, the sound frequencies were picked up by the electrode. Hartline then bent the snake into a U with the bottom of the U at the exact middle of the lung. He injected fluid into the lung at the bottom of the U, leaving the rest of the lung air-filled. Again he sent sound frequencies from the posterior end. This time the transmission was stopped where the fluid had been injected.

There are many mysteries about snakes that have been built into the folklore of peoples all over the world. Perhaps nothing has fascinated people more than the snake's forked tongue flicking in and out of its mouth. The tongue has incorrectly been seen as a poisoning instrument; it has also been associated metaphorically with evil, as in "to speak with a forked tongue." In prosaic fact, the snake's tongue is a highly developed sensing instrument, probably indispensable in leading the snake to prey or mates.

Snakes have a good sense of smell through their well-developed nostrils. But this sense is greatly augmented by the use of the tongue in relation to a special organ, the Jacobson's organ, which is found in a rudimentary stage in other animals but has reached a highly useful state only in snakes. Located in the roof of the snake's mouth, the Jacobson's organ is composed of two cavities lined with the same kind of cells that line the sensing part of the nose. This remarkable organ works in conjunction with the tongue to give the snake a chemical sampling of its environment. The flickering tongue acts as a busy scout, picking up small particles from water, earth, and air. As the tongue is withdrawn into the mouth, the forked tip is pressed into the cavities of the Jacobson's organ, which both smells and tastes the particles the tongue has picked up. The Jacobson's organ gives the snake extraordinary sensory powers. The snake can quite literally get a taste of the neighborhood, a taste so well-defined that it can follow the trail of its potential prey or of its potential mate.

Some of the most highly evolved snakes are the Crotalidae, or pit vipers—the rattlesnakes and their relatives. Pit vipers have all the sense organs of other snakes, as well as additional aids of particular use in the hunt for prey. These aids are the pits, special heat receptors located on either side of the head between the nostrils and the eyes. The pits look, in fact, like an extra pair of nostrils. All snakes have the ability to sense warmth, for like other animals including man, snakes have "touch" receptors and "heat" receptors scattered over the surface of their skin (which, because of its toughness, one finds it difficult to think of as sensitive). But the highly developed pits of the pit vipers are distinctive and fascinating. Each

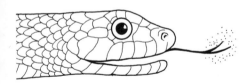

1. Tongue is flicked out to pick up chemical particles from the air.

2. Tongue is withdrawn to a point under the Jacobson's organ for taste-smell analysis.

20

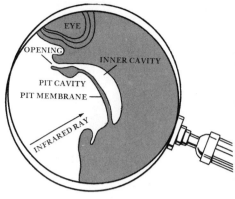

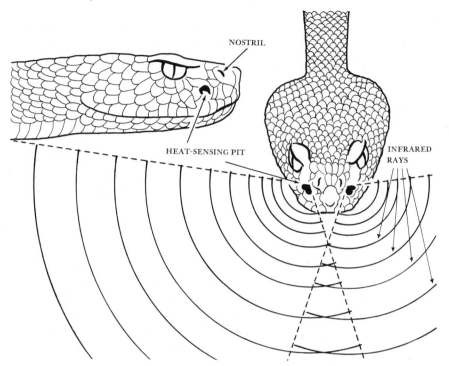

NOSTRIL

HEAT-SENSING PIT

INFRARED RAYS

EYE

OPENING

INNER CAVITY

PIT CAVITY

PIT MEMBRANE

INFRARED RAY

pit is actually made of two separate cavities. The larger one lies on the snake's nose just behind and generally below the level of the nostril, and opens forward. Behind this larger cavity is a smaller one, barely visible to the naked eye. The two cavities are connected internally, separated only by a thin membrane that has nerve endings so extraordinarily sensitive to warmth that pit vipers can detect minute differences in temperature between the air in the front cavity and the air in the rear cavity. The forward-pointing pits on either side of its face produce overlapping fields (as in the overlapping visual fields of human eyes); thus the pit viper can sense an object whose temperature differs from its surroundings and accurately judge the distance between itself and the object. The heat-sensing ability of a pit viper is so great that it can react to differences of temperature as small as one fifth of a degree Centigrade. Blindfolded, the snake will still strike with uncanny accuracy at warm-blooded prey.

Long thought to be unique in possessing their "pit organs," the

General Characteristics

21

pit vipers are now known to have company. Pythons and boas, including the rosy boa of the American West, have the same kind of organs in pits among their labial scales. This fact, conclusively established by Robert Barrett, P. A. F. Maderson, and Richard M. Meszler (1970), indicates that pythons and boas use the same heat-sensing ability as an aid in hunting and striking prey. A particularly noteworthy aspect of this discovery is the fact that *all* members of the family Boidae have this heat-sensing ability, whereas among the viperlike snakes only the pit vipers have it. One wonders if further studies will reveal that species from other snake families have similar organs.

Feeding

In killing prey, snakes use three methods. Nonvenomous snakes (by far the greater number) may simply grasp their prey and swallow it alive, as does a garter snake with a frog. Or the nonvenomous snake may throw two or three loops around the prey and kill or immobilize it by constriction that prevents breathing, as does a rosy boa with a wood rat. Venomous snakes, of course, make full use of their venom by striking at the prey, embedding fangs, injecting venom, then withdrawing to wait until the prey drops dead. Occasionally a rattlesnake may fail to retrieve a gopher or small rabbit it has killed simply because the rodent has strayed into rocks or a hole before death overtakes it.

Whatever the snake's method of killing, all snakes approach the actual feeding process the same way. They swallow their prey whole, whether it is egg, pig, or cricket. From the time of its birth (most young snakes will feed on insects) to the meal before it dies, the snake will normally approach its food so that it can be swallowed headfirst. The snake works the expandable jaws around the prey's body, moving its teeth forward by a kind of rotary chewing motion that brings first one side of the jaws then the other into play. During this process the snake releases enzymes in its mouth that begin the digestive process even as the food is being swallowed. If the food is considerably larger than the snake's head, as it frequently is, the ligaments attaching the jaws expand allowing the jaws to engulf the food.

Once the food has passed through the mouth, the eating process is continued by a process of alternate muscular contraction and relaxation that forces the food through the esophagus into the stomach, where, for a few hours or days, as digestion takes place, it remains as a noticeable bulge in the snake's body. If the snake is disturbed by an enemy while eating, it usually will regurgitate its food immediately, for the process of eating is a slow one and generally would greatly hamper a snake trying to flee an enemy or to defend itself.

The mating of snakes is not simply the result of a chance encounter followed by a casual entwining. This is not to say that snakes show evidences of romantic love like lions or humans, nor are they monogamous like wolves. Except for the period of hibernation, snakes can mate anytime during the year. In the American West, however, the principal mating season is usually in the spring, in late April or May, not long after snakes have left the winter's den. Then the female, through release of scent, lets it be known that she desires a mate and males seek the female out. The object purely and simply is copulation—not a lasting relationship. Copulation done, the mates will part, each going its own way. However, in many species courtship behavior becomes ritualized and may even include formal battles between males—battles which culminate in the submission of one male to the other, not in bloody violence or death. In several species of snakes, these battles for supremacy or breeding territory may become as stylized as the elaborate courtship dances of some birds. Courtship behavior has been identified in at least some species of nearly all the families of snakes (Shaw, 1951). No one knows whether all species engage in ritual battles among males, for this behavioral aspect of herpetology has not been sufficiently studied. Few references to male combat between snakes are to be found in earlier literature, probably because many observers didn't realize what they were seeing. For example, in *Death Valley* (Stanford University Press, 1930), W. A. Chalfant comments: "Another rattler found in the higher elevations in the Death Valley watershed is the reputedly rare tiger rattlesnake. Nineteen are said to have been killed in a single season in a canyon of the Panamints. The nearest to the Valley floor that we hear of any having been found is on the slope down from Towne's Pass, *where two were killed while standing partly erect with their heads near together, apparently playing* [italics added]."

Mating

What Chalfant was describing was a ritualized combat between male snakes, probably the Panamint rattlesnake rather than the tiger rattlesnake, which looks much like the Panamint but has not been found in Death Valley.

Whether the male snake has to fight or not, it does not find a female by relying on vision or hearing. It must track the female by using nose, flicking tongue, and Jacobson's organ. When the male finds the female, a kind of love play often takes place during which the male rubs its head along the female's body, exploring it with its tongue.

Snakes, like other reptiles, fertilize internally. Copulation takes place when the male snake injects sperm through one of its hemipenes into the oviduct of the female, which opens into the female's cloaca. If this all sounds "just like humans," consider that the hemipenes, possessed by both lizards and snakes are unique. Other male reptiles have a single penis, but a male lizard or snake has a pair of hollow copulatory organs, the hemipenes, which are turned outside-in behind the cloaca, near the base of the tail, until the male is ready for copulation. At that moment one of the hemipenes, the one nearest the female, is erected and thrust through the male snake's cloaca into the female's, as the snakes quite literally entwine.

Fertilization in snakes normally takes place in spring or early summer just before eggs mature within the female's body. Many snakes are oviparous, meaning that after fertilization they lay eggs that subsequently hatch: other snakes are ovoviviparous, meaning that after fertilization the eggs remain inside the female's body until they hatch, after which the young are born live. The oviparous snakes lay their eggs, generally seven to ten in number, in sand, humus, moist earth, rotting logs, or the like, depending on the habitat and species. The eggs are always laid in material that will provide warmth from exposure to the sun or from internal heat generation, and will ensure sufficient moisture to keep the eggshell pliable. Few oviparous snakes care for their eggs. Once laid in proper incubating material, the eggs are forgotten, left to hatch by themselves. In the one or two species that do provide some care for the eggs, the female coils around them during at least part of the incubation period.

Many oviparous snake species have natural safeguards to assure

SNAKES OF THE AMERICAN WEST

the fertilization of eggs. One female may copulate with several males over a period of time. In some species females are able to store sperm, establish an internal sperm bank, so to speak, that can be drawn upon days, weeks, or months after copulation at a time when the female's egg producing cycle is favorable. In spite of such safeguards, however, infertile eggs are occasionally produced and laid.

In snake eggs a developing embryo lies at the egg's center. Attached by an umbilical stalk to a yolk sac that provides its primary food supply, the embryo is encased by another sac called the amniotic sac. This sac is filled with fluid that bathes the embryo and protects it from sudden shock. Another envelope, the allantois, surrounds both the yolk and amniotic sacs. The allantois starts its development as an outgrowth of the embryo's lower gut. As the embryo gets larger and the yolk shrinks, the allantois also grows. The allantois performs two functions: it is storage bladder for the embryo's waste products, and it conveys oxygen to and carbon dioxide from the embryo. Finally, around embryo, yolk sac, amniotic sac, and allantois is still another enveloping membrane— the tough protective chorion. Lying next to the egg's outer shell, the chorion also encases albumen, some water, and perhaps some food for the embryo.

Birth of Young

After a few weeks to a few months of incubation, depending on species, the young snakes are ready to enter the world. For this difficult journey the young of oviparous snakes are left to their own devices, the chief one of which is the egg tooth, a sharp protrusion on the snout used to break open the tough shell that envelops the young snake. The job is not easy. The young snake must rely on instinct and the effectiveness of its equipment to enter the open world. If it fails, the snake dies. No one will help it emerge, and if it succeeds, it has only assured its survival temporarily. Relying solely on instinct for guidance, through the many trials that await it, the small, newly hatched snake is immediately on its own. It will probably never see its parents; nor would it recognize them if it encountered them.

Even the live-born snake goes immediately from the vicinity of its mother. In a sense ovoviviparous young are not born live in the same way as a mammal which is born attached by a placenta to its mother. In effect, the live-born snake emerges from an egg that has been carried by the female until the day of hatching: each fully developed embryo is covered only by a thin, clear membrane from which the young snake emerges.

A few species of snakes—for example, garter snakes—are viviparous. The young are connected to the mother by a primitive placenta, which provides nourishment to the developing young before they are born live.

In most temperate regions, including the American West, snakes are generally hatched or born in late summer, so that in August or early September observers may see many newborn snakes. The first task confronting these young snakes is simply to hunt for enough food, generally insect larvae and insects, to survive the first winter. In this and subsequent hunts they are apparently aided by a genetically coded ability to find the kind of food that is particular to their species. Conducting a number of significant studies of several species, Gordon M. Burghardt (1967) found that newly born snakes, unfed from the moment of their birth, could differentiate readily between cotton swabs dipped in distilled water, foods their species did not eat, and foods their species preferred. In most instances the youngsters would attack the cotton swabs that, chemically, to their tongue and Jacobson's organ said "this is your kind of food."

The young snake will grow rapidly after the first winter. A rattlesnake, for example, may double its length in the first year. Obviously, rate of growth varies from species to species and in relation to climate, availability of food, and other factors. The growth of a snake continues throughout its life, but each year that growth lessens, until, in an old snake, it becomes almost impossible to measure.

Hibernation   Throughout its life the snake that lives in a cold or temperate climate returns each fall to a den, or hibernaculum. There, with others of its kind and probably with snakes of other species, it spends the winter in the sleep of hibernation. Its metabolic processes are lowered, and it lives on the fat of summer until the thaws of spring signal that it is time to leave the den. The hibernaculum cannot be just any hole in the ground; it must meet certain conditions of temperature (above freezing), dryness (not too humid or moist), and ventilation (enough for air, but not so much that the temperature drops below freezing). Experiments conducted by the Japan Snake Institute in building dens for captive snakes cost the lives of many snakes before a synthetic hibernaculum was successfully built. Hibernation, in fact, is a dangerous state. Even under ideal conditions some snakes do not survive the winter.

What is an old snake? Life-span is almost impossible to determine in wild snakes, for few of them live the life-span possible for captive individuals of their species. They fall prey to enemies—most often man. Zoo records can give some indication of how long snakes might live if well fed and secure from enemies. In the reptile house at the San Diego Zoo, which holds many longevity records for western snakes, records show that large snakes can live as long as twenty-four years, and smaller species tend to live from fifteen to twenty years. A list of longevity records is found in Appendix I.

Life-Span

Chapter 3
»»»»»

KEEPING SNAKES AS PETS

At the age of greatest curiosity about themselves and the natural world—generally in the young teen period—many boys and girls want to keep a pet snake. This desire is common even in highly urbanized areas where wild snakes are no longer seen. Parents, unless they are unusually forbearing, are generally horrified. Fortunately for snake populations, then, only a few youngsters actually get to keep pet snakes. Many more snakes are kept by adults who like bizarre pets, even though snakes can hardly be called affectionate.

Every village, town, or city in the United States has a population of captive snakes, a surprising number of which are venomous. For instance, not long ago in San Diego an adult cobra escaped from a private collection kept illegally by a man living in one of the city's most crowded residential areas. This collection was kept for commercial purposes, ostensibly to provide venoms for anti-venins, and contained a number of deadly snakes including kraits, more cobras, and vipers. Because wild animals cannot legally be kept by private persons in San Diego, the entire collection was confiscated and turned over to the zoo.

Often snakes that are alien to a particular area are released by their captors in inhospitable terrain. They will eventually starve to death, and before dying will introduce a discordant note into the local ecology. Such releases normally arise out of the captor's guilt feelings. Noting that his "pet" won't eat or is otherwise languishing, the captor releases it and with its departure banishes his own guilt.

Unfortunately, these loose exotics pose a serious environmental problem. The local plants and animals, whose evolutionary development has established an intricate network of relationships with one another, may be disturbed or even completely devastated when confronted with a totally strange animal, whose habits their evolution has not taken into account. There are numerous instances in natural history of this problem of the alien animal—mongooses in Hawaii, rabbits in Australia, goats on the Galápagos Islands—all of which have partially or fully wiped out some native plants and animals. So far no major ecological imbalance has resulted from an alien snake. Yet one day perhaps a male and female will be released and breed, or a pregnant female will escape and produce her litter, and then. . . . Better by far is the practice of turning unwanted alien creatures over to the nearest major zoo equipped to handle them.

Snakes do not make good pets. They are not affectionate, can learn no tricks, and seldom move around like tropical fish to display their beauty. Moreover, they cannot be fed simply by tossing in some horsemeat. Their diets are often quite restricted in nature. And snakes must be kept in well-constructed cages, for if a snake can work its head through an opening, it will escape. Then, if the snake is captive in a residence, begins the difficult search—behind chests, inside the furniture (within coiled springs is a favorite spot), up in the walls, or in at least one instance, in the toilet bowl.

However, since no amount of discouragement will prevent some people from keeping a pet snake or snake collection (as the authors did when they were young), some words of advice may help. If the snake is purchased from a pet shop, the buyer should make certain that the snake has eaten in captivity and that appropriate food is readily obtainable. Otherwise the owner will have to undergo the mounting sorrow that a conscientious person must feel as he watches a living creature slowly starve to death. Since it is difficult to be absolutely certain about the health and habits of snakes bought from a pet store, potential owners are better advised to capture their own native snakes—paying heed, of course, to local and state laws protecting wild animals. Such captures permit either effective care and feeding or, failing this, the release of the snake either at the place where it was captured or in a similar habitat. We cannot stress this procedure too strongly. Snakes, fortunately, can live so long without food that an owner can ascertain whether or not his pet will feed in captivity and still have enough time to return it to the wild if it refuses to eat. Such releases should take place before the captive snake is so weakened that it can't hunt, and the release should be made when the air temperature is neither so hot that the snake is in danger of perishing nor so cold that it can't move. Early morning and late afternoon are generally the best times for release.

Capturing

The actual capture of nonvenomous snakes is comparatively easy unless one is hesitant about picking them up by hand. Few snakes, except perhaps the elusive and deceptive racers and whipsnakes, can move fast enough to get away from a determined pursuer. Some of the larger nonvenomous snakes, however, can cause lacerations by biting, and any bite by an animal creates the danger of infection. Consequently, snake hunters are well advised to use a snake stick when hunting larger nonvenomous snakes and, of course, venomous ones. Two types of sticks are commonly used, neither of them the forked stick of legend.

Commonly a snake hunter will use a four-foot, sawed-off broom handle to which an angle iron is fastened at one end, forming an elongated L. The bottom of this L should protrude from the broom handle some four or five inches. The iron should be smoothed to facilitate hooking it under a snake's belly. This stick serves two purposes. The bottom of the L can be pressed down across the snake's neck, pinning it to the ground so that the snake hunter can grasp it immediately behind the head to avoid being bitten. Or the stick can simply be used as a hook to scoop the snake from the ground into a sack or container. This hooking technique should not be used with venomous snakes unless the hunter is scooping them into a large standing container like a trash can. Otherwise the person holding the snake sack might be placed in sudden jeopardy should the venomous snake slip from the L.

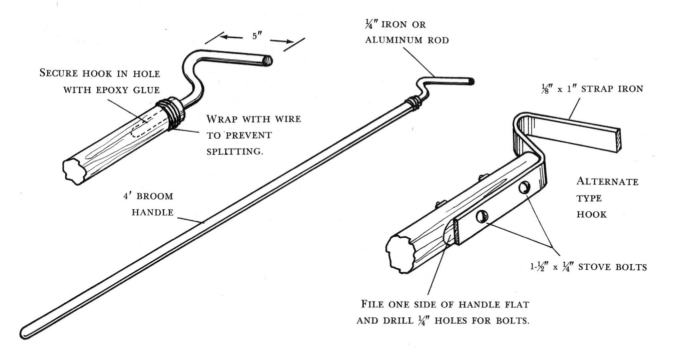

SECURE HOOK IN HOLE
WITH EPOXY GLUE

← 5″ →

¼″ IRON OR
ALUMINUM ROD

WRAP WITH WIRE
TO PREVENT
SPLITTING.

⅛″ x 1″ STRAP IRON

4′ BROOM
HANDLE

ALTERNATE
TYPE
HOOK

1-½″ x ¼″ STOVE BOLTS

FILE ONE SIDE OF HANDLE FLAT
AND DRILL ¼″ HOLES FOR BOLTS.

A second type of stick is used more often for venomous snakes. This stick, four to five feet long, has a wire, nylon, or leather loop attached to one end of a broom handle in the following manner. At one end securely rivet, staple, or nail to both sides of the broomstick a piece of tin about five inches long, providing a tube through which the wire or cord will be drawn. The tube should not be so large as to allow much play in the loop nor so small as to interfere with closing it. On the bottom side bend the tin over to remove any threat from sharp edges. Secure the loop wire or cord by rivets or nails on the side of the broomstick opposite the tube. Along the same side as the tube fasten at intervals several staples to a point about three-quarters of the way up the broom handle. Splice the section of wire, cord, or leather that will serve as the loop with a stiffer wire that will extend through the tin tube and up through the staples along the length of the handle. At what is now the top end of the snake stick, bend this wire into a small finger loop that will be used to operate the device. The completed stick should work smoothly. Hold the pole in one hand and manipulate the loop at the bottom by pulling the wire up or pushing it down with the finger

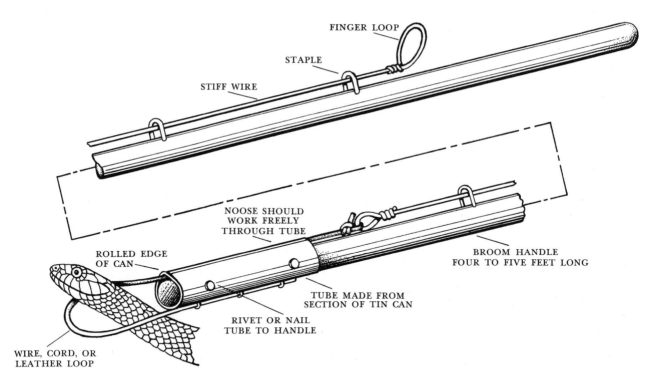

FINGER LOOP

STAPLE

STIFF WIRE

NOOSE SHOULD
WORK FREELY
THROUGH TUBE

ROLLED EDGE
OF CAN

BROOM HANDLE
FOUR TO FIVE FEET LONG

TUBE MADE FROM
SECTION OF TIN CAN

RIVET OR NAIL
TUBE TO HANDLE

WIRE, CORD, OR
LEATHER LOOP

loop at the top of the pole. The device is now ready to capture a venomous snake. The bottom loop will be passed over the snake's head and drawn tightly around its neck. By holding the tightly drawn snake stick in one hand and grasping the snake's tail with the other, the hunter can push the snake headfirst into a sack or container. Once the snake is securely in, he can release the loop and tie off the sack or close the container.

In the field, most captured snakes are kept in large mason jars if the snakes are small or in sacks if they are larger. The lids of the mason jars should be perforated from the inside out to provide air. Flour sacks or pillow cases make the best snake sacks. Such sacks should be of stout, closely woven material that has not even the smallest hole in it. Given a hole into which it can poke its nose, the snake will enlarge it to escape. Once after a desert snake hunt for the San Diego Zoo, the authors were driving home, their wives chatting pleasantly in the back seat of the automobile, when a sidewinder rattlesnake escaped on the floor of the back compartment in just this manner. One could only conjecture how long it remained there before it was discovered not far from the women's feet.

SNAKES OF THE AMERICAN WEST

Collecting sacks should be sufficiently long so that a knot can be tied in the top of the sack itself. If the top is simply tied off with string or drawcord, imprisoned snakes can often force exit. They cannot, however, wind their way through a knot in the bag itself.

Keeping captured snakes poses some problems. Small snakes can be kept in an aquarium remodeled into a terrarium. The top should be covered with screen or glass that allows ventilation. Sand with rocks, bark, and other objects can be placed in the bottom along with a small, shallow water container. The owner should be aware, however, that the small snake will either burrow in the sand, hide under the rocks or bark, or curl up in the water dish, depending on its species. A word of caution: *no snake should be placed for more than a few minutes, five at most, in a place where it cannot get away from direct sunlight.* At temperatures that people and other animals can endure and perhaps even enjoy, most snakes will die horribly, their blood heated beyond tolerance. A glass-fronted cage or terrarium heats rapidly, and inside temperature rapidly becomes greater than that of the room around it. Glass cages therefore should be kept in shade with only very brief exposure to the sun.

Housing

Larger snakes must be kept in specially built cages, preferably glass-fronted, with access from the rear or top (such cages are commercially available). Wire mesh cages can be used, but they must have a fine enough mesh or screen so that the snake cannot enlarge a hole with its probing nose. A good cage for snakes up to six or seven feet in length would be about three feet wide, two feet deep, and one and one-half feet high. It should have a glass front and a back of solid wood, plastic, or metal, hinged about halfway down with two fasteners at the top. In this top portion of the back—the door to the cage—should be a fine screen or series of small holes to provide ventilation. The two fasteners should be independently operated, to assure a tight fit when the cage is closed. Inside, the bottom of the cage should be covered with sand or gravel, again perhaps with some rocks or bark, and a shallow water dish (one does not want to run the risk of a pet snake drowning). If by some remote chance the pet snake is venomous, the cage should have a lock on it along with some indication—a red seal or skull and crossbones—that the inhabitant can bring death to cage openers.

To assure a constant temperature in the snake cage, the owner can use a simple heater. A seventy-five- or one-hundred-watt bulb should be placed in one end of the cage eight to ten inches above the bottom surface and opposite any shelter, such as rocks, log, or box, provided for the snake. The temperature at the cool end of the cage should not go above 80° F. If it does, the owner should either reduce wattage or put a reflector on the light; the reflector is a good idea anyway.

Feeding

Compared with most other animals, snakes do not eat often, but they do not adapt easily to foods that are strange to them. Since snake diets range from crickets to lizard eggs, depending on the snake, pet fanciers may find the problem of feeding a difficult one. However, many snakes—gopher snakes, kingsnakes, boas, and others—do eat mice and rats, which are relatively easy for the snake keeper to obtain. He can raise mice himself, livetrap them, or buy them from a supplier such as a pet store. Of course he may find it difficult as he stands there, cute little mouse in hand, snake waiting, to make the sacrifice. Or, he may, as one of the authors did, have a mother whose soft heart is so touched by the shivering little mouse in a cage that she will release it while the snake owner is away at school.

Raising mice is comparatively easy, if a bit messy and smelly. Livetrapping them can be fairly easily accomplished if the snake owner lives near a vacant plot of land with enough cover and food to assure field mice. The simplest trap is made of a two-pound coffee can, a conventional mousetrap, and a section of wire mesh. On to the "snapper" of the mousetrap affix securely the patch of tough wire mesh large enough to overlap the opening of the can. Then at the open end of the can fasten the mousetrap to one side, bait holder inside, so that the mesh, when the trap is sprung, will tightly cover the opening, trapping whatever is inside. The bottom of the trap is the side of the can to which the trap is secured. When the trap is set and baited, the wire mesh will lie parallel to the ground in front of the trap. The bait will be inside the can; mouse touches bait and—bam!—it's a prison.

In serving mouse to snake, the new pet owner will generally make the mistake of throwing the mouse into the cage alive and hardy. Alive the mouse should be, but it must be stunned. Otherwise the snake may bruise its nose striking at the lively mouse, missing, and hitting the sides of the cage. Stunning the mouse can best be accomplished by grasping it by the tail and knocking its head against a hard surface, such as the edge of a counter or the floor. If this process seems cruel, it should be remembered that the decision to keep pet snakes embodies the decision to feed them.

Pet garter or water snakes will normally prefer frogs to mice. The pet owner, therefore, may have to spend some time frog hunting to keep his pet fed. Some pet snakes, including the voracious garter snakes, can be induced to take specially prepared raw meat strips or balls, particularly if this food has been given a "wild" odor through such methods as grinding in some frog meat or earthworms. Since movement attracts snakes to prey, strips or balls of raw meat can be given movement by sprinkling live mealworms on top. The meat, on a flat dish, with several undulating mealworms on top, may appear live to the hungry snake.

Snakes will not eat if the cage temperature is too low. Ideally feeding should take place when the cage temperature is from 80° to 85° F. The owner—and others in the room—should avoid making sudden movements that may distract the snakes being fed. Feeding should take place once every week or ten days, assuming that the snake gets its fill at every feeding. That "fill," of course, depends on the size of the snake. A four- or five-foot gopher snake may take three or four large mice at a feeding.

Snakes periodically shed their skin in captivity, just as they do in the wild. They can be helped during shedding in two ways. First, rough objects—stones, bark, branches—should be placed in the cage so that the snake can rub against them to loosen the old skin. Second, the snake should be supplied with a place to bathe or should be covered with a wet towel to help it recover the moisture lost through the skin during the shedding process. The shed skin, by the way, may be a source of infection to the snake and should be removed from the cage immediately after it is shed.

Shedding

Diseases   Snakes suffer from various afflictions or diseases. Captive snakes commonly are attacked by almost microscopic mites, which gather between the scales or around the snake's eyes and suck the snake's blood. Unchecked, mites multiply rapidly. Moreover, mite-infested cages may remain the breeding places for future mite generations for years, even when uninhabited by snakes. Mites are more than parasite pests; they are vectors for various diseases as well. In all probability, malaria is spread to snakes through mites. To combat mites, the pet owner may use the commercial preparation Dri-die, a fine silica powder that removes the protective wax on a mite's body so that it dries to death. Some pet owners have successfully checked or eradicated mites with organic phosphate insecticides of various types, but it must be noted that perhaps all and almost certainly some species of snake are themselves affected by the chemicals. At least one young snake fancier learned to his sorrow that DDT spread on a snake to kill mites kills not only mites but snake as well. Mites must be checked, however. In addition to transmitting diseases to a snake, they can kill the snake by sucking its blood.

Another frequent disease of captive snakes is commonly called mouth rot, although it may be referred to also as canker mouth. This unpleasant disease is an infection caused by omnipresent bacteria, which invade the snake's mouth tissues because the snake has injured itself rubbing against wire mesh or striking at a lively mouse, missing, and hitting the cage. Unless checked, mouth rot will kill the snake. If the disease has not advanced too far, a preparation called Sulmet will cure it. The surest cure, however, even in advanced cases, is ascorbic acid (vitamin C) given through hypodermic injection under the snake's skin. This treatment should be given by a veterinarian.

The list of other disorders and diseases of snakes is long: they may be infested with flukes or other parasites, have pneumonia or tuberculosis, contract salmonella, come down with enteritis, or suffer from impactions of the bowel. Most of these illnesses are more than most pet owners can cope with and require the help of a veterinarian. If a previously healthy snake refuses food, shows signs of distress or pain, becomes listless and sluggish, or suffers discharges from around the nose or mouth, the owner should take his pet to the vet.

If by chance the captive snake lays eggs that the owner believes are fertile, he can attempt to hatch them the way it is done in zoos. Place a dampened paper towel on the bottom of an old-fashioned crockery jar. Then place the eggs carefully on the towel, separating them so that they have air space around them. Over the top of the jar place a sheet of glass. Irregularities in the top surface of the jar will provide air. The jar should be kept at an even 80° F. If the eggs do not become unduly wrinkled, but rather appear firm and "alive," then the pet owner may in two or three months' time have the pleasure of watching each tiny snake enter the world by cutting through the shell with the tiny egg tooth at the end of its nose.

Hatching Eggs

PART TWO

» » » » » »

HARMLESS SNAKES

Chapter 4

»»»»»

THE SLENDER
BLIND SNAKES

Travelers by night along many blacktopped desert roads in the American Southwest, particularly during late spring and early summer, will occasionally see snakes on the road, especially if they slow down and look carefully. The most difficult snakes to spot are slender wormlike creatures from six to sixteen inches long, frequently called worm snakes, but more properly referred to as blind snakes, slender blind snakes, or in the Old World, thread snakes. They are classified by scientists in the family Leptotyphlopidae, genus *Leptotyphlops*. Of the fifty species of *Leptotyphlops*, only two are found in the American West—the Texas blind snake *(Leptotyphlops dulcis)* and the western blind snake *(Leptotyphlops humilis)*. These species are distinguished by superocular scales; the Texas blind snake has superocular scales, but the western blind snake has none. Each has some subspecies. Blind snakes are unusual and fascinating creatures, though by no means are they glamorous in coloration or action.

Anatomical Characteristics

The slender blind snakes are probably fairly common but are so secretive in their habits that they are seldom seen by man. The untrained observer, in fact, not infrequently confuses these snakes with worms, although if he looks at them closely, he will note that they are usually larger than earthworms and that they are covered by quite hard, shiny scales. If he has the curiosity to pick one up, he will find it feels different from an earthworm—it is firm and dry (not slimy) rather than soft and moist. He will find also that the blind snake's defensive reaction is similar to that of many other snakes; it will immediately release through its cloacal opening a foul-smelling musk, which is stored in paired glands in the tail. If in spite of the offensive odor, the observer continues to hold the snake, he will find that the slender creature may try to prick him with a pinpointed spine that points straight back with a slight downward angle from the tip of its tail. This spine is harmless, for it is nonvenomous and too short to effectively break the skin.

The snakes of both species are small, slender, almost translucent, and colored pink, gray, or brown on top with a slightly lighter underbelly. Head and body are covered with unusually tough scales overlapped like armor plate and almost uniform in size over the whole body. In most other snakes, scale sizes may differ considerably in relation to location on the snake's body—for example, the scales on the belly may be larger than those on the back.

The slender blind snake's head is blunt and rounded. There is virtually no discernible neck. To the herpetologist the skull may properly be characterized as "massive," meaning that the bones have greatly developed and solidified as part of the snake's adaptation to burrowing.

The Leptotyphlopidae are in fact blind, having rudimentary eyes, each covered with an unmodified scale. They spend most of their lives underground, burrowing in sand or loose soil or living in crevices among rocks. Like the earthworms with which they are sometimes confused, they are most frequently seen above ground immediately after a rain, although they come out at other times, particularly in the late evening or night. Above ground the slender blind snake is restless, as though it is uncomfortable. It moves along the surface in serpentine fashion, occasionally slipping sideways, for its body is completely round, unlike most snakes, which have flattened bottoms that allow more of the snake's body area to touch the ground surface. As an aid to movement above ground, particularly on smooth surfaces, the slender blind snake uses its tail spine. It sticks this spine into the surface and then pushes itself forward by shoving against it, much as a skier might use one pole.

Among the several interesting features of the slender blind snake is a well-developed pelvic girdle (List, 1966). To the student of evolution this is exciting, for it indicates that the slender blind snakes, or their immediate progenitors, once had legs. The pelvic girdle is so well developed that its basic components are easily recognizable. In addition, there is a vestigial femur ("thigh bone") at the extreme end of which is a tiny spur. On occasional specimens this spur protrudes through a pore just behind the snake's anal opening. Some other species of snakes—the boas, for example—have vestigial femurs, but they are not so well developed as those of the slender blind snakes. Moreover, in most snakes that generally have anal spurs, the spurs are most often possessed by the male snake only. But among the leptotyphlopids spurs seem to run to females.

The fact that some snakes have remnants of a pelvic girdle and femur, however rudimentary, provides support for the theory that snakes evolved later than lizards and once had much better defined limbs, probably not unlike the limbs of modern lizards. Such remnants of limbs are found only among those snakes that scientists place at this lower end of the evolutionary scale among snakes. The more highly developed species of snake are, so to speak, all snake and no lizard. Nothing of their evolutionary past remains as a useless appendage; all of their organs efficiently contribute to their actions as snakes—hunting, killing, mating.

The slender blind snakes have another distinguishing and unique anatomical feature. They have teeth only on the lower jaw. The upper jaw is smooth. This anatomical curiosity is one of the main features that distinguishes the Leptotyphlopidae from the Typhlopidae, the other family of blind snakes, none of which are found in the American West. The typhlopids, displaying one of those quirks in nature that seem part of a larger cosmic plan, have teeth only in the upper jaw, the exact opposite of the leptotyphlopids. This fact has led at least one wag among herpetologists to suggest that the two families be crossed to give their offspring a full set of teeth. And indeed there is a family, not in the American West, called Anomalepidae that appears to be intermediate between the Typhlops and Leptotyphlops and has a full set of teeth.

Some scientists, pointing to all these anatomical curiosities, have proposed that the slender blind snakes are really legless lizards (even though unlike any other of the true legless lizards). Other scientists believe that the slender blind snakes should be placed in an entirely separate suborder of reptiles, neither quite snake nor quite lizard. The use of modern analytical laboratory techniques, however, has allowed some preliminary work on the karyotype—the chromosome structure—of the slender blind snakes. Their karyotype, it turns out, is quite unlike that of a typical lizard. It resembles much more the karyotype of the Colubrid or Crotalid snakes. So for the time being at least these slender blind creatures will continue to be called snakes.

Predator-Prey
Relationships

Blind snakes have been preyed upon by virtually every predatory animal. They have been found in the stomach contents of animals as diverse as coyotes and rainbow trout. They are eaten by owls, hawks, roadrunners, and thrashers. Observers have found them trapped in black-widow webs and stung to death by scorpions. They are probably eaten commonly by both the Arizona coral snake and the night snake, and quite possibly by other snake-eating snakes as well. In brief, they are preyed upon from all quarters.

In their own eating habits the slender blind snakes are highly specialized (Smith, 1957). They prey on certain ants and termites. They prefer eggs, larvae, and workers—they avoid the soldiers. In approaching a termite worker, the snake attacks from the rear, grasping the abdomen; the snake works its jaws rapidly over the termite's body until the hard head is reached. Then the snake rubs or presses its prey against the ground, sometimes vigorously, to break the termite's head off. One Mexican species of slender blind snake, *Leptotyphlops goudotii phenops,* forces out the contents of the termite's abdomen, then regurgitates the rest. Workers, however, are not primary food; slender blind snakes prefer ant "brood"— the larvae.

The *Leptotyphlops* have in their specialization picked a prey that will no doubt be widespread and abundant as long as there is life on earth. Moreover, snake will be able to follow ant until the final moment, for in its hunting the slender blind snake does not rely on blind luck or knowledge of ant or termite habits. Through ingenious research, a team of scientists, Julian F. Watkins, II, Frederick R. Gehlbach, and Robert S. Baldridge (1967) demonstrated that *Leptotyphlops dulcis* is able to follow the pheromone trails of the raiding columns that army ants send out on nocturnal missions. A pheromone is a chemical that, when released by one animal of a species, brings about a behavioral response in other animals of the same species. Examples are found in the scents male wolves use to mark their territorial boundaries, or in the odors emitted by female luna moths when they are ready for courtship. The pheromones of ants and termites are equally effective. For centuries small boys and other curious creatures have marveled at the ability of blind insects like ants to follow a trail almost single file. The secret is that the ants mark the trail with a pheromone scent, something much more effective than seeds, buttons, or string.

Long ago, apparently, the slender blind snakes learned to follow the pheromone trails of ants. Thereafter they no longer hunted by chance. A blind snake out hunting proceeds until it crosses a pheromone trail; it then follows that trail, ignoring all ants encountered on the way, moving inexorably toward the ants' nest. In the nest the snake will feast on its principal food—ant larvae. This ability to follow the ant pheromone trail spells survival for blind snakes, which have no other means of locating prey.

The structure of an ecosystem is seldom simple, as Watkins, Gehlbach, and James C. Kroll (1969) demonstrated. Delving more deeply into the ant-trailing abilities of the slender blind snakes, they found a most intricate web of relationships involving slender blind snakes, ant warriors, snake-eating snakes, and snakes competing for ant brood. One of the first questions posed was: Why didn't the ants attack slender blind snakes bent on the destruction of the ant brood? The answer is: They do, but they generally get repelled by the slender blind snake's defense. Attacked by ants, the snake contorts itself, writhing about on the ground as it voids an offensive cloacal discharge. The writhing allows the snake to coat its body in the foul matter it has voided. During the process the snake, normally dull brown on top and pinkish on the bottom, becomes an overall silver color through a change in light refraction brought about by shifting the angle of individual scales to the snake's body. Apparently, this shift allows the snake to coat itself between scales at places more vulnerable to attack by ants. In any event, the ants are repelled and for a while at least leave the brood-seeking snake alone.

A second question posed by Watkins, Gehlbach and Kroll was: Since the slender blind snake is more vulnerable while hunting on the surface, what defense does it have against such ophiophagous, or snake-eating, snakes, as the ringneck snake or milk snake? The answer has an ironic twist to it. Partially the slender blind snake's defense, which doesn't always work, consists of the same writhing, cloacal-voiding, body-coating action that repels the ants. But partially the defense comes from taking advantage of the fact that the ophiophagous snakes are repelled by secretions laid down by the ants. In other words, the slender blind snakes hide behind a screen of offensive secretions—their own and their prey's.

But what about competitors, other snakes that include ant brood in their diets, ground snakes or black-headed snakes, for example? Again, with the exception of juvenile ground snakes, competitors are repelled by both ant secretions and cloacal discharge from the slender blind snakes. Juvenile ground snakes apparently develop an aversion to ant secretions with age, but while young, they move into the ants' nests just as slender blind snakes do.

The Blind Snakes
1

The Texas blind snake *(L. dulcis),* which attains a maximum length of around thirteen inches, occurs from southern Kansas through Oklahoma, Texas, and New Mexico into southeastern Arizona in the United States. It is found also in many parts of Mexico. There are three subspecies of *L. dulcis,* only one of which occurs in the American West. This subspecies, the New Mexico blind snake *(L. d. dissecta)* ranges from southern Kansas and Oklahoma through southern and central New Mexico to southeastern Arizona.

The western blind snake *(L. humilis),* which sometimes grows to be sixteen inches long, ranges from southwestern Utah, southern Nevada, and adjacent California through southern Arizona, southwestern New Mexico, and into southwestern Texas (it is also found in parts of Mexico, including the peninsula of Baja California). Of

NOTE: *Marginal numbers correspond to the numbered photographs beginning on page 294.*

the seven subspecies of the western blind snake, three are found only in Mexico, but four live also in the American West.

An enterprising young herpetologist could make a substantial niche for himself as a scientist and perform a valuable service for herpetology by doing a thorough study of the classification of the slender blind snakes. This classification (taxonomy) is in great need of study and possible revision.

Scientists collecting the slender blind snakes look for them under rocks, in loose soil, or in rocky crevices. The Texas blind snake is most generally found under flat rocks on hillsides in moderately sandy, semiarid prairies. They have been found, however, in many different situations: on floating debris in a cornfield during a flooding by the Rio Grande, active on an Arizona lawn after a brief rain, in leaf mold, among roots of trees or shrubs—most commonly immediately after a rain. These snakes are not rare; in one instance a collector found thirteen specimens under a single sandstone slab twelve by fourteen inches and about two inches thick. The slab lay in tall prairie grass country with a hilly terrain and ground still moist from recent rains. Within such habitats the Texas blind snake can be found at altitudes ranging from sea level to 5,000 feet in elevation.

The western blind snake is found in terrain similar to that frequented by the Texas blind snake, although the western blind snake may also be found in somewhat more arid situations. Snakes have been caught in spider webs or brought in by domestic cats in the middle of heavily populated La Jolla, California. More frequently, however, the western blind snake has been taken in desert and grassland in sandy, loamy, occasionally gravelly soil, among roots, under rocks, or in rocky crevices. A necessary ingredient appears to be the presence of some moisture. The snake is seldom found in sandy flats, dry lake bottoms, or alluvial fans; it is more usually seen in the vicinity of streams—even dried-up ones. Most often the vegetation associated with the western blind snake's habitat includes mesquite, mountain ash, cottonwood, or ocotillo. Driving slowly on blacktopped roads through such country after dark in May or early June, one can observe blind snakes by looking carefully

The Slender Blind Snakes

Habitat

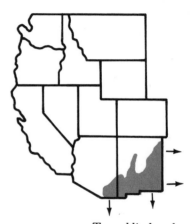

Texas blind snake

Western blind snake

for them in the headlights. They do not reflect quite as much light as most other desert foothill or desert snakes, and because they are small, probably many are overlooked.

Recently a scientist collecting scorpions in Arizona discovered a rather startling fact about the western blind snake. Using an ultraviolet black light, in the rays of which scorpions show with fluorescent brightness, the scientist found not only scorpions but also eight specimens of blind snakes (Hulse, 1971). They didn't fluoresce as brightly as scorpions, but could nonetheless be seen readily from ten feet away. In the black light their rostral scales shone bright blue while the rest of the body glowed pale green.

Reproduction

The slender blind snakes are oviparous, and the females lay clusters of five, six, or even seven eggs in the summer months. Interestingly, all species of *Leptotyphlops* possess only one oviduct, the right one, a peculiar anatomical characteristic they share with the *Tyhlops* and with the unrelated black-headed snake, *Tantilla*. Most female snakes have two oviducts, the left being considerably shorter than the right. Evolutionists, speculating on why certain burrowing snakes have lost the left oviduct entirely, think in terms of the advantage given to the gravid snake by being smaller in girth. Slenderness would facilitate burrowing through the earth; consequently, natural selection in burrowing snakes would tend to bring the gradual loss of reduction in size of organs that increased girth or gave the snake no particular advantage—as, for example, eyes.

Field observations of slender blind snakes show that they tend to be more active during the months of May and June. This activity is probably associated with the mating season, for it is known that spermatogenesis (the production of reproductive sperm cells) in the male snakes reaches its peak during these months.

A clue to reproductive behavior of slender blind snakes was discovered by paleontologist Claude W. Hibbard (1964). In Meade County, Kansas, Hibbard found a colony with more than six clutches of eggs in cracks in the wall of a fossil-bearing quarry in a gully. The clutches were about two and one-half feet below ground level and three feet into the crack. There were three female snakes, two of which were coiled on clutches of five and six eggs respectively. Three more unattended clutches, all of them disturbed, were also in the crack. Even more fascinating was the fact that old eggshells from clutches of years gone by were found below the new clutches, solid evidence that this was a regular den, a kind of maternity ward for slender blind snakes.

Hibbard reckoned there were uncountable numbers of older eggs, thirty-one fresh eggs unattended, and eleven attended eggs in the den. He later demonstrated that this colony was not an isolated phenomenon. He found four New Mexico blind snakes in a similar crack in a fossil deposit on the banks of an arroyo. All four of the snakes were gravid.

Distinctive, small, secretive, and full of anatomical curiosities, the slender blind snakes are of keen interest to science. They are, however, not among the snakes most laymen are likely to encounter or be interested in. After all, not many people get excited over a small snake that eats ant eggs and spends most of its life underground. C. B. Perkins, former curator of reptiles of the San Diego Zoo, captured a four-inch specimen, one of the smallest on record. The most curious aspect of this capture was the fact that the tiny snake was found crawling into the reptile house of the San Diego Zoo, which until then had none on display.

Chapter 5

» » » » » »

THE BOAS

For many people the word *boa* conjures up the mental image of a giant snake, a huge crushing constrictor that spends much time draped like a thick vine over a jungle branch. But even when applied to some of the largest members of the family—the anaconda or the boa constrictor—this image is somewhat distorted. When it is applied to the inoffensive boas that live in the American West, it is far from the mark.

The family of boas and pythons, thought by many to be jungle snakes, actually has representatives in many parts of the world. Many members of the family are relatively small snakes, two or three feet long. The largest member, the reticulated python, grows to a length of thirty-two feet. The boas are primitive snakes; they possess a vestigial pelvic girdle and rudimentary hind limbs represented by small single bones covered by a horny spur that protrudes from the snake's body in front of the cloaca. Male boas appear to use the spurs to stroke the female during courtship. Unlike most snakes, boas have two working lungs; the right one is larger than the left. Boas are ovoviviparous—that is, the eggs are hatched inside the female's body and the young are born live. Boas kill prey by means of constriction, tightening their coils around a victim until it dies of suffocation. Boas do not "crush" their prey to death.

In the western states there are two major species of boas, belonging to two separate genera: the rubber boas and the rosy boas.

The most widely distributed of western American boids is the rubber boa *(Charina bottae)* with its three subspecies.

The rubber boa probably ranges farther north than any of the other boids, although one or two of the Asian boas may reach the same parallel. It also endures cold better than most snakes; it has been found at altitudes as high as 9,000 feet.

Charina is often called the two-headed snake because it has a short blunt tail that resembles its head. This "two-headedness" produces some amusing results. The San Diego Zoo, for example, has had in captivity three honest-to-goodness two-headed snakes, all California kingsnakes. There one day the herpetologist Laurence M. Klauber encountered a zoo patron who was not at all impressed by the real two-headed kingsnake. This patron had seen a rubber boa, and, Klauber observed, he "thought the two-headed king snake unworthy of notice, since both heads were at the same end."

There are, needless to say, no snakes with a head at each end. But the rubber boa helps to keep the legend alive by behaving as though it had two heads. Its tail is shaped like a head, and when the snake is threatened, it may roll itself into a protective ball with its real head inside the coils and the tail sticking out. The false head is then moved about in the air as though it were in fact a head. To bring a final touch of verisimilitude, the snake will sometimes actually strike out with its tail as though, infuriated, it was going to bite its enemy. The advantage of such behavior—long ago preserved by natural selection—is to confuse predators into striking at the snake's tail while its vulnerable head and neck lie protected beneath its coils.

Much legend has accrued to this tail. For reasons not wholly known, hunters among the Thompson Indians of British Columbia, in part of the snake's range, wore the tail as a charm to protect them from grizzly bears, an extraordinary burden for any charm. The reason they assigned such potency to a snake's tail is lost. Perhaps,

The Rubber Boas
2

sometime in the tribe's past, a hunter observed the reflex muscular spasms in the tail of the snake that had been killed and concluded that the tail was a seat of magical life force—hopefully transferable.

The name "rubber boa" is quite fitting. Heavy-bodied and blunt at both ends, the snake resembles a tubular section of rubber. Adult rubber boas are plain brown on their backs and yellowish on their bellies. The young are pinkish or light brown on top, light yellow on the belly. The dorsal scales of this snake are small, smooth, shiny. Like the other boas, male rubber boas have anal spurs. Female rubber snakes may also have anal spurs.

The rubber boa is principally a burrowing snake, although it is also a capable swimmer and tree climber. Its burrowing activities, by the way, make it a poor pet if sand is placed in its cage, for the snake will immediately bury itself. Slow moving, giving the impression of deliberation, the snake never attempts to bite people who pick it up—one of the reasons, undoubtedly, it is often captured. Fortunately for the species, it is seldom seen during the daytime, except on cloudy days. Mostly it is active at twilight or at dawn or goes abroad at night. However, rubber boas have been seen basking in the sun in places as far removed from one another as Monterey, California, and the mountains of Montana. Remember that all snakes lack built-in temperature regulation and must adjust their blood temperature by alternate movement from shadow to sun and back again. Thus these basking snakes were probably trying to raise their blood temperature to aid their ability to move. Interestingly, though, adaptation to its extensive range, a large part of which covers colder temperate regions, has given the rubber boa the ability to continue movement at temperatures that would immobilize many other snakes. Specimens have been taken with body temperatures (reflecting air and surface temperatures around them) as low as 54° F. One specimen escaped capture by burrowing into a snowbank; such behavior would render most other snakes immobile.

At the other end of the scale, the rubber boa reaches its critical high temperature—a body heat beyond which the snake's locomotion becomes disorganized—at around 100.4° F. This is a lower maximum temperature than most snakes have. In brief, the rubber boa's operating temperature range is highly suitable to the colder temperate areas it usually inhabits. One field observer noted that the rubber boa's ability to stand lower temperatures than the Northern Pacific rattlesnake in the same habitat (in this case near Sand Flats, Calaveras County, California) allowed the two species to search for food at different times of day, and therefore these two competitors for food did not jostle one another while hunting.

The rubber boa, which like other boas is a carnivore that kills its prey by constriction, is not at all finicky about what it eats. One specimen, for example, was caught while swallowing a spiny lizard, which is named for its prickly back scales. A captive rubber boa ate a small Great Basin rattlesnake: this fact indicates that mutually exclusive activity periods, such as those described by the observer of Sand Flats, would benefit the rattlesnake. A captive mother rubber boa ate one of her three offspring immediately after it was born. Another rubber boa, two feet long, ate a nine-inch wandering garter snake and then tried to eat a second garter snake twenty-eight inches long—four inches longer than itself. The boa's method of attack was to bite the garter snake a short distance behind the head and then enfold it in constricting coils.

Analysis of the stomach contents of wild-caught rubber boas reveals that they eat insects and small birds as well as lizards, snakes, and small rodents. In spite of this apparent lack of selectivity, however, the captive rubber boa—given a choice between insects, lizards, or newborn mice—will probably take the mice.

The rubber boa is usually found in a moist habitat within its extensive range. It is found often among pines and other conifers in the forests. Its tree-climbing abilities have often been observed. One snake was seen twelve feet above the ground in the hole of a stump, but only because a female chipmunk called attention to it by her noisy chatter. It turned out that the hole contained a chipmunk nest with several young, the probable target of the boa's climb. When the rubber boa climbs, incidentally, it mainly uses the sinuous "caterpillar" method of locomotion.

Some specimens of rubber boa appear to be more than ordinarily attracted to water. One herpetologist caught a specimen half-submerged in a small mountain stream amoung yellow pines near Boise, Idaho. Later, in captivity, this same snake spent long periods half-submerged in the water dish in its cage.

Reports about the capture of this snake tend to follow the same pattern everywhere in its range: under rotting logs among ponderosa pines in the San Bernardino Mountains; beneath rocks or logs particularly near slide areas among yellow pines in the Mission Mountains of Montana; under surface objects or in rotten logs in the yellow pine forests in Deschutes County, Oregon; sometimes under pieces of loose bark on a fallen tree, or under bark that has fallen to the ground.

The rubber boa bears its young live, generally three or four at a time. Most reports indicate that the young are born in late July or August, although one litter under observation was born in mid-September. The four young in this litter all shed ten days after birth, but refused insects and worms offered to them as food. Another newly born snake, with its umbilicus still bloody, was found near Parvin, Washington, in late November. The combination of such a late birth date and the northern latitude at least raises the possibility that the young snakes are capable of surviving their first winter without taking food.

The other boa found in the American West is the often extremely beautiful rosy boa *(Lichanura trivirgata).* There are three subspecies.

The Rosy Boa

3

Adults of this species may reach a length of forty-four inches in the females, somewhat less in the males. Heavy-bodied like all boas, the rosy boa has a triangular-shaped head, as viewed from above. The rosy boa is easily distinguished from the rubber boa by the presence on the top of its head, between the eyes, of many small scales, instead of the large plates found on the rubber boa. Male rosy boas always have anal spurs; females have them occasionally. The bright, shiny, almost metallic scales of rosy boas range in color from the uniform dark brown found on snakes along the coastal side of mountain ranges to the strikingly contrasted color scheme of the desert boas. Desert boas often have three chocolate brown stripes with serrated edges, set against a beige background. From the reddish brown in this snake, which seems to give a rosy or even pinkish cast on occasion, comes the name "rosy boa." Albinism occasionally occurs in rosy boas. L. M. Klauber reported an albino coastal rosy boa *(L. t. roseofusca)* caught in San Diego County, California.

In contrast with the rubber boa, largely a burrower, the rosy boa is terrestrial, spending most of its time above ground except when it is hiding in rock crevices or cracks. Wherever it is found, the rosy boa shows a distinct preference for rocky haunts and bouldered areas. In the desert the snake is seldom seen in areas free of rocks and generally is found in the desert foothills. Some specimens of the coastal rosy boa have been taken in chaparral without rocky outcroppings or boulders, but it is much more commonly found in rocky areas. Observers have noted that the snake appears to use fissures in the rocks both as a resting place and, somewhat as the chuckwalla lizard does, for defense. It is extremely difficult to dislodge a rosy boa that has wedged itself into a crack in a boulder. There is no evidence, however, that it puffs itself up the way a chuckwalla does by taking in great quantities of air. In addition to favoring rocky terrain, the rosy boa tends to like streams and desert oases.

The three subspecies vary somewhat as to the maximum altitude at which each may be found. In Inyo County, California, the desert rosy boa *(L. t. gracia)* has been found at the 3,800-foot level, at which there is some snowfall during winter. The coastal rosy boa *(L. t. roseofusca)* has been found quite commonly at the 3,000-foot level in the Santa Ana Mountains of southern California. No real study has been made of the maximum altitude at which the Mexican rosy boa *(L. t. trivirgata)* may be found.

The docility of the rosy boa has made it a favorite of people who like to keep pet snakes, even though it does not eat particularly well in captivity. Its popularity as a pet, combined with the tendency of some people to kill any snake they see, has reduced rosy boa populations in the American West. Though it is slow-moving and docile under most conditions, the rosy boa is capable of astonishing speed when it attacks and throws its constricting coils around a mouse or bird. Indeed the docile nature of the rosy boa appears to develop with age. In at least one captive-bred family of boas, the newborn young were extremely aggressive at first and struck savagely at their captor, their mother, and one another. For six weeks this aggression continued. Then, as they were regularly fed, their savagery diminished, and they became completely docile, except when attacking prey.

Like rattlesnakes and other heavy-bodied species, the rosy boa quite frequently uses rectilinear (caterpillar) locomotion, moving over the ground in a straight line. The rosy boa shares one habit with the rubber boa, notably the defensive move of coiling into a ball with its head inside. Not all rosy boas use this defense; and none of them wave their blunt tails as though they were heads (even so, the rosy boa is sometimes called a two-headed snake for the same reason that the rubber boa is). The rosy boa also employs a defense common to many snakes: it discharges a foul-smelling liquid from scent glands near the cloacal opening.

The coiled-ball defensive posture sometimes produces amusing results. John Burnham, a friend of L. M. Klauber, tells of finding a rosy boa stretched out on a hillside. Prodded by Burnham's foot, the snake coiled into a ball and, having nothing to hold it back, rolled down the slope. It is tempting to think that this was a deliberate escape procedure, but actually the snake was probably as surprised by the roll as Burnham was. The relationship of this incident to the legend of the hoop snake is obvious. Had not Burnham been a thoroughly trustworthy and sober observer, he could easily have "seen," and sworn to it afterwards, that the snake took its tail in its mouth and rolled down the hill like a hoop.

Rosy boas are mostly nocturnal or crepuscular (active at twilight), although they are frequently observed in full daylight, especially during spring, and are quite often abroad on overcast days or immediately following rain showers. They have been caught in driving rains.

A constrictor, like all boas, the rosy boa eats small mammals, birds, and snakes; apparently it seeks prey smaller in proportion to its head than do most snakes. During spring the rosy boa probably carries out many raids among litters of young rats and mice. Favoring smaller prey, it must eat more at one sitting, so to speak, or eat more frequently; this need suggests that a nest full of young wood rats would suit the snake's purposes ideally. This conjecture is further supported by the fact that the rosy boa practices dual constriction; it is capable of holding two or even three small mammals simultaneously in its constricting coils. One rodent can be constricted in a loop at the lower part of the snake's body, a second farther up, and so on. One observer saw a twenty-two-inch snake constricting two small rats while seeking a third. During the hunt, incidentally, the snake's normally somewhat cumbersome, slow-moving appearance is transformed. In striking and throwing its coils, actions that can assure its continued survival, the rosy boa moves with the speed of a boxer's jab.

Occasionally in its search for food, a snake can come upon frustration not of nature's doing. One specimen was caught while haplessly trying to swallow a deer mouse that was firmly caught in a trap. As there was no way to extricate the mouse, the snake was trying to swallow trap and all.

Although rosy boas prefer rodents, they also will eat birds, and one captive specimen even preferred nestling birds to young mice. Occasionally rosy boas eat other snakes. At the San Diego Zoo a captive specimen ate one of a brood of sidewinder rattlesnakes.

Rosy boas are live-bearing, and like the rubber boa, they bear young in the fall. In one of the most unusual and valuable series of observations ever made on captive snakes, the herpetologist John F. Kurfess (1967) was able to watch the conception, birth, and subsequent growth of a brood of coastal rosy boas. Kurfess placed a young male snake in a cage with a female on May 29, 1963. At first the female evaded the male. Not wishing to hurry the process, Kurfess separated the two snakes. He placed them together again nineteen days later. This time the female was more receptive. During the courtship preliminaries the male slowly and deliberately flicked his tongue rapidly over most of the female's body. The female responded with several flicks of her own. Since the female proved ready to receive advances, the male gradually assumed a position on top of the female. Then the male brought his anal spurs into play, moving them rapidly back and forth, stroking the female on the rear part of her body above the base of her tail. Slowly the female responded, twisting the rear portion of her body to one side into the mating position and elevating her tail. During the ensuing copulation the snakes remained motionless for a half-hour; then they separated.

Within a week the female went into a tight, circular coil, with her head on top, beneath a lamp in the warmest part of the cage. There, in a temperature of 78° F., she remained completely inactive, taking neither food nor drink, a common characteristic of gestating snakes. Her position, Kurfess noted, was the same one that pythons assume while incubating their eggs. On October 26, after 131 days of gestation, five young were born, a normal litter for a species that generally bears five to ten young at a time. Kurfess believed that these young were conceived by the copulation he witnessed, although there exists the remote possibility that the female had stored sperm from a previous mating in the wild (the ability to store sperm for later use is characteristic of some female snakes). The day after giving birth, the female resumed her normal pattern of eating. At birth, the young averaged 13.85 inches in length, again normal for rosy boas. These young snakes (the same ones noted above for their youthful aggressiveness) grew rapidly. Nine months after their birth they averaged 29.15 inches in length, having more than doubled their length. During the same period the young father added only 9.5 inches to his length, growing from 18 to 27.5 inches long, and thus was shorter than his offspring.

Chapter 6

» » » » »

TWO PRIMITIVE COLUBRIDS

By far the largest family of snakes in the world is the Colubridae. The family includes snakes familiar to everyone—racers, bull-snakes, garter snakes—and it includes some less well known, among them, even in the American West, some species that are mildly venomous (but not harmful to human beings).

Among the smaller and less well known colubrids—less well known because they spend most of their lives concealed beneath stones, boards, or other objects—are two of the most primitive: the ringneck snake *(Diadophis punctatus)* and a fairly close but unique relative called the sharp-tailed snake *(Contia tenuis)*. These two species are the subject of this chapter; other colubrids of the American West are dealt with in the following seven chapters.

So unique is the sharp-tailed snake that it is placed in a monotypic genus, meaning that the genus has only one species (Stickel, 1951). This classification, however, has been applied only recently. *Contia* was once a catchall genus in which taxonomists placed any small colubrid snake that they couldn't otherwise assign and that exter-

The Sharp-Tailed Snake

4

nally resembled the sharp-tailed snake. At one time or another *Contia* has included snakes now assigned to the American genera *Opheodrys, Seminatrix, Sonora, Chionactis, Conopis, Toluca,* and *Pseudoficimia,* and the western Asian genus *Eirenis.* Thus from a worldwide distribution of many snakes, the genus *Contia,* through taxonomic ingenuity, has shrunk to the point where it comprises just one snake of a fairly limited geographical distribution in the American West. It remains now only for some enterprising herpetologist to demonstrate that *Contia tenuis* shouldn't be a *Contia* at all, and the formerly large genus will be done away with entirely.

For those who wonder how an animal is assigned to a particular species or genus, the sharp-tailed snake can serve as an example. In classifying a snake, such external characteristics as length, shape, coloration give the first clues to a snake's relationship to other snakes. Then the taxonomist studies scale patterns, numbers of scales to a row, numbers of rows, and so on until even minute differences in scale arrangements have been resolved—for the scales on a snake, while not quite so distinctive as fingerprints on a man, are sufficiently differentiated to distinguish species or subspecies from one another. In addition skeletal and other anatomical studies are made to determine possible similarities to and differences from other species. For example, twenty years ago studies of *Contia's* hemipenes, teeth, and jaws established that *Contia* is quite unique and of unknown relationship, although a progenitor could have been a snake like the ringneck snake. Geographical distribution must also be considered in classifying a new species or subspecies. Finally, using all the tools of modern science, the taxonomist makes a study of blood serum and the specimen's karyotype—that is, the number and arrangement of chromosomes. The sharp-tailed snake's karyotype resembles those found in racers, rat snakes, and others of the Colubrinae, one of several subfamilies of the Colubridae.

A small snake, like the ringneck snakes with which it is so often associated both geographically and scientifically, the sharp-tailed snake reaches a maximum length of nineteen inches. It bears long, sharp teeth and a sharp spine at the end of its tail (hence its common name). Like the slender blind snakes, the sharp-tailed snake may probe grasping human fingers with this nonvenomous spine, but it is so tiny that it can't effectively prick the skin.

Contia is easily identified because of its belly markings of distinctive crossbars of alternating black and cream. These belly markings contrast with its reddish brown or gray back, which many times has a line of yellow or red on each side. The tail appears to shade into red.

A snake with a greater-than-average tolerance for low temperatures, *Contia* has a wide distribution and altitude range, which in many northern areas parallels that of the rubber boa. *Contia*'s tolerance of cold is shown by some specimens taken near Beegum, Shasta County, California, in February where the temperature averages around 50° F. These snakes—by no means torpid or sluggish—had cloacal temperatures of 52° to 61° F., which is low for snakes in general. Food in their digestive tracts indicated that they had recently eaten, and thus were sufficiently active to hunt and kill. Much cold country occurs in the sharp-tailed snake's range, which, at altitudes up to 6,600 feet, extends from the vicinity of San Luis Obispo, California, northward through the Sierra Nevadas and in spots along the coast into British Columbia, including Vancouver Island. The northernmost record comes from McGillivray Lake near Chase, British Columbia. Throughout most of this range the distribution is spotty, being generally confined to moist habitats. Occasionally, however, the sharp-tailed snake is found in arid surroundings, notably on the floor of the Central Valley, California—but even here it frequents the moister areas.

The type of distribution that finds a species in places other than what appears to be normal habitat is not really unusual. In the course of its history, the species may follow streams and spread out from ancestral habitats. Originally a frequenter of mountains and mesas, perhaps, it descends as it follows the water it requires until it has reached arid plains or deserts. There, if moisture and food supply are still to be found, it adapts to new surroundings, perhaps becoming subtly different in coloration, but otherwise retaining its specific characteristics. Perhaps for this reason *Contia*, normally a snake of higher altitudes, has been found at such diverse places as Wheatland, Yuba County, California, and near Sloughhouse and along Arcade Creek, in Sacramento County, California. Equally surprising for a species expected in moist grassy meadows among cedars and pines, the sharp-tailed snake has been observed at an altitude of 6,300 feet in Kings Canyon National Park and in the famous Mariposa Grove of big trees at an amazing 6,600 feet in Yosemite National Park.

Sharp-tailed snakes apparently are gregarious. The naturalist Joseph Slevin and others have reported numerous instances of finding several snakes in the same immediate area. Once Slevin found eight specimens under a single log near Carlotta, in Humboldt County, California; and in Comptche, Mendocino County, California, he exceeded this record when he found eleven sharp-tailed snakes under a small pile of boards. Other reports include a group of twenty-three near Lebanon, Linn County, Oregon, and forty in one small area of Alameda County, California.

Although land developers cause depletion of many snake populations, they actually help to increase populations of the sharp-tailed snake. In fact, wherever in its range houses are built and the conditions of moisture are met, the sharp-tailed snake probably increases in numbers. This increase occurs because its food supply also increases, and it, being both secretive and small, is able to remain hidden from human eyes.

Because of its eating habits, the sharp-tailed snake is the gardener's friend. *Contia* has highly specialized food selection; it concentrates on just one kind of prey—garden slugs. *Contia's* long, sharp, well-spaced teeth are particularly adapted to grasping slugs. Consequently, where slugs have increased, the sharp-tailed snakes have spread, no matter how "civilized" the area. Forty sharp-tailed snakes were taken from a backyard and adjacent vacant lots in a downtown residential area by Joseph Colaci and some friends (see S. Cook, 1960); the area was surrounded by shopping centers, housing developments, and superhighways. The snakes were found under such objects as used tires and chunks of concrete slab. Present, of course, were weeds and slugs.

One aspect of *Contia's* propensity to eat slugs is particularly fascinating to evolutionists and other students of animal adaptation and behavior (Cook, 1960). The habitat and distribution of the sharp-tailed snake sharply correlates with those of a genus of slugs *(Arion)* that was originally native to Europe. In short, the principal food of a native snake is a creature that did not exist in the American West two or three hundred years ago. Yet the sharp-tailed snake so favors *Arion* as prey that it will steadfastly refuse other food offered to it. In one experiment the herpetologist William Woodin, former director of the Arizona—Sonora Desert Museum, tried to induce four sharp-tailed snakes to eat earthworms, mealworms, termites, Jerusalem crickets, millipedes, centipedes, crane-fly and other larvae, and salamanders—all to no avail. Yet all four snakes readily ate small slugs. The only identifiable remains in the stomachs of sixty-seven preserved snakes were those of slugs (S. Cook, 1960).

Sharp-tailed snakes have been captured during every month of the year, but logically enough they are most often abroad when slugs are most active. Frequently this activity comes during the first warm spells in late winter following rains. In California activity increases to peaks in February, March, and April, and then again in November. In Oregon a single activity peak comes in April or May; this single peak probably also characterizes the isolated populations in Washington and the populations in British Columbia.

The ringneck snake, a distant cousin to the sharp-tailed snake, is found in the same habitat and has remarkably similar seasonal activity. Yet the two species have different food preferences and so there is no competition between them (Zweifel, 1952). The ringneck snake pursues salamanders; the sharp-tailed snake chases slugs—if going after slugs can be called a chase. The one discordant note that enters this otherwise harmonious illustration of similar animal species occupying different ecological niches in the same habitat is the fact that ringneck snakes may occasionally eat sharp-tailed snakes in lieu of salamanders.

Contia is oviparous. The two to nine eggs, laid in summer, hatch in the fall. The best information to date on the egg-laying habits of the sharp-tailed snake comes from three observers, Edmund D. Brodie, Jr., Ronald A. Nussbaum, and Robert M. Storm (1969), who found an amazing aggregation of eggs and young from five species of reptiles on a talus slope only one mile south of Corvallis, Oregon. Here were 51 lizard eggs, 294 snake eggs, and 76 snakes. Among these were forty-three eggs of sharp-tailed snakes—forty-one hatched, one unhatched, one spoiled. Six of the hatchlings were still in cracks of rock outcroppings six to twelve inches below the surface. Curiously enough, one clutch was in a soil cavity and another in some grass roots six inches below the ground. The clutches contained two, three, four, eight, and nine eggs respectively.

The wonder of this discovery is that so many eggs and so many reptiles of so many separate species were involved. It appeared that in human terms this select and hallowed ground was dedicated to the perpetuation of several reptile species. A more prosaic explanation was offered by the discoverers: The talus slope in which eggs and snakes were found was the only southward-facing (therefore more sun-warmed) slope in an area where sites suitable for egg laying had been greatly reduced by several nearby housing projects on the outskirts of a growing city.

The Ringneck Snake

5

Perhaps the most common snake in the American West, or for that matter in the United States, is one few people have seen, even though its common haunts are backyards and gardens. It is a small snake, most often dark gray on its upper side, but with a ring of bright yellow around its neck immediately behind the head. This ring gives it the common name ringneck snake *(Diadophis punctatus)*. On occasional specimens the ring may be missing; some of these atypical specimens may even be black on their topside. But the more typical ringneck snake has in addition to its "necklace" a further touch of brilliance, an orange yellow underbelly, which on some specimens is coral to red in color, and frequently is spotted irregularly with black dots. On the dull background color of a typical ringneck snake, the orange or red underbelly and the yellow ring on the neck stand out like freshly enameled porcelain. The color contrast is made even more bizarre when the snake is disturbed, for an alarmed ringneck snake may thrust its tail up into a conical coil, prominently displaying the orange undersurface.

This habit, by the way, leads to some interesting speculation. Typically a ringneck snake may defend itself by biting, discharging musk, feigning death, or displaying its tail (Gehlbach, 1970). One wonders what leads the snake to choose feigned death, which requires a totally passive posture, instead of displaying the coiled tail, which in appearance is threatening. Biting and discharging musk are last-ditch defenses, normally undertaken when a snake is seized in jaw, bill, or human hand. But when the decision between feigned death or threatening posture is being made, the snake still has some room to maneuver. It is probable that the ringneck snake's choice is programmed genetically in relationship to the nature of the attack. Over a period of thousands of years some snakes in a species survive because they have acted successfully, by bluffing or otherwise, in the face of the enemy; these "successful" chromosomes are passed on to the snakes' progeny. In addition, one type of defense may work against one type of enemy, a second against another type; through natural selection the more effective behavior becomes instinctive, a part of the genetic heritage that programs the behavior of future generations. It has been theorized that the coiled-tail bluffing defense of the ringneck snake, for example, developed for primary use against birds, since many other predators lack red vision. Any bluff, of course, is designed primarily to buy time. Momentarily disconcerted by the threatening display or feigned death, the predator pauses in its attack or even breaks it off altogether, giving the bluffer a chance to escape. If the bluff fails, the threatened snake must use its direct methods of defense—biting or discharging musk.

The use of tail coiling by the ringneck snake has, at least in Florida, another puzzling aspect (Myers, 1965). Two differently colored varieties of *D. punctatus* occur in Florida. One, on the peninsula, has a reddish underbelly and characteristically uses tail coiling when disturbed. The other, found in northern Florida, has a yellow underbelly and does not use tail coiling. In the area between North and South the bellies vary from yellow to red and some yellow-tailed specimens do not use tail coiling. The question, of course, is: Why this variation in behavior in separate geographical zones? Moreover, if this is the case between separate races of *D. punctatus* in one part of the country, are similar disparities to be found in other parts, as in the American West, where some authorities recognize eight separate subspecies of *D. punctatus?* In the growing science of ethology (the study of animal behavior) snakes should not be neglected.

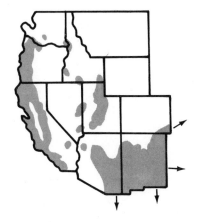

The ringneck snake, which varies in length from twelve to thirty inches, is found over much of the American West, ranging from southern Washington and Idaho to northern Baja California and Mexico from sea level to altitudes of 7,000 feet. Included in its range is Santa Catalina Island off the coast of California. It ranges eastward to the Atlantic and Maine. There are eight subspecies in the American West.

Two Primitive Colubrids

In all but the regal ringneck snake *(D. p. regalis)* the subspecific differences are measured in the count of scale rows and slight differences in coloration. The Pacific ringneck *(D. p. amabilis),* for example, has fewer rows of scales than the San Bernardino *(D. p. modestus).* The San Bernardino has conspicuous black spots on its belly; the northwestern *(D. p. occidentalis)* has few. The regal ringneck does differ quite markedly from the others, so much so, in fact, that some authorities consider it as a separate species, *Diadophis regalis.* A larger snake, reaching two and one-half feet in length, it is a paler gray, often with a blue green cast. It is found in New Mexico, southern Utah, and Arizona, but also ranges into central Texas and into the Mexican state of Veracruz.

The ringneck snakes prefer a moist habitat, but like *Contia tenuis* may be found in moist areas of arid regions. The ringneck snake is a common inhabitant of towns and cities, living in gardens, backyards, and vacant lots under rocks and old boards.

Often in such places several ringnecks will be found under a particular rock or board. Seeking to determine whether or not this was accidental—the result of random selection—Harold A. Dundee and M. Clinton Miller III (1968) set up an experiment. Covering the bottom of a seven-foot-wide livestock watering tank with sand, they placed at regular intervals around the inside of the tank's perimeter twelve slate-colored plates under which ringneck snakes could hide. Several times they released simultaneously up to forty snakes in the center of the tank. After a few minutes the snakes would seek shelter—but not randomly. Rather, they tended to form groups under some plates while leaving others uninhabited. Moreover, after several experiments it became clear that plates under which aggregations formed were apparently marked by a pheromone so that snakes could more readily find the plate where the other snakes gathered. Such aggregations, Dundee and Milton conjectured, may be purely social or they may have some other motivation, such as a need for moisture when moist earth is found only under a few surface objects. But the undeniable fact is the ringneck snakes are deliberately social during periods other than hibernation. The search for moisture may help explain why they are much more commonly found in spring than in summer, when they tend to become subterranean.

The ringneck snake's diet consists of earthworms, salamanders, small frogs and lizards, perhaps some insects, and small snakes. Although it uses partial constriction in subduing prey, some observers speculate that it may also have a weak venom, which is harmless to man. The causes of this speculation are two: it has enlarged, sabrelike teeth at the rear end of its mouth, teeth which on other snakes are accompanied by mild venom; and one observer reported a burning sensation after being bitten. The presence of venom would not be strange, since, as we discuss in chapter 14, venom itself probably evolved from salivalike fluids that contained enzymes for starting digestion of foods being swallowed.

Ringneck snakes are egg-layers. Little is known about their mating time, but four to six eggs are probably laid sometime between late May and early August. It is thought that females usually lay one clutch a year. The herpetologist Raymond L. Ditmars believed the ringneck snake to be "one of those serpents that stand midway between the viviparous and the egg-laying snakes [actually ovoviviparous], as the eggs contain large embryos when deposited and hatch in less than half the time required for the development of the eggs of the majority of snakes." And in a letter written by Arthur Erwin Brown in 1891 comes this observation: "In August, 1891, two small *Diadophis punctatus,* evidently newly born, appeared in a case containing several adults. No indication of eggs had been observed, nor were any fragments of egg membranes found when the young were first seen." Mr. Brown goes on to state his belief that the ringneck snake is normally egg-laying, but that captivity produced abnormal ovoviviparous births of the two young observed. Most recent observations, and they are scanty, confirm that *D. punctatus* is an egg-layer. In one observed hatching, eggs from a fifteen-inch mother were deposited June 28 and were hatched August 8. The young, breaking out of eggs that measured one and one-half inches long, were themselves four and one-half inches in length. They had a much darker ground color than the adult snakes, being almost black. Their rings were yellowish white.

Chapter 7

»»»»»

SNAKES WITH STRANGE NOSES

Limbless, all snakes have had to make tools of their bodies in order to accomplish feats other animals handle with paws and feet. On several snakes the particular part most used as a tool is the nose. Frequently the nose becomes a specialized drill for burrowing in soil and sand or a spade for rooting out prey. On the two primitive colubrids discussed in this chapter—and on several more highly evolved snakes described in later chapters—the nose becomes such a dominant feature that it gives the snake its common name.

One of these snakes, the western hognose snake *(Heterodon nasicus)*, belongs to one of the few subfamilies in the large and taxonomically cumbersome family of colubrids. The subfamily of the hognose snake is called the Xenodontinae. In it are several snakes similar in many ways to the hognose snake—including the genera *Lystrophis* of South America and *Xenodon* of the American tropics.

To the unenlightened observer the western hognose snake looks and acts like the most venomous of snakes. Thick of body, the hognose snake has a sharply pointed head that ends in a pugnacious-appearing, turned-up snout. The dull body, made so by keeled scales, is covered with dark blotches that increase its venomous appearance. Its coloration, however, is only part of an act that shows the greatest bravado in snakedom.

When it is encountered in the wild in a place where it cannot readily escape, the hognose snake will very likely threaten its suspected attacker with apparently uncontrollable anger. Flattening its head and neck to further add to its ominous appearance, it will hiss or blow loudly and strike out savagely toward the attacker. Again and again it will repeat this action in an altogether convincing performance that has earned it the names "puff adder," "death adder," "sand viper"—all more dramatic surely than the unflattering name "hognose snake." The act, however, is not over. If the attacker persists undeterred by the striking and hissing, the hognose snake shifts to "scene two." Ceasing its threatening approach, it now acts as though it had been severely injured. Its mouth falls open. Strength leaves its body. A convulsion starts that ends with a twitching of its tail. Then, adding the final touch to a great death scene, it turns over on its back and lies perfectly still, mouth gaping, to all appearances lifeless. The act is convincing. Picked up, the snake will dangle loosely; draped over a fence, it will hang limp, inanimate, dead. But before giving an Oscar for the great performance, consider one flaw. For reasons no one can adequately explain, the hognose snake plays dead *only* on its back. If, after it has "died," it is turned on its belly, it will promptly come to life long enough to flip over so that it is once again belly up. Each time it is flipped over it will turn back, no matter how often. This part of the act is inexplicable. One can understand the threatening attitude and simulated death, for the hognose snake generally inhabits country that is flat and sandy with much open space. In this kind of terrain it is likely that the snake will be caught in the open, particularly because it is fond of sunning itself on the sand. With shelters few and far between and predators many, this harmless snake developed defensive reactions that misled an enemy and either drove it off through the threatening pose or caused it to lose interest through the simulated death. If an observer withdraws some distance when a hognose snake is playing dead and watches patiently, he will be rewarded by seeing the snake turn over onto its belly, raise its head

The Western Hognose Snake

6

to survey the situation, and then move off toward shelter. Captured and placed in a cage, the hognose snake may feign death once or twice, but then it will cease this defensive "fixed action pattern." Interestingly, its subfamily relatives from the genus *Lystrophis* in South America use the same pattern of threat and feigned death.

Apparently, then, the whole two-part act is genetically programmed (it is inconceivable that hognose snakes teach one another how to act fierce and play dead). And we can readily grasp the reasons for the program. But what causes the flaw? What causes the snake to ruin an otherwise perfect imitation of death by the habitual practice of flipping over onto its back each time it is turned over? Perhaps like the orange tail of the ringneck snake, the pale underbelly of the hognose snake has served to startle and drive off bird predators. Perhaps predators in general are more repelled by the paleness of the belly than they would be by the pale brown or yellow back with its black blotches. Perhaps, finally, many predators do not accept an imitation of death that displays the snake in its normal posture, but are properly confused when it convulses into an unnatural belly-up position.

In spite of its dramatic ability, the western hognose snake is as inoffensive to man as a snake can be. It can seldom be induced to bite, and its bite is not dangerous to man. Possibly its threatening pose has worked against it with human predators, for unknowing people are inclined to kill creatures they believe threaten them. What is more prominent in human nature, in fact, than the desire to play the hero? Many an inoffensive creature has fallen before human weapons not so much because it constituted a real threat, but because its death could be seen as an escape from danger, which becomes both a topic of future story telling and a memory that adds meaning to life.

In the American West the western hognose snake is found mainly in the eastern half of Montana, Wyoming, Colorado, and New Mexico. One subspecies, the Mexican hognose snake *(H. n. kennerlyi)*, comes into the southeastern part of Arizona, but is found mainly in Mexico. East of the Rockies the western hognose snake is found over much of the Midwest and Texas. It is generally found in scrublands, with many rocks and much sand. It is a burrowing snake, and the sharply keeled and upturned rostral is used like a kind of

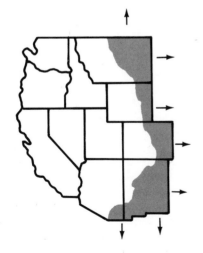

drill. Digging it into the earth, the snake twists its head in a semi-rotary motion to loosen the soil. As a burrower, however, the hognose is not truly a subterranean dweller like the slender blind snake; rather, it burrows in its search for food.

Ranging in length from around 8 inches at hatching to a maximum of 35¼ inches in a fully developed adult, the snake typically is pale brown or yellowish with a series of closely set, darker blotches on the back and two rows of smaller alternating blotches on the sides. The head, paler than the body, is strongly marked with bands of dark brown, two across the top of the head, others from behind the eye to the angle of the mouth. Each temple has a wide blotch or band of the same color; between these is a short dark bar. A distinguishing mark is the black on the underside of the hognose snake's tail. The eastern hognose snake *(H. platyrhinos),* whose range may overlap that of the western hognose in Colorado, lacks this black pigmentation on the lower surface of its tail.

The hognose snake specializes in eating toads, although it will also eat salamanders, frogs, lizards, birds, and small mammals. There is even one record of a hognose snake stealing eggs from a turtle's nest.

As a toad eater, the snake has some special equipment. On each side at the rear of its upper jaw, it has enlarged, fanglike teeth that serve at least two purposes and possibly a third. The long, sharp, curved teeth serve to deflate toads, which defensively blow themselves up when under attack. The teeth also hold prey firmly during the swallowing process.

In a paper published in 1960, Arthur N. Bragg threw some doubt on the previously accepted idea that the hognose snake is nonvenomous. Accidentally bitten on the left thumb by a western hognose snake, Bragg suffered both pain and swelling in the hand. An experiment performed by Wayne H. McAlister (1963) showed that tissue taken from the salivary gland of the eastern hognose was fatally toxic to small toads within twenty-four hours following injection. The most recent evidence comes from a 1964 study by Edward J. Kapus which shows that some hognose snakes have enlarged parotid glands (the glands that would be most concerned in the production of venom). If all this evidence is correct, the hognose snake is an example of a primitive stage in the evolutionary development of venomous snakes. The venom, if in fact it can be called that, would be useful only in subduing prey and not defensively, particularly against so large an animal as a man.

Perhaps the most interesting adaptation to toad eating, however, is the hognose snake's greatly enlarged adrenal gland, larger than that found on any other American snake. A few other snakes, notably some garter and water snakes and rattlesnakes of the genus *Sistrurus,* also have enlarged adrenal glands, though not so large as the hognose's. These snakes have one common habit: they include adult toads in their diets, and the correlation between enlarged adrenal glands and toad eating is a close one, as two scientists, Hobart M. Smith and Fred N. White (1955) found in an important study of the subject. Toads have extremely powerful poisons in their skins, which discourage most predators. These poisonous skin secretions, more potent in some species of toads than in others, have brought death to dogs, other mammals, even in one recorded instance a man (who thought he was eating a frog).

Complex in chemical composition, these skin secretions from adult toads have two effects: one element, epinephrine, accelerates the heartbeat of the predator, often to a lethal level; if this fails to kill the predator, then a second element, a digitaloid, slows the predator's heart perhaps to the point of death. Smith and White point out that a greatly enlarged adrenal gland could produce enough adrenalin to neutralize the actions of both elements. Consequently the capacity to secrete neutralizing amounts of adrenalin would enable an animal to eat toads. For the hognose snake, then, the greatly enlarged adrenal gland is supremely important. In fact, some hognose snakes would be unable to live in part of their range if they could not eat toads, which comprise up to eighty percent of their diet.

The hognose snake is oviparous. Mating takes place in late March, April, and May. Eggs are generally laid in June or July in clutches of from seven to thirty-nine, although sixty-one well-formed eggs were found in one female in Minnesota. Incubation takes from two to three months. At hatching the young hognoses, already fully equipped for a life of toad hunting and bluffing, are from six and one-half to eight and one-half inches long.

As one crosses the high desert during late afternoon, when the sun is coming in golden and aslant, the pastels of the land, no longer washed by the glare of noon, emerge with subtle beauty—pinks, light blues, tans, reds, rich but subdued, all painted in gentle harmony. These are the colors of most desert snakes—including the leaf-nosed snakes—which have evolved to blend with their desert surroundings.

Distinguished by a greatly enlarged rostral shield that folds back over the nose like a bent leaf, the two species of leaf-nosed snakes in the American West are similar in adult size—twelve to twenty inches—and scalation but differ markedly in the pattern of blotches on their backs. The spotted leaf-nosed snake *(Phyllorynchus decurtatus)*, with five subspecies, has more than seventeen blotches on its back set against a tan, white, pink, gray, or yellowish background color. A second species, the saddled leaf-nosed snakes *(P. browni)*, with four subspecies, has fewer than seventeen blotches (not counting those on the tail) that resemble saddles, generally set against a pink or cream background. The ranges of the two species overlap in several areas, mainly in Arizona, and Sonora and Sinaloa, Mexico, but there is no evidence of crossbreeding between them. Males of both species have keeled dorsal scales; otherwise the leaf-nosed snakes are smooth.

Two of the four subspecies of the spotted leaf-nosed snake are found in the United States, often in association with the kind of country that produces the creosote bush. One cannot say definitely that creosote bush and snake form a firm ecological association, however, since each one is also found in places where the other does not occur. In any event the spotted leaf-nosed snake ranges from southern Nevada to the tip of Baja California and eastward into southern Arizona, and Sonora and Sinaloa, Mexico, at altitudes up to 3,000 feet.

The clouded leaf-nosed snake *(P. d. nubilus)* has from 42 to 60 blotches on its back, excluding the tail, and 167 or fewer ventral scales on males, 178 or fewer ventral scales on females. The western leaf-nosed snake *(P. d. perkinsi)* has from 24 to 48 blotches, excluding the tail, with 168 or more ventral scales on males, 179 or more on females. This subspecies, by the way, was named after the late herpetologist C. B. Perkins, former curator of reptiles at the San Diego

Zoo. Perkins, a salty conversationalist, took delight in pointing out that males of the western leaf-nosed snake, his namesake, are proportionately better endowed sexually than most other snakes.

Two subspecies of the saddled leaf-nosed snake are found in the land of mesquite, creosote bush, paloverde, and the giant saguaro cactus, mostly in the vicinity of Tucson, Arizona, across the southern base of the Arizona Plateau in the Phoenix-Superior region, south into Sinaloa, Mexico, and west to the Tule Desert near Yuma, Arizona. (A third subspecies is found in Mexico.) The Pima leaf-nosed snake *(P. browni browni)* has blotches on its back that are much wider than the spaces between them, with 166 or fewer ventrals in the males, 179 or fewer in the females. The Maricopa leaf-nosed snake *(P. b. lucidus)* has blotches and spaces of roughly equal proportion with 167 or more ventrals on the males, 180 or more on females.

A strange fact about the leaf-nosed snakes is that they were originally described in 1868, yet from that date until 1922 were thought to be extremely rare. In that fifty-four-year span only ten specimens were caught and identified. Then in 1922, L. M. Klauber discovered a technique of snake hunting that showed that leaf-nosed snakes are really quite common. Noting an asphalt road near the Borego Desert east of San Diego, California, Klauber got to wondering. Desert snakes are mostly nocturnal. Their colors and patterns have evolved to blend with sandy desert surroundings, and therefore would stand out starkly against the black surface of an asphalt road. With his companions, Klauber drove slowly along the asphalt road at night, watching for snakes. In one night he collected enough leaf-nosed snakes to convince him that they were far from rare. In subsequent nights he collected more in one night than had been placed in museums during the previous fifty-four years. This technique, by the way, has since been widely used; it works so well, in fact, that countless amateurs and collectors for pet stores now pose a threat to snake populations in some desert areas.

With the large "leaf" on its nose the leaf-nosed snakes are hard to mistake. However, there are other desert snakes with enlarged rostral scales, so the classifier looking for distinguishing features will note also color, pattern, size, and—in the leaf-nosed snakes—large eyes with elliptical pupils. The leaf-nosed snakes are among the few North American colubrids with elliptical pupils.

Because of the shield provided by their leaf nose, and because they will dig into sand in captivity, the leaf-nosed snakes are considered burrowers, although not so efficient as the more highly evolved shovel-nosed snakes. However, burrowing alone would probably not allow leaf-nosed snakes to survive the fierce desert heat, for these desert dwellers cannot survive temperatures over 115° F. Burrowing might suffice in sand dunes or extremely loose soil, but the leaf-noses often occupy terrain with hard packed earth. In such country the snakes seek shelter in deep rock crevices, rodent holes, and other places, which enable them to escape the high surface temperature.

At night, and apparently only at night, the leaf-nosed snakes come out from the cool spots to search for food. Like many snakes in the American West, their period of greatest activity is during April, May, and June and between 7:30 and 10:00 P.M.

Little is known about the leaf-noses' eating habits except that in the spring they favor eggs of the banded gecko. The snakes are also given to eating small lizards and possibly insects. One young leaf-nosed snake, placed in a collecting bag with several geckos, ate the tails off two of them. Since the tails had not been previously dropped (a defensive habit of the banded gecko when attempting to elude capture), the leaf-nose was apparently an aggressor. Being relatively small, however, it could not cope with the full-grown gecko and had to be satisfied with the tail. Lest one gather the impression that the leaf-nose's predilection for gecko tails is that of a gourmet, like an ancient Roman eating peacock tongues, note that full-grown leaf-nosed snakes have been observed eating an entire gecko. Yet gecko tails, fat and juicy as they frequently are, may be an important food item. Out of twenty-one geckos caught in one night's collecting, five had recently lost their tails. Since these lizards are not given to the indiscriminate dropping of tails, the conclusion must be that the five tailless ones had been subject to attack by predators, perhaps including a leaf-nosed snake.

An oviparous snake, the leaf-nose lays from two to four eggs in a season, not a large number for so common a snake that is the target of many predators. Its greatest enemy is probably the glossy snake, a snake eater that occupies much of the same range and is active during the same periods.

As a defense against attack, the leaf-nosed snake uses a lesser version of the hognose snake's bluffing tactics. It assumes a coil, head drawn back ready to strike. If pressed, it lunges forward hissing, sometimes with its mouth open and its neck expanded vertically. It is, of course, totally harmless to man.

The leaf-nosed snake is one of the best examples of convergent evolution on widely separate continents. Until 1964 leaf-nosed snakes were held to be closely related to the Old World genus *Lytorhynchus,* the various species of which are distributed from North Africa to southwestern Asia. Placing snakes of the two species side by side, an observer would swear that he was looking at very close relatives. They are amazingly alike—roughly the same length in adults, with similar blotched markings, and above all the large rostral scale that folds back over the nose like a leaf. They even live in similar habitats—dry, arid, sandy, or rocky. Yet, they are separated from one another by a wide biological gap. This fact was demonstrated by Alan E. Leviton and Steven C. Anderson (1970), who made a detailed comparison of the bone structure of each. The skeletal structure, particularly of the skull, of *Phyllorhynchus* is clearly, even to the uninformed examiner, different from that of *Lytorhynchus.* Evolution has provided them with the same outward appearance, including the leaf nose, but within the skins are totally different snakes.

teristic is either a groove or a pronounced dark line running from the eyes to the point of the snout just above the mouth. Nature is seldom capricious in the way she equips her creatures. Natural selection assures that most anatomical features and markings of animals have some use that has helped the animal to survive on earth. For example, consider the markings and feathers of male birds and their role in attracting females; or consider the many examples of markings that provide camouflage or help to deceive the eye of a potential enemy, as in the stripes on a striped racer or striped whipsnake. But the grooves and lines running from eye to nose on whipsnakes and racers have been a puzzlement until recently. In 1971, Robert W. Ficken, Paul E. Matthiae, and Robert Horwich offered a fascinating hypothesis backed up by some facts.

Naturalists have for some time theorized that dark markings around the eyes of many animals have developed primarily to reduce glare, since such markings appear much more frequently in animals that inhabit desert or sparsely wooded lands with pronounced reflection from the sun. Ficken and his associates, however, noted that many animals, particularly fish, reptiles, and birds, have a distinct line of color or a pronounced groove running from or sometimes across each eye forward to a point just above the upper lip or bill. These lines or grooves converge to a point at or just ahead of the mouth. In considering lines or grooves of this kind, the researchers came up with an interesting conjecture. Suppose, they wondered, that these lines or grooves are sighting lines—like the sights of a gun—that enable the animal to draw a bead rapidly when grabbing for prey? The predator that misses too frequently when striking at or lunging for prey will eventually either starve or become too weak to reproduce. The more efficient predator will be one that can achieve a high score of successful strikes. The road to survival may, then, be measured in milliseconds, the difference in time between hitting and missing. Anything—such as a method of rapid sighting—that improves the strike score will help assure survival. Moreover, Ficken and his colleagues thought that the need for sighting lines would be more pronounced in creatures that fed primarily on fast-moving prey such as darting insects and scampering lizards. When North American songbirds were divided into six groups according to feeding habits, the group that fed on the fastest insects contained the largest number of birds with line-of-sight eye markings. Checking predatory fish against grazers and other non-predators showed that the predators much more often had line-of-sight eye markings. In brief, these conjectures may explain why racers and whipsnakes, among others, have markings or grooves from eye to nose.

Such sighting lines would not be necessary on animals such as cats, dogs, and higher primates, which have forward-directed eyes that produce stereoscopic (binocular) vision. Animals with grooves or sighting lines as a rule have their eyes located on the sides of their heads and therefore lack the depth perception provided by stereoscopic vision. The sighting lines or grooves may be necessary as a substitute for depth perception. The coursing racer or whipsnake that pauses, raises its head, and moves it slowly from side to side may be doing more than searching for food; it may be surveying the landscape by sighting in on rocks, shrubs, or trees.

Among snakes closely allied to the racers, one of the prettiest and most bewildering in effecting sudden escapes is the smooth green snake *(Opheodrys vernalis)*, sometimes called the grass snake because it is almost always found in meadow or grassy marsh. The smooth green snake is a slender snake; like the racers, its scales are smooth, regular, with the luster of fine satin. It is two-toned—pale leaf green on its back, greenish white on its underside and around the mouth. When dead, it turns bluish gray. Adults range in length from eleven to twenty-six inches but average around fifteen inches. Common in one subspecies *(O. v. vernalis)* through many of the midwestern States, from western Ohio and Indiana through Illinois, Iowa, and northern Missouri to eastern Nebraska and the Dakotas into southern Canada, the subspecies of smooth green snake in the American West *(O. v. blanchardi)* is limited to one large and several relatively small areas in the states of Idaho, Montana, Wyoming, Utah, Colorado, and New Mexico. (Isolated populations are also found in Texas.) The largest range runs down through the center of Colorado and New Mexico. The western subspecies is distinguished from the midwestern subspecies by a larger number of ventral scales, usually more than 131 in males and more than 140 in females.

Wherever they occur, smooth green snakes are associated with

The Smooth Green Snake

9

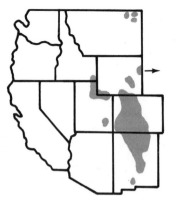

grass in moist areas from sea level to 9,500 feet. Although they spend most of the time on the ground, they will occasionally climb low trees or shrubs. Being grass-colored helps them to make bewildering disappearances. Sometimes given to sunning themselves on rocky ground in their habitat, the snakes play "now you see me, now you don't" with hikers who happen upon them; they glide so rapidly into the grass that the hapless observer may wonder if he really saw a snake at all. If he does capture one, the captor will find it gentle and inoffensive—not at all prone to the testy biting that characterizes most captured racers.

Over part of its midwest range the smooth green snake may occasionally be confused with the rough green snake. No confusion, however, should exist after a second look, since the rough green snake, as its name indicates, has keeled dorsal scales along seventeen rows in midbody, where its relative is perfectly smooth.

Of considerable ecological interest is the fact that the smooth green snake is an insectivore, the first of the relatively few snakes we shall consider (other than those eaters of ant and termite larvae, the slender blind snakes) that eat insects and spiders almost exclusively. Few other snakes show the smooth green snake's predilection for insects. Offered a juicy frog or salamander or tempted with an earthworm, a captive smooth green snake will not be moved; but served with a fat garden spider, grasshopper, or cricket, and the fast is over. Above all, however, *Opheodrys* favors larvae and caterpillars of several species of moths within its range. Like the slender blind snakes, then, it appears to favor a diet that will help to assure its survival, as insects will always be with us. However, eating the targets of insecticides like DDT may sooner or later give these snakes problems in reproduction.

An egg-layer, the smooth green snake apparently mates in the spring and deposits from three to eleven eggs, which hatch in late August or September. The young at hatching are about four and one-half inches long, being a dark olive color on the back and greenish white underneath. The herpetologist Francis R. Cook (1964) made some field studies of the smooth green snake that indicate that the females use communal egg depositories, generally in rotting logs or under flat stones in land bordering meadows or other moist grassy areas. One clutch studied yielded twenty-seven eggs, three of which

80

were bad. The remaining twenty-four comprised three separate clutches of eggs with embryos at slightly different stages of development. This finding conforms to the known fact that smooth green snake clutches average around seven eggs.

The communal depositories, which as we have noted are used by some other species, pose an interesting question. Why do females gather to deposit their eggs? Are the conditions of warmth and moisture necessary for incubation found in so limited a number of places that several females have to use the same depository? This seems unlikely. Indeed, the greater risk to the race lies in literally putting too many eggs in one basket. Survival would be more assured by individual egg-laying in diverse spots, since egg-hunting animals would not be able to wipe out so many embryos at a single sitting. What the communal laying probably shows is that smooth green snakes, like ringneck snakes and others, are sociable, coming together to perform functions important to the survival of the group.

Smooth green snakes were involved in one of the classics of herpetological literature, an account called, "Snakes from an Ant Hill," written in 1937 by Stuart Criddle, a farmer of Treesbank, Manitoba. Criddle's account gives some answers about the habits of hibernating snakes—but it also poses countless questions.

The story begins innocently, if unhappily, with the killing on September 25, 1934, of two smooth green snakes on an anthill. The anthill, located on Criddle's property, thereafter became the focal point of the unfolding story. It was a "flat mound about six inches high and three feet in diameter." Presumably, its occupants were black ants of the genus *Formica.* It was located in a stand of hazel and hawthorn scrub. Nearby grew oak and aspen, and not far away were willow swamps and muskegs. The anthill had openings that appeared normal save for the fact that some were larger than usual. Ants still crawled in the vicinity, although not in large numbers. Curious about the hill, Criddle dug out a few handfuls of dirt. Few ants were seen, but the digging turned up six red-bellied snakes. Returning the next day, Criddle found four more snakes. Even more drawn to complete an examination of the hill, Criddle got down to serious digging on October 6. What he found amazed him. Below the raised mound were lower galleries which to water level nearly five feet below the ground "were almost alive with snakes."

The Fast Snakes

In this one hibernaculum Criddle found 257 snakes—8 plains garter snakes, 101 red-bellied snakes, and 148 smooth green snakes. Larger snakes were nearer the bottom; smaller snakes were nearer the top, which suggests that the adult snakes arrive first at the denning place, with the young arriving later. There is a possibility also that young snakes, being able to warm faster, can leave the den briefly on warmer days to forage.

The Rough Green Snake
10

Larger than its smooth-scaled generic cousin, the adult rough green snake *(Opheodrys aestivus)* is from two to nearly four feet long. Because it has been found in Colfax County, New Mexico, the rough green snake must be included as a snake of the American West, but in fact it is more typical of wooded areas, particularly around water in most of the lower Midwest and Southeast—from sea level to 5,000 feet.

Green on its back with keeled scales, this slender snake is pale green, yellowish, or white on its belly. Death changes its marked green color to a dull gray or blue. The six- to eight-inch young rough green snakes are grayish green.

The largely insectivorous rough green snake prefers a leafy habitat where, either on the ground among the limbs of bushes or trees, its green body effectively blends into its surroundings. Favoring woods near water, it is frequently seen swimming. In the leafy wilderness it prefers, this snake searches for crickets, grasshoppers, caterpillars, and spiders—often moving easily along low limbs of dogwood, sumac, or other shrubs and bushes in its habitat. In the water it sometimes preys on frogs.

Oviparous, the rough green snake lays from four to eleven eggs that hatch in late August and September. Normally it comes out of hibernation in April and disappears again in late September or October.

The Racer
11

The racer *(Coluber constrictor)* is a species of snake whose range, not contiguous but in patches, covers most of North America from southern British Columbia to Guatemala, from the Atlantic to the Pacific. In base color the various subspecies show great regional variation. The blue racer is found in the Midwest; the black racer occurs in the East and Southeast; and the racer of eastern Texas and Louisiana, which is called the "buttermilk snake," is speckled. The most widely distributed subspecies of the American West, called the western yellow-bellied racer *(C. c. mormon)*, is brown or olive on its back and pale yellow on its belly. The eastern yellow-bellied racer *(C. c. flaviventris)* enters the American West in Montana, Wyoming, Colorado, and New Mexico.

The racer sometimes reaches a length of six and a half feet, although adults are generally two and a half to four and a half feet long. The scales are smooth and the anal plate, the scale just in front of the vent, is divided.

Uniform in color on its back, an adult racer differs markedly from a young one. The young, blotched with brown saddles on their backs, are sometimes confused with young gopher snakes. The blotches fade as the young snake grows, seldom appearing on a racer over a foot and a half long. This type of pronounced change from the young form to the adult is known as an ontogenetic or developmental change, and it poses several problems for natural science. First, until a species is thoroughly studied, ontogenetic change frequently causes taxonomic confusion. Younger and older western yellow-bellied racers were once thought to be two different species. The first specimen described was a young snake, typically blotched. Later, an unblotched adult was collected and was described as a separate species—by the same naturalists who had collected the juvenile.

Most perplexing, however, is the problem of why ontogenetic change occurs. The young of the green rat snake, like those of the western yellow-bellied racer, have brown blotches. Yet in both species of the green snakes the young are uniform green like the adults. All four species, then, have their green color in common, yet two of them have young which are a different color. One explanation has been advanced by herpetologist Joseph Copp. The young of the racer and green rat snake are normally hatched in the fall in places where leaves have turned brown and the grass has dried. Brown blotches would help the young snake stay alive by more effectively concealing it from predators. The green snakes, on the other hand, are hatched in moist grassy areas where the landscape remains green. The uniform green color would help conceal them from their many enemies.

The Fast Snakes

83

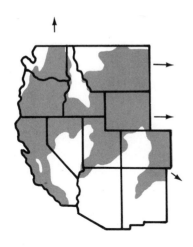

In choice of habitat the western yellow-bellied racer is extremely particular, favoring grassy areas within its spotty range. With the possible exception of eastern Montana, all of its range is on the west slope of the Continental Divide (including Santa Cruz Island off California)—generally not in thick forest or desert, but rather in chaparral and meadow or in grassy forest glades from sea level to 6,700 feet. The racer is highly territorial, quite often spending the active part of its life within a twenty-four or twenty-five-acre area, leaving its territory only to hibernate during the coldest months. During hibernation it favors crevices or caves in limestone outcroppings, choosing most often the warm southern exposure and there denning up with others of its kind. During hibernation its body temperature can drop below freezing, but it cannot survive being frozen solid.

Hibernation, in fact, is a dangerous process for snakes. The herpetologist Harold F. Hirth (1966) made an intensive study of ninety-eight snakes of three species, which he captured at the entrance of a hibernaculum in northwestern Utah. Caught, weighed, and marked, the snakes were released to complete their denning. The species studied were the Great Basin rattlesnake, the desert striped whipsnake, and the western yellow-bellied racer. When spring came and the snakes started moving out, Hirth recaptured sixty of them to check their body weights against what they had weighed in the fall. Adult snakes had lost an average ten percent of their body weight. Some young rattlesnakes, in their first hibernation after birth, had lost twenty-five percent of their body weight. Moreover, mortality among all three species had been high. Dead before they could crawl into another spring were thirty-nine percent of the whipsnakes, thirty-four percent of the rattlesnakes, and fifty percent of the racers.

Racers have been observed emerging from hibernation while temperatures were as low as 55° F. Actually the racer prefers higher temperatures than most snakes. It is a frequent sunbather, seeming to gather from the sun the energy that it will later use in the rapid final dashes that it makes in running down its prey. It does, of course, gather the ability to act. Found under a rock in the early morning while a chill remains in the air this fast snake will be sluggish, barely able to move. Later, warmed by the sun, blood flowing

HARMLESS SNAKES

freely to supply food and oxygen to its muscles, the snake will achieve its characteristic swiftness. Body temperatures taken by Henry S. Fitch (1963) of racers during peak activity were concentrated in the 93–95° F. range. He found, however, that for short periods the snakes could survive temperatures up to 113° F. although prolonged exposure to temperatures over 104° F. normally would be fatal.

As a hunter, the racer makes great use of both eyesight and speed. Coursing through grass or brush, it occasionally pauses, head raised, looking for movements, then moves smoothly on until at one pause prey is sighted. A short swift dash, prey seized in mouth, pressed down by the snake's body, swallowed—and the hunt goes on. The racer, belying its specific name *constrictor,* does not use constriction; rather it simply bites the prey, and then pins it to the ground to secure it for swallowing.

It would be difficult to imagine a less selective predator. In one study of stomach contents it was found that racers had eaten a total of 1,357 food items representing more than 50 species of insects, reptiles, and mammals. Judging by this count, the favorite prey species were crickets, grasshoppers, camel crickets, katydids, racerunners, leopard frogs, moles, and white-footed mice. Insects greatly outnumbered vertebrates, but the bulkier food items were vertebrates. Among the species eaten were birds and some small snakes including, in unconscious cannibalism, juvenile racers. It appears that racers, taking what they can get, have a seasonal variation in diet, with more mice and moles on the menu during spring and early summer and more crickets and grasshoppers included during late summer and fall.

Speed and deception are the main defenses of the racer. Its first reaction is to flee. When threatened, it will often immediately seek a downhill slope in order to increase its escape speed. If a stream is nearby, it may swim to safety; or if the country has low trees or brush, it may climb to concealment. Sometimes, come upon suddenly in grass or brush, the racer resorts to deception. Thrashing about violently, it seeks to focus the enemy's attention onto a specific small patch of ground; then silently, on the snake equivalent of tiptoe, it glides away from the focal area. The enemy, convinced that the snake is still there, searches vainly. Occasionally, quite boldly, the racer will circle around the enemy and observe him from some hidden vantage point directly opposite the place the diversion occurred. Cornered or caught by an enemy, the racer normally thrashes about vigorously, striking and biting with great energy and force.

Aside from the omnipresent enemy, man, the racer is beset by many natural enemies, particularly the red-tailed hawk. Other hawks, barn owls, and among mammals, the striped skunk see the racer as a desirable meal. The skunk is an especially bad enemy, for it feeds on adult racers, offspring, and eggs.

Racers breed during May after courtships that frequently see two males offering themselves to one female. The amorous male lies on or alongside the female he desires. Every so often he ripples his abdominal muscles and presses his vent against hers. In tantalizing fashion the female may glide rapidly to another spot, the male trying his hardest to maintain contact with her while this continues. Once in a while, almost as though he cannot stand the frustration, the courting male leaves the female's side and moves completely around her. But shortly, he returns to his previous position and goes on with his hopeful muscle flexing. The signal of acceptance comes when the female raises her tail. Coitus then takes place for several minutes during which the female subjects her lover to a final indignity. Slowly she moves along the ground dragging him behind her.

Eggs are laid in clutches of about seven, normally from mid-June to early August. Curiously, the racer shows a geographical variation in the size of its clutches: the western yellow-bellied racer averages nine to a clutch, the eastern yellow-bellied racer averages twelve, and the northern black racer lays about seventeen to a clutch. The eggs are deposited in the earth, generally in the tunnels of moles or other fossorial (burrowing) mammals. After an incubation period of nearly fifty-one days, the young emerge. At hatching they average about eleven inches in length. Immediately upon emerging the young must beware of the countless predators that would like very much to eat them. These predators, alas, include the same adult racers that produced them.

If the coachwhip *(Masticophis flagellum)* were venomous, it would be a dangerous snake indeed, for it is one of the few snakes in the American West (or anywhere else) that will aggressively pursue an animal, or man, that threatens it. This aggression generally comes only when the snake feels hopelessly trapped; like other snakes, the coachwhip will first attempt to flee from an enemy. And flee it can at great speed, either on the ground or into the branches of shrubs or trees, sometimes high above the ground, for it is a good climber. Not uncommonly, it will seek the cover of an animal burrow. But when cornered, the coachwhip does not wait passively for the enemy to approach. Rather, in man's greatest tradition of courage, it moves toward the enemy.

Anyone seeing a coachwhip for the first time would instantly know how it got its names, both the English "coachwhip" and the Latin *"flagellum,"* which means "whip." The snake is long and slender, and its long tail is so colored and scaled that it suggests the braided rawhide of a whip. In earlier times this resemblance bred outrageous stories about the coachwhip actually using itself as a whip. In one of the first accounts of snakes in the United States, Captain Thomas Walduck wrote in 1714, "there be likewise . . . Snakes made like a Coachwhip as long and as small, that will twist their head round a horse's leg, and with their tayl lash a horse with great violence untill ye blood comes. . . ."

Ranging in adult length from three to eight and one-half feet, the smooth-scaled coachwhip shows up in many different colorations. Quite commonly it is pink, reddish, tan, or gray with black crossbars on the neck; occasionally it is black.

Its range is extensive, covering almost all of the southern half of the United States from coast to coast and southward to Sinaloa, Durango, Querétaro, and northern Veracruz, Mexico. It is also found on many islands in the Gulf of California: Espíritu Santo, Cerralvo, San José, Monserrate, Carmen, Coronado, San Ildefonso, and Tiburón and on the Isla Santa Margarita off the outer coast of Baja California. A diurnal, or daytime, creature, the coachwhip will frequently be the only snake abroad at midday, prowling for food in scrub desert while other species have sought shelter from the heat.

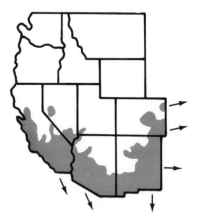

The coachwhip's habitats are many: creosote bush and mesquite flats in the Colorado Desert, Joshua tree country in the Mojave Desert, sagebrush and grass in the Great Basin, short grass prairie in eastern Colorado and New Mexico. Occasionally the coachwhip is found in wooded areas, but nowhere does it appear to like heavy chaparral or forest, preferring more open area. One does not think of it as a mountain snake, yet it has been taken as high as 7,700 feet in the Wet Mountains of Colorado.

The wide variety of color patterns in the coachwhip is dramatically illustrated by the differences within and between three of the principal subspecies. One of these is called the red racer *(M. f. piceus),* found over much of southern California, southern Nevada, the extreme southwest corner of Utah, and southern Arizona, thence southward into northwestern Sonora and northwestern Baja California. This subspecies is known in two distinctive patterns of coloration. Typically it is a light red with black or dark brown cross-bands on the neck (even perhaps the first fifth of the body) and horizontal white stripes with black borders on the side of the head. In south-central Arizona the second phase of the same subspecies is entirely black on its back. (It is often called the western black racer in this region.) In southeastern Arizona a mixed phase may be found; the forward portion of its back is black and the lower half of the back is pink or red with some brown intermixed.

The lined whipsnake *(M. f. lineatulus)* is found in the extreme southeast of Arizona and southwest of New Mexico, and thence southward over much of the Mexican plateau. Unlike the red racer it has no neck markings and no horizontal stripes on the sides of its head. Distinguished by the longitudinal black streaks on the forward part of its back, it exhibits little variability in color pattern.

The western coachwhip *(M. f. testaceus)* is found over much of New Mexico and eastern Colorado, thence eastward and southward over the Great Plains and the east coast of Mexico. This subspecies is usually tan, although occasionally it is red or pink in Colorado, New Mexico, and Trans-Pecos Texas. Uniform narrow- and wide-banded patterns occur.

Two other subspecies of coachwhip have been accepted by most herpetologists. The San Joaquin whipsnake *(M. f. ruddocki)* is light yellow to olive on its back with a dark head and faint or absent neck-bands. This subspecies, found in the San Joaquin and Sacramento valleys of California, has a relatively constant color pattern. The banded red racer *(M. f. cingulum)* is extremely variable in color pattern. Sometimes it may be reddish brown with widely separated pairs of pink crossbands along the rear portion of the body; sometimes it may be a uniform reddish brown or black. Snakes with lighter colors will tend to have a single light band behind the head. The banded red racer ranges from extreme southern Arizona south to southern Sonora excluding the Gran Desierto of the northwestern corner of the state.

Of the seven subspecies of the coachwhip, a sixth occurs in the American West, barely entering the United States in southern San Diego County, California. This subspecies, *M. f. fuliginosus,* the Baja California whipsnake, extends throughout Baja California except for the extreme northeastern corner. It is another highly variable subspecies in color pattern characteristics, coming in a light and a dark phase, the latter of which is the only one represented in the American West.

The bewildering variety of color patterns in the various subspecies of the coachwhip have probably helped it survive and extend its range. The polymorphism in color pattern obviously helps the species adapt to differing surroundings. Even the one subspecies, the San Joaquin whipsnake, that has a uniform color helps to bolster this observation, for this color, uniformly light in hue, matches the light-colored dried grass so characteristic of the San Joaquin and Sacramento areas of California during late spring and summer, the peak of this particular subspecies' activity.

Like most of the racers and whipsnakes, the coachwhip has a varied diet—mice, rats, young rabbits, birds and their eggs, various lizards, other snakes including rattlesnakes, young turtles, and insects such as grasshoppers and crickets. In one recorded instance a coachwhip was found eating carrion, the carcass of a nighthawk. The coachwhip, like the racer, hunts by coursing through its habitat, pausing now and then, head raised, alert to movements that might betray a prey animal.

Stanley deTreville, while camped near Palm Springs, San Diego County, witnessed an unusual encounter between a red racer and a jackrabbit. Lying on a cot under some mesquite in the morning sun, deTreville saw the snake, a four-footer, gliding through the creosote brush not twenty yards away. In its mouth was a young jackrabbit. Behind the snake, apparently pursuing it, was a full-grown jackrabbit, probably the mother. The snake took refuge on the lower limbs of a creosote bush not far from where de Treville lay. The mother rabbit remained in the vicinity until de Treville, a moment or so later, rose from his cot. Both snake and mother rabbit then fled, the snake without its prey which, when de Treville reached it, was dead.

The herpetologist Arthur I. Ortenburger, author of a definitive study on racers and whipsnakes (1928), one morning came upon a coachwhip snake that was swallowing a relatively large western diamondback rattlesnake. Ortenburger succeeded in pulling the dead rattlesnake from the coachwhip's mouth, but the latter escaped before it could be captured.

The coachwhip is oviparous. Mating probably takes place during April and May. Females lay up to two dozen eggs, although the average clutch contains eight to eleven. In the laboratory incubation has required from seventy-six to seventy-nine days.

The coachwhip's wide range, high tolerance of heat, and great speed of movement are factors that may help to assure its survival in spite of the constant encroachment of civilization. Its greatest threat comes from highways cut through its range, for no snake is fast enough to escape an onrushing car.

The Striped Racer

13

The stripes of the striped racer *(Masticophis lateralis)*—one cream or yellow line on each side of its back from neck to vent—play a more than decorative role. They aid the snake in escaping its enemies by so impressing themselves on the retina of the observer that the eye sees them at a particular spot for an instant or so after the snake has moved away. The experience is somewhat akin to viewing a naked light bulb and then, after closing one's eyes, still seeing the image of the light bulb. The striped racer's stripes are nowhere near so bright as a light bulb, of course, but the optical illusion is the same. One can imagine the frustration of a red-tailed hawk or golden eagle that has swooped down to snatch up a tasty snake only to find itself clutching dried grass as the snake, now several feet away, moves rapidly off to shelter.

Adult striped racers range from two and one-half to four feet in length, with occasional specimens growing to five feet. On the major subspecies, the California striped racer, *M. l. lateralis,* the snake's topside is a blackish brown or black with yellowish stripes, about one scale row wide, on either side. Curiously, striped racers in the San Francisco area have broader stripes, up to two scale rows wide, that are orange in color. This restricted subspecies, the Alameda striped racer *(M. l. euryxanthus),* has an orange belly anteriorly. On most striped racers the underbelly is cream or light yellow and on the underside of the tail pink shades into coral. Its scales are smooth, with seventeen rows at midbody.

The striped racer's range closely parallels the chaparral country of California and Baja California. Generally it is found west of the Sierra crest at altitudes up to 6,000 feet from northern California to central Baja California. Its range extends to the desert foothills in southern California. In country that has much manzanita and scrub oak, the striped racer is often seen foraging or sunning well off the ground in the brush. Like all the whipsnakes, it seems quick and alert, the possessor of great reserves of nervous energy. As it courses through brush or grass, it raises the forward third of its body slightly off the ground, pausing to move its head from side to side as though it were a radar device to detect food or enemies.

The striped racer has great prowess in eluding capture. Partially this ability comes from the illusion provided by its stripes, an illusion so effective that human hunters aiming to seize a striped racer by the neck frequently find themselves holding one by the tail, a position that allows this invariably scrappy snake to bite the hunter on the hand. But the snake uses more than illusion, it also uses its great speed and agility, not infrequently avoiding capture by climbing into manzanita or similar underbrush so thick that pursuit is impossible. And, like the racer, the striped racer uses deception when an enemy surprises it. It may thrash about to achieve the same diversion the racer achieves, fixing the enemy's attention onto one spot while it moves quietly away to another. The effectiveness of these escape methods has been indicated through an experiment conducted by Henry S. Fitch (1949). He marked twenty-six striped racers and released them. In subsequent hunts over the same area none was ever recaptured.

No great specialist in diet, the striped racer eats insects, frogs, lizards, other snakes (including rattlesnakes), birds, and rodents. When prey is sighted, the striped racer simply grabs it, pins it to the ground, and without constricting begins to swallow the creature

The Fast Snakes

live. Like most snakes interrupted while eating, a disturbed striped racer will regurgitate food during the swallowing process in order to achieve a fast escape from whatever disturbed it.

Mating season for the California striped racer comes in April and May. A captive pair in the San Diego Zoo were observed mating on April 1 and 8. The female laid eggs on May 27. Incubation, under laboratory conditions, took just over three months.

As a kind of footnote on littering, there appeared in the Santa Barbara, California, *News-Press* (May 20, 1959) a story and picture of a striped racer captured through what can only be described as its curiosity. Coursing through the chaparral that characterizes the Santa Barbara foothills, the snake came upon an empty beer can with two openings punched in one end. The snake crawled into one of these openings, found itself in a cul-de-sac, and started to crawl out the second. Perhaps the turn was too sharp or perhaps the keen edge of the opening caught the snake's scales, but in either event the snake could not escape. It died there, ignominiously, half-in, half-out of the beer can in the messy wilderness left by men.

The Sonora Whipsnake

14

The Sonora whipsnake *(Masticophis bilineatus)* is principally a Mexican snake, occurring in the American West only in the extreme southwestern portion of New Mexico and in the southern half of Arizona. Thence at altitudes up to 6,100 feet it ranges southward in Mexico to Oaxaca. In size Sonora whipsnakes range from three to four feet long—with exceptional specimens reaching five and one-half feet. In the subspecies *M. b. bilineatus* the ground color of the back is olive, bluish-gray, or light gray brown, shading into a yellowish color or lighter gray brown on two thirds of the body toward the tail. The head of this snake is a study in contrasts. The top of the head will tend to be the same color as the back. This color is bounded by a black line that runs from snout to neck just under the eye on both sides of the head and across the front of the nose. The mouth is lined in white or cream, and above the black line there may be a cream line pointing back from the snout toward the eye. On the forward third of its body along both sides, a well-marked Sonora whipsnake has both dark and light stripes: a narrow white stripe about one and a half scale rows wide and two or three narrower black stripes. The white stripe tends to be longer than the others. Flecks of darker coloration on the scales toward the rear of this snake's body give it a streaked appearance. The underside is pale yellow, paler forward, deeper aft. A few black dots may fleck the chin.

Another one of the climbing whipsnakes, the Sonora whipsnake is so often found in the acacia, paloverde, and other brush and trees in its favorite habitat—the lower mountain slopes up to the pine-oak belt—that some authorities call it arboreal. One associates it with rocky slopes and stream beds where saguaro cactus and ocotillo abound. Its food consists mostly of young birds and lizards, both of which it hunts from May, when it first appears on the desert foothills, to October, when presumably it leaves for hibernation.

A second subspecies of the Sonora whipsnake is found in the American West. This subspecies is called the Ajo Mountain whipsnake *(M. b. lineolatus)*. Patterned much like the major subspecies, it is a darker snake with a much narrower light stripe—a pinstripe—along each side. This subspecies is found confined to the northern branch of the Alamo Canyon in the Ajo Mountains, Pima County, Arizona. Interestingly, this snake has been a frequent victim of what has come to be known as the Ajo trap. The trap is a hole (in Spanish, *tinaja*) in the floor of Alamo Canyon on the west side of the Ajo Mountains. Described by M. Max Hensley (1950), who took a number of specimens there, it is approximately five feet long, three and a half feet wide, and four and a half feet deep, most often filled with stagnant water. Steep sides deny exit to the hapless mammal or snake that slides into the hole. On one occasion Hensley found ten Ajo Mountain whipsnakes there, eight of them dead. Eight days later he again visited this natural trap and found two more specimens there, one of them dead. On a final visit two weeks after, seven more Ajo whipsnakes were found, of which three were dead. This experience leads one to wonder how many snakes or other animals this trap had captured over the years—and, for that matter, how often natural traps like this one exist. One does not ordinarily envision a hole in the ground as playing such a vital role in the ecology of a region. Without motivation, indifferent as fate itself, it lies there accepting weak and strong alike. Yet if a population had been seriously reduced, just such an ordinary hole could conceivably bring death to the final breeding members of a species of animals.

The Fast Snakes

While the Sonora whipsnake is oviparous like its relatives, little is known of its breeding habits.

The Striped
Whipsnake
15

As though the whole group of racers and whipsnakes weren't confusing enough, another common snake, the striped whipsnake *(Masticophis taeniatus)*, looks and acts like the striped racer. They are in fact close relatives, but the striped whipsnake is much more widely distributed and the ranges of the two species do not overlap. The striped whipsnake differs markedly from other whipsnakes because it possesses fifteen rows of scales at midbody, whereas most others have seventeen. Sometimes attaining a length of six feet, the striped whipsnake is black, dark brown, or dark gray on its back, frequently with a bluish or olive cast. Along each side runs a cream or white stripe, down the middle of which runs a narrow black line. Below this combination run additional black lines, the total effect being a thoroughly striped side. The snake's belly is white or cream in the vicinity of the neck, changing to a more yellowish tone along midbody, finally merging into a coral pink in the region of the tail.

In the American West the striped whipsnake is represented by one subspecies—the desert striped whipsnake *(M. t. taeniatus)*. It ranges from central Washington, southward in the Great Basin bounded by the Cascades and Sierras to the west and the Continental Divide to the east. Its range crosses the Continental Divide into New Mexico, runs down through the Western portion of Texas, thence south into Mexico as far as Michoacán. Normally associated with the seemingly endless sagebrush flats of Nevada or the piñon and juniper forests, this snake has nonetheless been taken in the mountains at altitudes as high as 9,400 feet.

Many of the whipsnakes are particularly attracted to rocky streams, whether running or not. The striped whipsnake is no exception. Also, like most of its relatives, it is a daytime snake that spends much time climbing bushes or trees. Its slenderness makes it suited for an arboreal life. One snake hunter, noting that the striped whipsnake seemed bolder off the ground, commented, "When chased, it climbs into a sagebrush and sticks its head out threateningly." The interpretation, "threateningly," of course, can be seen as the reaction of a man who had probably been bitten by this testy snake, which like all the whipsnakes defends itself vigorously even to the point of endeavoring to bite with chewing motion. A snake sticking its head from a bush may simply be observing. The "threat" may be only in the eye of the beholder. On the other hand, if the snake hisses loudly or strikes, the observer can hardly be blamed for seeing a threat. The snake may be responding to a genetically keyed escape program, part of which is designed to confound the pursuer long enough to provide time to flee.

The striped whipsnake hunts lizards, snakes, and small mammals. It has been observed in the wild eating a western diamondback rattlesnake. Oviparous, the female deposits four to eight eggs probably in late June or July; specimens captured as late as June 20 have carried eggs that appeared nearly ready for laying.

Close relatives of the racers and whipsnakes, the patch-nosed snakes are distinguished from their relatives in two ways: they have an enlarged rostral scale, sometimes as extreme as the "leaf" of the leaf-nosed snake, that gives them their common name; and they have a pronounced stripe down the center of their back as though it had been painted on to mark where the backbone runs.

The Western Patch-Nosed Snake
16

The western patch-nosed snake *(Salvadora hexalepis)* is associated with bushy desert, chaparral, and rocky washes and streams. Where it lives and hunts one sees creosote bush, galleta grass, Joshua trees, and sagebrush, although occasionally it goes to higher altitudes, having been taken as high as 7,000 feet. Its range is from west-central Nevada south to the tip of Baja California and includes the coastal regions of southern California, much of Arizona, southern New Mexico, and western Texas; on the Mexican mainland, it is found to southern Sinaloa and in Chihuahua and Coahuila. It also occurs on Tiburón and San José islands in the Gulf of California.

It takes a trained herpetologist to determine the difference between sexes of most snakes. But the western patch-nose—handily for the interested layman—has an external difference. On males the scales above the vent and at the base of the tail are keeled. Females have no keeled scales or, in exceptional cases, extremely weak keeling. Thus, if one can catch a western patch-nose, he can tell which sex he has caught. Catching one, however, is very difficult; for this snake, like its racer relatives, is slender, fast, and deceptive.

The base color of the patch-nosed snake is light gray to grayish beige. Against this ground color are placed three stripes: a beige or yellow stripe about three scale rows wide running down the center of the snake's back, and on either side of it broad lateral stripes two to four scale rows wide of a dark olive brown or blackish brown. But great variety may be found in both the stripe patterns and color. In one subspecies, the coast patch-nosed snake *(S. h. virgultea),* the center stripe is much narrower. Another subspecies, the desert patch-nosed snake *(S. h. hexalepis),* has two more dark stripes, one on each side about two scale rows wide. The Big Bend patch-nosed snake *(S. h. deserticola)* has these same additional stripes, but they are only one scale row wide. Finally, the stripes may be obscured or broken by crossbars, a condition that exists with the Mojave patch-nosed snake *(S. h. mojavensis).* On their bellies the patch-nosed snakes are a relatively uniform white, sometimes suffused with dull orange, especially toward the tail.

In the broad daylight of May and June, when lizards are scampering or sunning themselves and small mice are gathering grain, the patch-nosed snake is most active. This is a period of mating and hunting—and lizards and mice are principal items on the patch-nosed snake's diet. Another favorite food is eggs—in this case, lizard or snake eggs. On a field trip in Sonora, Mexico, Joseph Copp came upon a juvenile patch-nosed snake in the process of swallowing a lizard egg. Near the snake lay two other eggs and a hollow spot in the sand that, when dug out, yielded several more eggs. Without question, the patch-nose had dug out the buried clutch, probably using lateral motions of its head. On the free edges of the rostral, grains of sand still clung, adhering there because of dampness in the sand below the dry, sun-scorched surface. Copp conjectured that the enlarged rostral scale on the patch-nosed snake (and that of the leaf-nosed snake, which has a similar fondness for reptile eggs) has developed mainly for rooting out sand and soil to get to the eggs of reptile nests, for neither leaf-nose nor patch-nose is primarily a burrower.

As a possible ironic touch to the patch-nosed snake's inclination toward reptile eggs, it is itself an egg-layer. Consequently, although a female patch-nosed snake lays with her four to ten eggs a pheromone scent that "warns off" hungry snakes of the same species, the chances are that from time to time adult patch-nosed snakes root out and eat eggs of their own kind.

The western patch-nosed snake and its close relative, the mountain patch-nosed snake *(Salvadora grahamiae)*, provide a fascinating example of different species living in almost entirely different habitats within much of the same geographical range. The mountain patch-nosed snake is found mostly at altitudes of 4,000 to 7,500 feet in the mountains of southeastern Arizona, north-central New Mexico, and central Texas, thence southward to Querétaro, Mexico. Through most of this range the western patch-nosed snake is also found, but at altitudes below 4,000 feet. Where the western patch-nose is a snake of sage, cresote, and Joshua tree, the mountain patch-nose is found on rocky slopes or in grassy glades among stands of cedar and pine. Apparently the mountain patch-nose suffers distress from lower desert altitudes and seldom descends below 4,000 feet except in the humid eastern portion of its range, where it is found down to sea level on the prairies of Texas.

The Mountain Patch-Nosed Snake
17

Generally smaller, adults being twenty to thirty inches long, the mountain patch-nose is slightly different from the western patch-nose in pattern and color. Down the center of the back of the mountain patch-nose runs the same three-scale-wide stripe in white, grayish white, or yellow—lighter than the greenish, bluish, or gray ground color on its sides. Bordering this stripe are light brown, dark brown, almost black, or sometimes bluish or olive brown stripes two or slightly more scale rows wide. These appear darker on the mountain patch-nose so that the lighter center stripe stands out even more. Sometimes a narrow dark stripe runs down each side on the third scale row.

The generally recognized subspecies of the American West, *grahamiae*, lacks the narrow stripe. The Texas patch-nosed snake, *S. g. lineata*, generally has the stripe. For this reason some herpetologists argue that *lineata* must be seen as a distinct species, even though famed herpetologist Charles Bogert noted intermediates between *S. g. grahamiae* and *lineata* in southern Chihuahua and Durango.

How then does the mountain patch-nosed snake actually differ from the western patch-nosed snake? So far we have noted two differences: the mountain patch-nose is generally smaller and its coloration pattern, much the same otherwise, has a more pronounced center stripe. The real differences, however, lie in scale patterns. The raised rostral scale of the mountain patch-nose is not nearly so well defined as that of the western patch-nose. The large chin shields toward the rear of the head are in contact or separated only by a single small scale, whereas the western patch-nose has two or three small scales between chin shields. Finally, the mountain patch-nose has eight upper labial scales (those behind the rostral on the upper "lip") to the western's nine. In diet, mating, and egg-laying the mountain patch-nose is much the same as the western.

The genus *Salvadora* provides in itself an interesting study of evolutionary development. The raised rostral scale is the key element. One Mexican and Guatemalan species of the patch-nose, *Salvadora lemniscata*, has a rostral scale that is not noticeably different from that of most snakes. Gradually, moving northward, following what some evolutionists believe was the fanning out of snake species from their primitive beginnings in Mexico, the various species of patch-nosed snakes show more and more pronounced rostral shields, culminating in the highly developed rostral of the western patch-nosed snake. The raised rostral, it should be remembered, helps the snake dig out reptile eggs. It is in that way better equipped to survive than a snake without the pronounced rostral patch.

Chapter 9

» » » » »

SOME FARM SNAKES

Most harmless snakes—and most snakes are harmless—benefit man through their eating habits. But some snakes, including several discussed in this chapter, benefit man more than others, largely because they are bigger or, following the mice and rats, they are attracted to agricultural areas. Some of these "farm snakes" are among the commonest of snakes, yet largely through ignorance, they continue to be persecuted by man.

Occasionally snakes get bad reputations by adding to their largely rodent diets such delicacies as baby chicks. The corn snake, for example, is sometimes called the chicken snake. The farmer or rancher whose fields harbor corn snakes must weigh the relatively small cost of a few chickens against the economic benefits brought by the snake's extensive destruction of mice and rats. Probably the relative value of the few chickens sacrificed would be less than the cost of poisons required to kill the additional rodents that would result from the scarcity of corn snakes.

The rat snakes are members of the widespread genus *Elaphe*, which has European, and Asian representatives. Eight species of these long, slender, secretive snakes occur in the Western Hemisphere

The Rat Snakes

but only three are found in the American West. Rat snakes are distinguished by weakly keeled dorsal scales and the fact that their heads are quite distinct from their necks. With many snakes it is difficult to tell at a glance where head ends and neck begins, but with the rat snakes it is easy. Characteristically, the rat snakes eat rodents and are therefore drawn toward agricultural areas where rodent populations, with bountiful repasts available, have sleek coats and large litters.

THE CORN SNAKE

18

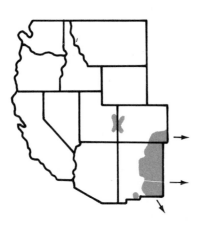

The corn snake *(Elaphe guttata),* one of the most widespread of the rat snakes, is found over a large part of the United States and Mexico. It ranges from Eastern Utah and central New Mexico to the Gulf and Atlantic coasts, and from southern Nebraska to Querétaro and Veracruz, Mexico. In the American West the corn snake is found along the Colorado River in Utah, Colorado, and in mountainous regions of eastern New Mexico. At altitudes that reach above 6,000 feet, its strictly wild habitat typically is a place where streams run down rocky courses or along rich river bottoms; it inhabits hills where rocks are scattered and lives among pine and cedar forests. It has received its common name, however, from its presence near cornfields, toward which it has migrated as agriculture has invaded its range. Most of the time it spends underground in rodent burrows, so corn snakes may be plentiful in an area but seldom seen.

Adult corn snakes average about three feet in length, although a large individual will sometimes attain six feet. Of the three subspecies of *Elaphe guttata,* only one, *E. g. emoryi,* called the Great Plains rat snake, is found in the American West.

Corn snakes vary greatly in color. Generally the Great Plains rat snake has a light grayish brown ground color. Along the back, not including the tail, are oval, brown or dark gray blotches with darkened edges, forty-two to fifty-five on males and forty-four to fifty-five on females. Of course, for a person who encounters a corn snake in the wild, the effort to count blotches on a fairly fast-moving snake would result in some frustration. Yet, exterior markings that help to differentiate sexes are so few among snakes that when they occur they must be noted.

If the snake's backbone lies north to south, these oval blotches are elongated from east to west. On either side of the dorsal blotches are two rows of smaller blotches, similarly colored, alternating with one another and the dorsal blotches. On its underside the corn snake has more than 245 belly scales, each white or cream with two dark spots so arranged that they give the belly a checkered appearance. The final characteristic, although not always present on the corn snake, is the pair of elongated neck markings, the same color as the body blotches, which unite between the eyes to form a forward-pointing spearhead.

The corn snake, like the other rat snakes, is likely to be particularly offensive when captured. As we have seen, many snakes discharge musk anally as a defense. However, the rat snakes—and the water snakes and garter snakes discussed later—use anal discharge as a chief line of defense, firing off great quantities from their musk glands when they are first handled. The resultant odor is persistent, sickening, and most foul. Later, if accustomed to captivity, the snakes are less inclined to discharge musk.

The corn snake is oviparous. Mating probably takes place in May and June, egg-laying in July, and hatching in September. One captive specimen in the San Diego Zoo laid fourteen eggs, probably an extremely large number, since other clutches contained five and four eggs respectively. Deposited on July 8 and 9, these eggs began hatching on September 18. The young measured about nine and one-half inches at birth. Until they reach adult size, the young snakes eat frogs, lizards, and young mice.

Slender, green or olive in back color, the green rat snake *(Elaphe triaspis)* is occasionally confused with the smooth green snake. The differences, however, are marked. The green rat snake has weakly keeled scales, whereas the smooth green snake is smooth. And, for those who like to count, the green rat snake has twenty-five or more rows of scales to the smooth green snake's fifteen. Mainly, however, the hiker, camper, or snake hunter is not likely to encounter both snakes in the same area. The green rat snake, sometimes called the neotropical rat snake, is a Central American and Mexican species that, like the vine snake, extended its range into the mountains of southern Arizona that used to be the home of Apache Indians— namely the Baboquivari, Pajarito, Santa Rita, and Chiricahua ranges. To these same places came other tropical forms now seen

THE GREEN RAT SNAKE

19

no more—the ocelot and the jaguar. The green rat snake remains. To the south it lives along the slopes of the Mexican highlands ranging as far as Costa Rica.

The subspecies of the green rat snake found in Arizona is *E. t. intermedia.* Adults measure from two feet to slightly over four feet in length. Green or olive on top, the underside is cream, marked only by a slight touch of yellow. When distended, the scales may give the impression of being bordered with black.

Surprisingly little is known about the behavior of the green rat snake. It is a snake of the mountains, having been taken above 7,000 feet. The few herpetologists who have studied it believe it to be chiefly crepuscular, a snake that does its hunting in late afternoon or evening. Among the pine, sycamore, walnut, cottonwood, and wild grape of the Arizona mountains it is well camouflaged. Efforts to find and capture it have often led herpetologists to frustration. A fast snake, it apparently takes to the trees in seeking escape. One Arizona pioneer noted that he had seen a large green snake that goes through the tops of trees like a "bat out of Hades." Scattered field observations have indicated that its principal prey is rodents— particularly wood rats—and birds.

THE TRANS-PECOS
RAT SNAKE

20

Another largely Mexican snake that barely extends its range into the American West is the Trans-Pecos rat snake *(Elaphe subocularis).* It bears the specific tag *subocularis* because there is a row of small scales, known as suboculars, under each eye. More popularly this snake is called the H snake because running along either side of the center of its back are twenty-eight parallel black or dark brown markings that are frequently joined or nearly joined to form an H. Sometimes the lateral poles of the H's join toward the neck to form fore and aft stripes. These markings are set against a yellow background color. The underside is olive buff, turning white on the neck.

Ranging northward from southern Coahuila and central Durango, Mexico, the Trans-Pecos rat snake is found as far north as Carrizozo, Lincoln County, New Mexico. Whereas the green rat snake favors the mountain forests, the Trans-Pecos rat snake favors the creosote, yucca, mesquite, and ocotillo among the rocks of the high desert; it has most often been captured at altitudes between

1,500 and 5,000 feet. Like all rat snakes, *E. subocularis* is slender, almost racerlike in appearance, with extraordinarily large eyes made to appear larger by the surrounding scales. Adults are from nearly two feet to six feet in length.

The Trans-Pecos rat snake is one of three species of snakes in the American West that regularly practices dual constriction in subduing prey. Two rodents can be smothered simultaneously in the snake's coils. The action is rapid. The first victim, seized in the snake's jaws on the first lunge, is rapidly enfolded in a constricting coil and moved toward the snake's tail. In a flash the snake seizes the second victim and throws an anterior coil which will constrict it while the first victim is being smothered in what is now a posterior coil. This practice, also used by the rosy boa and the gopher snake, may be an adaptation to the habits of certain mice that all three snakes prey upon. Significantly, these mice of the genus *Peromyscus* often run in pairs. Dual constriction, therefore, provides the snake with the capacity to capture a pair at once. The snake's ability to get two for the price of one gives it a slight edge in the competition with other predators for the same food supply.

Herpetologists studying the Trans-Pecos rat snake have uncovered two interesting, though unrelated, puzzles. One of these puzzles stems from the study of karyotypes (Bury et al., 1970; Baker et al., 1972), the number and arrangement of chromosomes, a study that is central in trying to understand genetics and evolutionary development. Most snakes in North America, from boas to rattlesnakes, have what geneticists call a diploid (2N) chromosome number of thirty-six. There are some minor departures from this norm. One garter snake, *Thamnophis butleri,* has a 2N of thirty-seven; one *Elaphe obsoleta,* a generic relative of the Trans-Pecos rat snake, had thirty-five; and the lyre snake *(Trimorphodon biscutatus)* has a 2N of thirty-eight. Astoundingly, however, and full of profound implications, *subocularis* has a diploid of forty, a great departure from the norm in the forty-four distinct species studied. Outside of North America, other marked departures in diploid number have been found, in one instance twenty-four, in two instances fifty. The major question raised, and so far unanswered, is this: Does the higher diploid number show *subocularis* to be at a more advanced or at a less advanced state in evolution? Only the stark fact remains:

in karyotype the Trans-Pecos rat snake is unique among North American snakes.

The second puzzle provided by *subocularis* comes from this snake's role as the only known host for a species of hard tick, *Aponomma elaphensis* (Degenhardt and Degenhardt, 1965). This symbiotic relationship is fascinating in several ways. The tick is the only one of its family found in North America. Its closest described relative is an Australian species which apparently uses the wombat as a host. Though the tick in captivity is able to obtain nourishment from other species of snake, it is unable to reproduce on these secondary hosts as it does on *subocularis*.

Students of the relationship believe it is derived from the habits of *subocularis*. Individual snakes spend much time deep in rock fissures, probably returning after each hunt to the same resting place. Moreover, the Trans-Pecos rat snake is not diurnal, hunting almost exclusively at night. These conditions make *subocularis* a better host than any other species of large snakes in the area, for the tick would not survive long in intense sunlight and requires a moist, dark place to deposit its eggs.

Probably the two, snake and tick, provide a good example of coevolution. Diverging from their respective ancestors, they have evolved to their present state, each influencing the other's development. How great this influence has been no one can say. In one aspect of the relationship, however, the snake is apparently the loser. As they engorge themselves with blood, the ticks move toward the snake's tail from which, finally, they drop to deposit eggs. On older, larger Trans-Pecos rat snakes this action of the blood-sucking ticks eventually causes the tip of the snake's tail, deprived of nourishment, to mortify and drop off.

The Glossy Snake

21

The glossy snake *(Arizona elegans)* is indeed an elegant snake. One almost pictures it as a turn-of-the-century dandy whose well-tailored summer clothes have a smooth gloss to them. If snakes could wear spats and carry a cane, the glossy snake, one feels, would have both. This smooth-scaled snake, whose body reflects glisteningly any nearby light, is sometimes called the elegant bullsnake, for it can be confused at first glance with the gopher snake (also called bullsnake). It differs, however, by having smooth dorsal scales where the gopher snake's are keeled and by being a much lighter color than the gopher snake.

Adult glossy snakes are from slightly over two feet to four feet ten inches long. Their basic coloration is much like that of a gopher snake whose pattern has faded. Although there is a great variation in patterns among the various subspecies of the glossy snake, the ground color is always light brown, pinkish brown, buff, cream, or yellowed gray. Against this ground color, running down the middle of the back, is a row of thirty-six to eighty-three blotches—reddish brown, tan, or dark gray. These median blotches normally alternate with rows of smaller blotches running down each side. The impact of the glossy snake's color patterns is not visually startling. It is more like the faded coat of paint on an old piece of furniture made rich by the addition of a coat of varnish.

A gentle snake, the glossy snake rarely attempts to bite. In the American West it is nocturnal, seldom being seen when the sun shines unless a farmer plows it up. Such an uncovering happens fairly often, for the burrowing glossy snake frequents rodent burrows or its own tunnels. Two or three feet underground during the daylight hours, it can be unearthed only by plows or bulldozers. Attracted to agricultural areas in its search for food, it unwittingly exposes itself to earth-clearing blades.

At night the glossy snake crawls out of its burrow, generally between 7 and 11 P.M. when the air temperatures are between 70° and 90° F. Then it searches for food: lizards, smaller snakes, mice, moles, almost any small rodent. Judging from one field observation, certain lizards can spell trouble. An adult glossy snake found dead near Azusa, California, had protruding from its neck the spines of a fully grown horned lizard that it had attempted to swallow. In this case hunger had apparently overcome caution, for adult horned lizards with their bristling collar of thorns are not often preyed upon by wandering snakes.

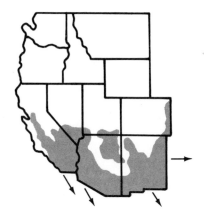

Within its range, the glossy snake lives in a variety of habitats. It is found all through the southwestern United States from central Kansas and Oklahoma to central California and from northeastern Colorado to Mexico. In Mexico it is found both in Baja California and on the mainland, in Sinaloa, Sonora, Durango, Chihuahua,

Zacatecas, San Luis Potosí, Coahuila, Nuevo León, Aguascalientes, and Tamaulipas.

Few snakes occupy the wide variety of habitats in which the glossy snake may be found. Being a burrower, it tends to prefer arid situations where sand or loam is available, one of the reasons it is drawn to agricultural areas where the soil has been worked. There appears to be some restriction on the altitude it prefers. Only one subspecies in the American West, *A. e. philipi* in Arizona, goes as high as 5,500 feet. (In Aguascalientes, Mexico, specimens have been taken as high as 6,200 feet.) Mostly glossy snakes prefer lower altitudes, where they are associated with whatever vegetation is predominant—blackjack oak and hickory, sagebrush, creosote and mesquite, Joshua trees, or thick coastal chaparral.

The nine subspecies of the glossy snake differ, often markedly, in color patterns and scalation. Six of these subspecies occur in the American West.

Glossy snakes are oviparous. Females lay three to twelve large eggs, with an average of eight, probably during May. A record of twenty-three eggs laid by one female hatched on August 26 after sixty-eight days of incubation. The young at hatching are from eight and one-half to eleven inches long.

The Gopher Snake

22

Found over almost all of the United States west of the Mississippi and widespread in the American West, the gopher snake *(Pituophis melanoleucus)* is often called bullsnake, no doubt because the original pioneer namer ran into a large individual—and a big gopher snake may be over eight feet long. Early reports, in fact, cited lengths of ten, eleven, even twelve feet—probably exaggerations, but one is tempted to believe that there were granddaddy snakes that, growing continuously as snakes do, reached these extremes. Herpetologists, after all, recognize that the larger snakes are more likely to be killed by automobiles and by rock-throwing, club-wielding humans—simply because large snakes are more easily noticed. In the primeval wilderness, having outwitted hawks, skunks, bears, and Indians—the successful snake, grown canny, might achieve gigantic size before an unlikely natural death. Such a possibility these days is remote, for the snake's vulnerability to its persistent, intelligent principal enemy, man, is far too great.

Yet estimates of snake sizes are almost always exaggerations, often by wide marks. Thus a four-foot snake may become six feet long when a person untrained in science subsequently tells of an encounter. Finally, we can rely only on actual measurement, but measurement is difficult since a live snake does not cooperate willingly in being stretched out to full length, and a dead snake, muscles relaxed and vertebrae separated, can be stretched out well beyond the live length of the same snake. In any event, returning to our bullsnake, an actual early measured length made in 1903 was eight feet three inches. This same snake was almost eight and one-half inches in circumference at the thickest point of its body. Normally adult gopher snakes fall into a three-and-a-half- to five-foot range with a few exceptional individuals growing larger.

Gopher snakes are large and relatively slow-moving, with a somewhat triangular head quite distinct from the neck. Confronted, the snake will coil defensively and flatten this triangular head so that it may look much like a rattlesnake. The resemblance, in fact, is probably not accidental, for in other aspects this nonvenomous snake resembles a rattlesnake. Although there is wide variation among subspecies, the gopher snake is most often marked on the back by a center row of black, dark brown, or reddish brown blotches that can readily be mistaken for the "diamonds" on a diamondback rattlesnake. Like the rattlesnakes, the gopher snake has strongly keeled scales. The gopher snake is likely to hiss loudly and extend its tongue for prolonged periods, moving it up and down as does a rattlesnake. Finally, the conclusive touch, the gopher snake vibrates its tail rapidly. There are, of course, no rattles on its tail, but in dry leaves or grass the vibrations can cause a rattling effect, particularly to the snake-fearing city dweller who isn't interested in taking the time to make a correct identification. Consequently gopher snakes suffer greatly at the hands of humans. So often is the gopher snake taken for a rattler that it's quite common along the roads in springtime to see a gopher snake that has been brutally killed. Curators of herpetology at zoos and museums in the American West are accustomed to making identifications of gopher snakes brought in chopped into several pieces. The only pleasant part of these experiences is to witness the relief that shows on the faces of the bite victims or their friends—since often the victims have already been taken to the hospital—when they find out the snake is harmless.

This particular cross the gopher snake has to bear was noted very early in herpetological literature. Writing in 1907, about the time the first automobiles were being mass produced, Joseph and Hilda Grinnell, referring to the gopher snake, comment:

> This is the most often met with of all our snakes, and, taken on the whole, has the most favorable reputation with the ordinary run of people. Most ranchers and country people have learned to recognize in the gopher snake an efficient destroyer of those pests of the farm, gophers and squirrels, and accordingly seldom offer injury willfully.
>
> But with city people who now and then drive into the country it is different. The gopher snake has an unfortunate habit of crawling out into open roads, especially on warm spring days, evidently with the purpose of basking in the grateful sunshine. Along comes the city man with his instinctive but unreasonable fear and hatred for snakes in general, and he attacks the harmless and slow-moving gopher snake to the usual destruction of the latter. So often one sees the mangled remains along roadsides that it seems a wonder that there are any gopher snakes whatever left.
>
> It is very evident that snakes are far less common than they used to be twenty years ago; at the same time gophers and ground squirrels are in many districts more of a pest than ever before; and the reason is obvious. . . .

If one wonders why there are so many ground squirrels visible over much of the American West, he need only think of what has happened since the Grinnells wrote that passage. Where in earlier times city people now and then drove into the country, today they move out in caravans of campers and squadrons of trail bikes, spreading over the landscape like a mechanized plague, still largely with the same ignorance and unreasoning hatred, still inclined to destroy first and identify afterward.

Ironically, natural selection may have betrayed the gopher snake. For thousands of years selection apparently favored those gopher snakes that could best imitate rattlesnakes, perhaps because they could convince most predators that they were not to be trifled with. Now the very act that helped preserve the species may be dooming it—for it is too convincing to that aggressive and unrelenting killer, man.

The hiss of a gopher snake is worthy of special note. It may well register the highest decibel count of any hiss in snakedom. It is, in fact, such a notable hiss that the gopher snake's generic name *Pituophis,* meaning "phlegm serpent," refers to the hiss. The loud noise is made possible by a special modification of the glottal region of the trachea (Martin and Huey, 1971). Two separate portions of the trachea, just behind the glottis, enlarge like small balloons, and in front of them ahead of the glottal opening a vertical fin of cartilage stands in the air stream to create more sound as air is expelled. In a sense the gopher snake's hiss apparatus is quite as remarkable as a rattlesnake's rattle.

Few snakes range more widely over the American West, or for that matter the entire United States, than the gopher snake. It can be found in all kinds of habitats—prairie grass, desert mesquite, pine forests of the mountains, and rich cultivated fields of the farm country; at altitudes to over 9,000 feet; from the Atlantic to the Pacific; from Canada to Mexico. It ranges well up into British Columbia, Alberta, and Saskatchewan and is found in Mexico to southern Sinaloa and central Veracruz. In many places a diurnal or crepuscular snake, it has adapted to crepuscular-nocturnal activity in hot areas, to take advantage of cooler temperatures. A measure of the diversity in this snake's habitat can be inferred from a census published in 1939 by L. M. Klauber, in this case of one subspecies, the Sonora gopher snake *(P. m. affinis).* Of 234 specimens captured (over several years), 7 were caught in orchards or vineyards, 104 in cultivated fields, 42 in grass, 17 in rocky desert, 54 in brushy desert, 6 in sandy desert, and 4 in barren desert. One notes, of course, the propensity of gopher snakes to be found in cultivated or grassy fields and brush where the gophers, ground squirrels, field mice, and other principal prey of the gopher snake abound.

Large and somewhat bulkier than many harmless snakes—although nowhere near so bulky as the rattlesnakes—the gopher snake normally has twenty-seven to thirty-seven rows of keeled scales at midbody. The body itself has a yellow or cream ground color with the aforementioned black, dark brown, or reddish brown

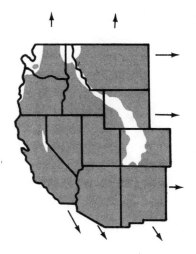

blotches. Smaller blotches, often in two or three rows, alternating, run down each side. Looking down on a gopher snake one sees a chainlike pattern with the dorsal blotches as the main links, joined by side blotches; most often there is a dark line running across the head in front of the eyes and other dark lines running from behind the eyes to the angle of the jaw. The belly is white or yellowish, frequently spotted with black. This most frequent pattern can have great variation, both in intensity and arrangement. Some specimens may be very dark; others, particularly in desert areas, are quite light. Sometimes what would be blotches, or links in the chain, on the normal gopher snake form lateral stripes. This pattern, in fact, is fairly frequently found on individuals in the Sacramento Valley and around San Francisco and Monterey in California.

Albino gopher snakes are not infrequent. In a notable experiment at the San Diego Zoo, C. B. Perkins managed a perfect demonstration of Mendelian genetics with an albino female gopher snake captured on May 27, 1940. The female, given the name "Blondy," was first bred to an accommodating normal male. The result was three eggs, two of which were hatched. The young appeared normal but carried, of course, the recessive genes for albinism. While the two young were growing, Blondy and her normal mate produced another clutch of five eggs, all of which hatched into normal-appearing youngsters. When one of the first two offspring, a male named "Sonny," reached maturity, he was placed with his mother; the normal male, his father, having performed an essential but undramatic part in the experiment, was relegated to the obscurity of the common gopher snake cage. The incestuous union of mother and son produced four eggs on July 3, 1945. One was infertile, but two of the remaining three hatched. The young snakes were perfectly formed albinos. Mendelian genetics would have it that of the four eggs laid, half should produce "normal" offspring. Perhaps through some strange happenstance the 'one fertile egg that didn't hatch would have been the normal snake. The final part of this experiment came in 1947. The ever willing Blondy was bred to her own grandson, Pinky, and the union produced five eggs. According to Mendel all five would be albinos. All five hatched. All five were albinos.

There are several subspecies of gopher snakes, among which

there is great variation in marking. One of the most interesting is the Santa Cruz Island gopher snake *(P. m. pumilus)*. This subspecies, found only on the California channel island of Santa Cruz, is a dwarf race. Closely resembling all the gopher snakes in appearance, it seldom grows longer than two and a half feet. Again one is amazed at the evolutionary process that fashioned a creature so well adapted to the requirements of its environment—in this case the restricted amount of space on a relatively small island. Strangely, though, three other subspecies of gopher snake on islands off the outer coast of northern Baja California are not dwarfs, even though one of these islands, South Coronado, is extremely small. These subspecies are *P. m. coronalis* (South Coronado Island), *P. m. fuliginatus* (San Martín Island), and *P. m. insulanus* (Cedros Island). In addition, *P. m. annectens* is found on Santa Catalina Island.

In their tongue-flicking hunts for rodents, lizards, small birds, and occasionally even other snakes, gopher snakes, like other snakes, frequently race abruptly into unexpected problems at the hands of man. The natural Ajo trap discussed in chapter 8 was as nothing compared with the man-made trap set by the San Francisco Water System, particularly in San Mateo County, California. Here three lakes, six miles long, serve as part of the water supply. In fairly large numbers snakes fall into the flume carrying the water. Down the flume they are swept, winding up in a concrete tower where heavy brush accumulates. In twenty-seven trips made between April 17 and June 20, 1949, one herpetologist collected 582 snakes, 165 of which were gopher snakes, in this case the Pacific gopher snake *(P. m. catenifer)*. These figures indicate how common the gopher snake was in those relatively recent days on the San Francisco peninsula; but considering the amount of construction that has taken place in the last twenty years, the figures would probably now be quite different.

Both field and laboratory reports of the courtship of gopher snakes indicate that it involves a highly ritualized male combat. As we have noted, combat between male snakes is fairly commonplace. The list of participating species includes representatives of the major snake families Colubridae, Elapidae, Viperidae, and Crotalidae. Boas and pythons (Boidae) have not been observed in combat, but this may simply be a failure in observation.

Various interpretations have been given. Early observers, of course, often mistook male combat for precopulatory courtship between male and female. There is still a possibility that in some instances male "combat" is actually homosexual in nature—although this interpretation has more validity applied to males confined in a zoo than to wild snakes. Pure territoriality or struggle for an exclusive prey-producing area is another possible reason for combat. Most likely, however, combat in wild snakes is caused by the effort to assert dominance over a small patch of ground upon which the winner can court a female snake. Perhaps, also, the females are attracted to winners and repelled by losers. Once again scents on the male snakes may differ once winner and loser have definitely been established.

In any event, gopher snakes have performed some of the best recorded combats between males. The fact that such combats took place is actually more exciting than the combat itself. Watching such a struggle is not unlike watching grass grow. A classic struggle between gopher snakes was described by the herpetologists Charles M. Bogert and Vincent D. Roth (1966). The two combatants were extraordinarily large, both over six feet long. They were Sonora gopher snakes *(P. m. affinis),* later established to be males. When first noticed near the town of Portal, Arizona, the two males were on a grass-covered bank near a house above the main part of town. The day was warm. They had evidently been at combat for some period, although how long no one could say. The snakes were completely intertwined in a good representation of the physicians' symbol, the caduceus. (It is tempting to believe that this symbol had its origin in an observed combat dance between males of the Aesculapian snake *Elaphe longissimus* in Greece. However, the original caduceus had only one snake; the symbol of two intertwined snakes was introduced in Roman times.) The combatants could not move through any of the normal means of snake locomotion. Instead, they moved very slowly forward in a corkscrew manner, the movement apparently being caused by the force each exerted on the other. Their heads, parallel to the ground, were close to one another, although neither made an effort to bite. Once in a while one would momentarily get the advantage so that the other was forced to roll over. Such victories were hollow, however, since the momentarily victorious snake was carried along in the rolling motion. Both snakes hissed loudly and repeatedly. For an hour the combat continued, and during this period the fighters corkscrewed ahead no more than ten yards. During much of this time the snakes were watched by several interested onlookers—yet, unfazed, they continued their struggle. The combat finally concluded when the owner of the home asked that the snakes be removed from the premises. For the observing herpetologists, of course, this was an unsatisfactory ending, for they would like to have seen that final untangling that could clearly establish a winner. Incidentally, no female snake was sighted in the vicinity of this struggle.

In actually courting the female, the male gopher snake continues his aggressive behavior. Commonly his approach is to seize her by the neck, biting quite fiercely, as he seeks to copulate. So bent on their mating objectives are these males that they are apparently not deterred by the most unfavorable of conditions. One herpetologist, while collecting, had placed two male and one female gopher snakes in a snake bag. Not long after, noting some threshing about by the snakes, he unceremoniously dumped them out. Without attempting to escape, the larger male began biting both the female and the probably somewhat bewildered smaller male who, after undergoing a few minutes of this treatment, decided to leave. The larger male, virile and victorious, scarcely paused; he immediately began a copulation that lasted twenty minutes. Later that same day, safely in a cage, he and the female copulated again. The final touch of irony to this story came when the female laid twenty-two eggs—none of them fertile.

Gopher snakes, not known primarily as burrowers or climbers, will both burrow and climb in their pursuit of prey. Mostly they eat mice, rats, gophers, rabbits, squirrels—all those cute little rodents that, unchecked by predators, multiply so rapidly, cause so much damage, and bring such a threat to human health. Occasionally gopher snakes eat birds and their eggs, and to raid a nest, they may climb a tree. To seek out rodents or perhaps find shelter from the sun, they may burrow. Gopher mounds, those bulkheads against the world outside the gopher's tunnel, pose no obstacle to a hungry gopher snake. Using its head as a tool, the snake will loosen the dirt of the mound, catch some in a loop behind the head, and pull it from the mound. This action will be repeated until the snake gains entry. Then, moving down the tunnel like a scaly nemesis, the snake clears out the gophers one by one.

As we have seen, gopher snakes are oviparous. Eggs laid in midsummer generally hatch between the middle of September and the second week of October. Perhaps more than some species the young gopher snakes, because they are larger—eight to twelve inches—than most snakes at birth, suffer at the beak, claw, and hand of predators. Few live long enough to see a second year. Few, in fact, reach their first winter.

A reader of general books on herpetology written before 1960 would be somewhat confused by the fact that the snakes now lumped under the term gopher snake used to be described as several different species. The change to one species is another demonstration that taxonomic studies are continually needed. The study that brought this lumping was performed by Hobart M. Smith and J. P. Kennedy (1951). On June 2, 1951, Kennedy captured a snake near Livingston, Polk County, Texas, in an area between populations of the pine snake, *P. melanoleucus ruthveni* and the bullsnake, then described as *P. catenifer sayi.* Significantly, the captured snake appeared to be an intermediate between the two. It had features of both "species." Smith and Kennedy proposed that *melanoleucus* and *catenifer* be lumped into one species, *melanoleucus.* This proposal was generally supported where other captured specimens showed the same intermediate characteristics.

There are six subspecies of the gopher snake in the American West.

Chapter 10

» » » » » »

KINGSNAKES AND THEIR RELATIVES

Probably no other group of snakes has accumulated over the years more goodwill among Americans than the kingsnakes. Many a person, asked if he knew anything about kingsnakes, would respond, "Why, certainly, they kill rattlesnakes." Some people seem to believe that kingsnakes have a warm spot in their hearts for mankind and kill rattlesnakes as a sort of gallant gesture, the same way porpoises purportedly drive sharks away from swimmers. Other people, less romantic, fancy that kingsnakes simply have a taste for rattlesnakes and seek them out above all other prey. Its reputation as a rattlesnake killer and the kingsnake's bold markings, which cannot easily be confused with rattlesnake markings, have helped to preserve kingsnakes from persecution by man.

Kingsnakes *do* kill rattlesnakes, but they do so instinctively as predators, for rattlesnakes are one staple of their varied diet. Kingsnakes are ophiophagous: they will eat any other snake, including other kingsnakes and—unbelievably—snakes longer than themselves. Several herpetologists in the field have come upon one kingsnake swallowing another slightly larger snake of the same species. Kingsnakes also eat lizards, mice, and birds; in short, they have about as varied a diet as a snake can have, including on occasion their own shed skin.

When attacking rattlers, kingsnakes are protected by their immunity to rattlesnake venom. The battle, nonetheless, is not always won by the kingsnake. Probably warned by a scent secreted by the kingsnake's skin, rattlesnakes that live in kingsnake country adopt a specialized defensive posture when a kingsnake attacks. When confronting a man or other animal, a rattlesnake will normally throw its body into the usual S loop, prepared to strike with fang and venom. Faced by a hungry kingsnake, the same rattlesnake pushes head and neck against the ground and backs rapidly away. Occasionally, if the kingsnake relentlessly follows, the rattlesnake will use a loop of its heavy body as a club and endeavor to pound at the kingsnake's head. Its only hope is to discourage the attacker, to make the kingsnake decide that the meal is not worth a buffeted head.

The rattlesnake, normally the death-dealing poisoner efficiently destroying its enemies and killing its prey, in this case turns coward and runs from the field. Of course, this type of encounter in no substantial way differs from any other encounter between predator and prey — between wolf and caribou, fox and hen, owl and mouse. One animal dies and in dying helps another to survive.

Kingsnakes are entirely confined to the Western Hemisphere, where there are about eight species, all moderate-size, found from southeast Canada to Ecuador. Their generic name *Lampropeltis* means "shiny skin." The description is apt, for their smooth-scaled skins give an impression of brilliance, glinting softly when the light strikes them. Their heads are not distinctively separate from their necks, but seem rather like to tapered extensions. Almost all kingsnakes are handsomely marked, some so beautifully that the most shuddering snake hater has to admit their beauty. Although often cantankerous when first picked up, defending themselves both by biting and releasing musk, they most often settle down in captivity and make good pets.

The common kingsnake *(Lampropeltis getulus)* is found from coast to coast. In the American West it ranges from southwest Oregon to the Mexican border. Missing the more northerly western states, it is found throughout California (including Catalina Island), the lower half of Nevada, southern Utah, western and southern Arizona, and most of New Mexico. It is also found throughout much of mainland Mexico to northern Sinaloa, San Luis Potosí, and northern Tamaulipas. It is found on many islands in the Gulf of California— Angel de la Guarda, Salsipuedes, San Lorenzo, Monserrate, Santa Catalina, and Cerralvo.

Adult common kingsnakes are generally from two and one-half to three and one-half feet long, although occasional specimens have been over six feet long. With only a little instruction anyone seeing a kingsnake can immediately identify it. What plays hob, however, with such identifications is that while the colors remain much the same—cream or yellow set against black or brown—the patterns vary greatly among the eleven subspecies in relation to geographic locations. Through much of its western range the common kingsnake is banded with fairly wide cream or yellow bands against black or brown. Around San Diego, California, about forty percent of one subspecies, the California kingsnake *(L. g. californiae)*, have a cream or yellow vertical stripe down the center of their backs, even though brothers and sisters from the same clutch of eggs are banded. These striped kingsnakes formerly were considered a separate species, but it is now known that they are just a color phase. L. M. Klauber and C. B. Perkins observed one clutch laid by a captive mother at the San Diego Zoo (Klauber, 1936). This one clutch was kept under carefully controlled conditions from the time of laying, where only this one mother could have been the layer, to the time of hatching. From the clutch at hatching emerged both striped and banded young, thus destroying the idea held then that the striped variety was a different species from the banded.

In much of Arizona the kingsnake may be spotted with cream to yellow spots. On some snakes these spots form bands; on others they are more generally distributed. In southern Arizona and Sonora, Mexico, the kingsnake is often completely black with no bands at all. As a matter of interest, one continues to find this variation in a single species of snake as one moves east: light-spotted markings in southern New Mexico into Texas; abundant spots down the middle of the back in the Midwest; another dark phase with light crossbands (sometimes absent) and some lateral spotting in the Appalachian region; distinct, chain-linked crossbands in the East; mottled

Kingsnakes and Their Relatives

markings in central Florida; light-colored, unbanded, and speckled on the tip of Florida. Albinos occur not infrequently in all color variants.

Banding, spotting, or speckles also mark the kingsnake's belly in many variations. One variant occurs at the north end of the San Joaquin valley, California, where individuals are black-bellied with pale crossbands that broaden on the lower sides to form lateral stripes.

Befitting a snake with such an extensive range, the kingsnake dwells in a wide variety of habitats from sea level to 7,000 feet. It may be found in pine forests, woods, swamps, along river bottoms, around farms, in thick brush, on prairies, or in the desert (where the bands tend to be whiter and the ground color darker). Not especially equipped for desert life, kingsnakes living in desert favor the beds of streams or the areas around water holes. It is, in short, a highly adaptable snake in both diet and habitat. This adaptability, along with goodwill from man, may assure its survival long after other large snake species have died out. Even around the constantly encroaching housing developments it is often the only fairly large snake that stays on for a while—until automobile traffic becomes so dense that no large snake can survive.

Most often a snake that is abroad during daytime or in the softer long-shadowed period of late afternoon, the kingsnake in desert country seeks shelter from hot desert sun by hunting at dusk or after darkness comes. It is a terrestrial hunter that will, if spurred by hunger, climb into bushes or trees to search for eggs and young birds. It kills its prey by constriction.

Kingsnakes are egg-layers; clutches of six to twelve eggs are deposited from mid-May to early August. From mid-July into early October the hatchlings emerge. They are about nine to twelve inches long.

Kingsnakes use two main modes of defense. If escape is cut off, the snake will coil and vibrate its tail. In leaves or dry grass this vibration can produce a sound like that of a rattlesnake's rattle. The kingsnake does not at all resemble a rattler, but its coiled intensity, punctuated by an occasional strike, and accompanied by the vibrating tail can give pause to the uninformed. In fact, one of the authors remembers that as a very young boy he had such an encounter with a common kingsnake (the picture of the snake is still indelibly there) and ran home crying. The snake escaped unharmed—the whole objective of its defense.

When picked up, the kingsnake may be docile, but more likely it will bite and discharge foul-smelling musk. Until recently herpetologists believed that this discharge of musk was entirely defensive in character. Now, however, some evidence points to another use. The musk smell may act as an alarm device, a kind of scent siren, to warn other kingsnakes that enemies are in the area. I. Lehr Brisbin, Jr. (1968), of the Savannah River Ecology Lab of the Atomic Energy Commission, ran across this possibility by accident. For a study of growth, he had captured a young female eastern kingsnake *(L. g. getulus)* less than two weeks old. For thirty-nine months this snake was kept isolated from all other snakes. Never during that time did it release musk. On May 5, 1967, Brisbin measured on the lab table a freshly caught Florida kingsnake *(L. g. floridana)*. Somewhat roughly handled, the snake discharged copious quantities of musk over much of the tabletop. After being measured, the wild-caught kingsnake was placed in a cage. The lab table was thoroughly scrubbed, rinsed, and dried. It still retained a slight odor of musk. Fifteen minutes later the female kingsnake was placed on the same table for measurement. Immediately, before being handled in any way, this sheltered snake began moving back and forth across the table in a most agitated manner. As it moved, it vibrated its tail rapidly. Half a minute after being placed on the table this snake, too, discharged musk—for the first time in its life. Brisbin concluded that this response by the female may have been sexual, since scent plays a large part in sexual behavior of many animals, including snakes. On the other hand, he noted, snakes, being unable to cry out or otherwise use vocal alarms as many animals do, might well use musk discharge as their counterpart of a blue jay's scolding or a squirrel's angry chatter.

"Sports" or "freaks"—unnatural, deformed, grotesque creatures—are found from time to time in all animal species. They may result from prenatal disease of the mother, unfortunate accidents, or some abnormality in the gene structure of the parents. Viewed with avid curiosity by many people, freaks, human or animal, fake or real, are unfortunately chief attractions of the circus, carnival, or roadside zoos. Thus even today six-legged cows, Siamese twins, (fake) horned snakes, and many other grotesques are displayed before people to whom perhaps the greatest satisfaction in seeing abnormality is in feeling relief at being normal.

Strangely, within the past nineteen years of its fifty-eight-year history, the San Diego Zoo has received four snake freaks, all California kingsnakes with the same abnormality: two quite distinct heads. If it were not, indeed, for the fact that these two-headed monsters, all captured young, came from widely separated points within San Diego County, one might suspect that they were offspring of the same genetically defective parents. The explanation, however, for the hatching of four such freaks in such a relatively short period must lie elsewhere, for the distances are too great for one snake to have traveled. Since four have been captured, one wonders how many others have hatched in the wild. The captured snakes, in this case, would undoubtedly live longer in captivity under the care of concerned zoo keepers, for being two-headed poses certain problems. The first problem comes when it is time to hatch. Hatchlings must use the egg tooth at the end of the snout to pierce the tough, leathery shell. One wonders how a two-headed hatchling, each head presumably cutting a slit in the egg shell with its own egg tooth, decides which head will lead the way out of the egg. Then comes the problem of moving. If one head wants to go east and the other west, the snake will be immobilized. This inability to move has observably frustrated two of the San Diego Zoo's two-headed snakes. The right head strives mightily to go right, the left to go left—each visibly straining, raising off the ground, with the skin at the juncture of the two heads stretched almost to the breaking point. Capturing and swallowing prey poses another problem, or rather two more. Fortunately, for the cannibalistic kingsnake, the distinct heads cannot quite reach one another; otherwise one might be confronted with the spectacle of a snake swallowing itself. Altogether, the problems of two-headedness cast considerable doubt on the ancient adage, "Two heads are better than one." Fortunately, in all four two-headed snakes, one head was clearly dominant, eating more often and dragging the other perfectly alert, tongue-flickering head passively along. Dudley, the right head of Dudley Duplex, the first two-headed snake at the San Diego Zoo, almost always swallowed the mouse even though Duplex, the left head, sometimes got hold of it. In 146 feedings Dudley ate 139 times, Duplex only 7. Fortunately for Duplex the food wound up in their joint stomach; but if snakes savor their food, Duplex missed a lot of gustatory pleasure.

All four of the two-headed kingsnakes have been, or are now, on display at the San Diego Zoo. Dudley Duplex I lived for six and one-half years, probably an extraordinarily long life for a two-headed kingsnake. Its death came from what amounted to a built-in time bomb. As it grew, each neck likewise grew until one day the growth pressure of one neck severed the main spinal cord and Dudley Duplex was dead. Still living are two more of Dudley's relatives, Dudley Duplex II and Nip-and-Tuck.

Ten percent of the letters addressed to the San Diego Zoo's reptile house concern the two-headed snakes. Often the writer apparently can't quite believe he has seen such a creature. One youngster wrote: "I like your animals at your zoo. I like the polar bears and tigers too. I like the snakes 'cause you have a two-head king snake. You have big turtles. *Is there a two-head snake?"* Many of the letters ask the zoo to support a person who has seen one of the two-headed snakes but can get no one else to believe him. A letter from northern California is typical: "Last evening I attended a cocktail party and entered into a discussion on snakes. I mentioned that I had seen your two-headed snake, and that it is the only one of its kind in captivity. Of course, no one believed me. (Perhaps I was seeing double last night, but I know I was completely sober when I was at your zoo)."

Beauty in any animal, as in a work of art, lies mainly in the eye of the beholder. Yet there is remarkable agreement, even among people who say "Ugh" at the mention of snakes, that the California mountain kingsnake *(Lampropeltis zonata)* is spectacularly beautiful. In this serpent, the adult length of which is slightly under two to slightly over three feet, nature has combined and arranged colors to achieve an aesthetic impact that seems to transcend mere evolutionary necessity. Black, white, and red rings form a continuous glistening pattern the length of the snake's body. The head is black on the nose and top and white toward the rear. Behind this is a black

The California Mountain Kingsnake

24

ring, then red, then black again, then white, and so on, in a vivid sequence of rich colors. The red is always bordered by black, the three rings forming what is called a triad.

This snake is found principally in both the coastal and interior mountains of California, although one subspecies ranges as far north as southern Washington. A snake of moist woods at altitudes up to 8,000 feet, the California mountain kingsnake is seldom encountered below the mountain forests, although it has been taken at sea level. It is not found in the desert. One looks for it among the pines or heavily thicketed chaparral, around rocky places, or in hollow logs. Mostly it hunts during daylight, but if the weather is warm, it may prefer to move about at night. Then its beauty is grayed by moonlight, obscured by darkness. One sees it best when it moves, a chain of bright colors against the dark brown of a rotted log, where sun dapples a carpet of pine needles on the forest floor.

Sometimes called the coral kingsnake because it is seen by some as an "imitator" of the venomous coral snake, it is completely harmless. Moreover, nowhere does its range overlap that of the coral snake. It does resemble two close relatives, the Sonora mountain kingsnake and the milk snake. Again, however, neither is found where the California mountain king is found. It also somewhat resembles the long-nosed snake which is found in its range, but seen side by side the two species appear quite different, notably in the arrangement of rings and intensity of coloration. On the long-nosed snake black and red rings alternate without the intervention of white and the colors are less intense because of the presence of off-color scales that break up the main color.

Like the common kingsnake, the California mountain kingsnake hunts a wide variety of prey—small mammals, young birds, lizards, other snakes. An egg-layer, this snake has seven subspecies, five of which occur in the American West. The others are found in Mexico. One of these, the Todos Santos kingsnake *(L. z. herrerae),* provides an extreme example of relictual distribution. Isolated in a relict population by geographic upheavals, confined to tiny, arid South Todos Santos Island off Ensenada, Baja California, far removed from its relatives in the moist mountains, this kingsnake has lost the red in its color pattern and has evolved so that in appearance it resembles its mainland cousin, the California kingsnake.

When one first sees the Sonora mountain kingsnake *(Lampropeltis pyromelana),* colored much the same as its cousin, the California mountain kingsnake, one senses that it inspired some of the colors and patterns used by the Navajo Indians in their art. Many a Navajo rug displays the same basic black, red, and white arranged in much the same way. In size an adult Sonora mountain king is from nearly two to about three and a half feet long. It ranges in the mountains from central Utah and eastern Nevada southward into Arizona and extreme southwestern New Mexico, into the Sierra Madre Occidental mountains of Mexico. One or two isolated populations occur at such places as the Egan Range, Nevada, and the Hualpai Mountains of Arizona. It is almost always found at altitudes between 2,800 and 9,100 feet.

The Sonora Mountain Kingsnake
25

The chief difference between this snake and the California mountain king is in the fact that the Sonora mountain king has a white or pale yellow snout. On those rare occasions when the snout is black, it is flecked with white. The black bands on this snake vary greatly in width, but almost always narrow noticeably or even disappear on the sides. It differs from the venomous western coral snake—found in parts of the same range and upon which it may prey—in having red bands bordered by black, whereas the coral has red bands bordered by white or yellow.

Another snake of mountain chaparral and forest, one associates the Sonora mountain king with pines, firs, and piñon in places near water. There it lives in dense places, difficult to reach, in thick clumps of brush, among fortress rocks, under fallen logs. It preys on lizards, other snakes, nesting birds, and small mammals. Oviparous, it has four subspecies, three of which are found in the American West.

Among the most persistent of snake legends is that of the milk snake. The story, told as fact by many dairy farmers, has it that the milk snake obtains a substantial part of its diet by milking cows or other milk-producing animals. The method described is quite simple: the snake climbs a leg, coils around it, stretches out its neck, seizes a teat, and sucks away. Naturally, such action is not seen as desirable by dairy farmers. The story goes well back in U.S. history. In the diaries of Lewis and Clark we find one account. Clark writes:

The Milk Snake
26

During the time I lay on the sand waiting for the boat, a large snake swam to the bank immediately under the deer which was hanging over the water and no great distance from it. I threw chunks and drove this snake off several times. I found that he was determined on getting to the meat. I was compelled to kill him—*the part of the deer which attracted this snake I think was the MILK from the bag of the doe* [italics added].

The plain fact is that *no* snake drinks milk or for any reason milks cows or other animals. When a milk snake *(Lampropeltis triangulum)* invades a barnyard, it is probably searching for some of the mice that proliferate around any kind of farm. It is not searching for milk.

"Milk snake" seems too pallid a name to describe this beautiful representative of the kingsnakes. Ranging over a large part of the United States, the various subspecies of the milk snake show great variations in color. Like the mountain king's, these colors are vivid —rings or saddles of red, orange, or sometimes reddish brown, bordered by black, and interspersed with yellow or white. Again, the black always borders the red or orange. On the milk snake the yellow or white rings almost always widen toward the belly.

As an interesting side note for the student of evolution, although it does not involve the subspecies of milk snakes found in the American West, milk snakes in the Southeast and South have much wider red bands than those elsewhere in the United States. In this same area ranges the eastern coral snake, which also has wide red bands. Did the milk snake evolve with wider bands to imitate the venom-carrying coral snake and thus achieve a measure of protection from attack? If not, how do we account for the fact that only in this particular area does the milk snake have wider red bands? This kind of question fascinates herpetologists and ecologists. The answers—if any can be found—will help man to come to terms with the natural world around him.

In adult length the milk snake ranges from a foot and one-half to four and one-half feet. It occurs mainly in the eastern portion of the American West: the southeastern portion of Montana, eastern Wyoming, eastern Colorado, and northern New Mexico. A fairly large isolated population of one subspecies is found in Utah. A small isolated population also occurs in northern Arizona.

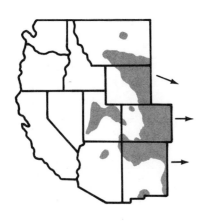

Extensive in range, varied in habitat, the milk snake, like the common kingsnake, may be able to survive longer than many species. Milk snakes may be found at altitudes from sea level to 8,000 feet, on prairies or in river bottoms, among pine forests or leafy wooded glades, on rocky hillsides or on dunes of sand, among fields of corn or in a peach orchard. They are seldom seen, for they are often nocturnal and during the day hide under boards or fallen bark, in rotted logs, or under rocks.

Four subspecies of the oviparous milk snake are found in the American West.

Closely related to the kingsnakes, the long-nosed snake *(Rhinocheilus lecontei)* is beautiful, gentle, and possesses, for a snake, a nose that rivals that of Cyrano de Bergerac. Long and even turned up in a slightly sneering way in one subspecies, the Texas long-nosed snake *(R. l. tessellatus)*, this nose is a tool for burrowing and digging out prey. Adult long-nosed snakes are from two to nearly three and one-half feet long. Sometimes confused with the California or Sonora mountain kingsnakes, the long-nosed snake is distinguished by being speckled over most of its body by off-color scales, white against black, black against red. This speckling has the effect of diluting and graying the beautiful ground colors—saddles of black lightly bordered by white with pink or red bands between. The underbelly is pale yellow or white, sometimes marked with a few dark spots. Like the kingsnake, the long-nosed snake's head is only slightly wider than its neck. The nose, however, is much longer and quite pointed. In certain parts of its range this snake frequently lacks the pink or red, being then banded in black and white not unlike the common kingsnake. There is one sure way to distinguish long-nosed snakes from kingsnakes. Kingsnakes have a double row of scales, the subcaudals, on the underside of the tail. The long-nosed snake is the only colubrid in the American West that has most of its subcaudals in a single row.

The long-nosed snake ranges from southwestern Idaho and southeastern Colorado through parts of Utah, most of Nevada, a large part of California from above San Francisco south (except in the High Sierras), Arizona, and New Mexico, and on down into Mexico as far as Nayarít, San Luis Potosí, and southern Tamaulipas.

The Long-Nosed Snake
27

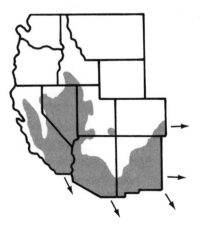

A fairly common snake, it is seldom encountered because it lives underground during the day, coming out in the evening or night-time to hunt. It prefers a brushy or rocky habitat, whether on deserts, prairies, or in coast chaparral. Although it is seldom encountered above 4,000 feet, it has been taken as high as 5,400 feet. Strangely enough for a snake of the lower elevations, however, it appears to tolerate lower temperatures better than many snakes, having been taken in air temperatures as low as 59° F. Hunting in the desert at night, Klauber reported one long-nosed snake that was blown across the highway by a strong, cold wind at a time when he saw no other snakes. Excepting its ability to burrow, the long-nosed snake does not seem particularly adapted to desert life. Much of its movement into arid lands apparently occurs after farmers have brought irrigation. Where irrigation exists in the desert, more long-nosed snakes occur. In the barren reaches few are found.

Clarence J. McCoy of the Carnegie Museum and Frederick R. Gehlbach of Baylor University published a study (1967) of the defensive tactics of the long-nosed snake. It uses a variety of approaches: it hides its head, rapidly coils the body, elevates its tail, coils its tail helically, vibrates its tail, and, when picked up, will probably both defecate and discharge musk anally. Many harmless snakes, as we have seen, use one or more of these defenses, each for a particular reason. The head, being the snake's most vulnerable part, must be protected. Rapid coiling, even thrashing, serves as a diversionary measure. In fact, with snakes marked in bands like a kingsnake or long-nosed snake, a continuous coiling and uncoiling can deceive the eye. It can, for example, make the snake appear larger than it actually is. Elevating the tail may warn off a particular kind of predator such as a color-conscious bird, or it may simply keep attention away from the much more vulnerable head. Vibrating the tail makes a noise that warns off hoofed animals and may provide some extra protection by similarity to the rattlesnake's behavior. The defecation and musk discharge are at least disconcerting and at most mildly sickening, and are likely also to warn other members of the species that an attacker is near.

In defensive display, long-nosed snakes (probably only females) often discharge blood through the cloaca or the nose when they discharge musk. This peculiarity, found in some female kingsnakes, is shared by few other snakes. Its exact purpose remains a mystery. McCoy and Gehlbach established that such discharge is not from an injury and concluded that it may be either a "physiological side effect" or that the blood may actually provide additional discouragement to the attacker, although they found no special poisons in the blood. Horned lizards in defense emit blood from their eyes. From experiments with such blood sprayed on dogs and cats, L. M. Klauber concluded that it caused a "discomfiting effect." Very possibly this discomfiture also occurs when the long-nosed snake uses blood. But why does this bizarre behavior occur only in females? If this is invariably true, there may be a peculiarity in the female's construction that brings mild bleeding when the snake is greatly agitated.

Insects, lizards, small mammals, and the eggs of reptiles are the food of the long-nosed snake. Among lizards, whiptails of the genus *Cnemidophorus* are particular favorites. Within the same habitat the western patch-nosed snake also often eats whiptails. Yet strangely, seeking the same foods, the two species probably never run across one another while hunting. The western patch-nose, a daytime hunter, is fast moving and catches the moving lizards. The long-nosed snake, an evening or nighttime hunter, is relatively slow moving. It probably uses its nose to dig out lizards sleeping under a layer of sand. Being a burrower, the long-nosed snake can dig out nests in the manner described for the patch-nosed snake. Long-nosed snakes are not selective in their egg-eating habits, and they may well devour eggs of their own kind during the period of vulnerability between laying in early June and hatching in August. There are two subspecies of long-nosed snakes in the American West.

Chapter 11

» » » » »

WATER SNAKES
AND
GARTER SNAKES

In the great game of nature called "Adapt or Die"—a game played not in a single lifetime but over many generations—some snakes have adapted largely to a terrestrial or subterranean existence, or to a combination of both. The food they seek and their hiding places are on or under the ground. But food and hiding places exist also in the waters of the earth, in the lakes, ponds, and running streams. Here live fish, crayfish, water insects, tadpoles, frogs—often in great numbers. Here, too, live some small mammals, and others come to drink. The watery places, moreover, offer many shelters from predators—ancient stumps and logs with hollow recesses, under-water piles of rocks and boulders full of crevices and caves, piles of rotted vegetation, and burrows of aquatic mammals.

In the logic of nature, therefore, one would expect to find in the lakes, ponds, and streams snakes adapted to the aquatic life—good swimmers, like all snakes, but ones adapted to prey on water-dwelling animals. Such snakes do, in fact, exist. Called the natricine snakes, they include the true water snakes, those of the genus *Natrix*, and the garter snakes, perhaps the most abundant and certainly the most wide-ranging snakes on the North American continent. Mostly these snakes depend upon water for their food supply and move on or die out when swamps are filled, ponds drained, or streams radically changed by dams. A few of these snakes, though natricines by structural classification, have adapted to a wholly terrestrial existence.

So distinctive are the natricine snakes that they are a separate subfamily—the Natricinae—of the Colubridae. Like the genera *Elaphe* and *Coluber,* they have a worldwide distribution, being found in Europe, Asia, Africa, northern Australia, and North America. They are distinguished from other snakes by vertebral differences, wide ventral scales, and nonvalvular nostrils. A few herpetologists, in fact, still believe they should be placed in their own family.

The Water Snakes

In the United States one thinks of the true water snakes as inhabiting the swamps and waterways of the Southeast. Here, in fact, most of them do live, inhabiting places like the Everglades of Florida. Here, too, they have shown remarkable adaptability, even in one instance to salt or brackish water amid tangled mangrove roots.

But two species of the genus *Natrix* extend into the American West. Like most of their relatives they are heavy-bodied, dull in color, usually considered ugly, vicious snakes that are frequently, and incorrectly, called "water moccasins" and killed forthwith. Unlike the true water moccasin, or cottonmouth *(Agkistrodon piscivorus),* which is a venomous pit viper, found only in the Southeast, water snakes are harmless, though they bite savagely when picked up.

In addition to being confused with the moccasin, water snakes have suffered at the hands of man for another reason. They are fish eaters—not exclusively, but undeniably. Some sportsmen, therefore, resent them as competitors for game fish and kill them so that more fish may survive. Such heedless tampering with natural predator-prey relationships has almost invariably brought results exactly opposite to those intended. The fish saved by killing water snakes are slower and less intelligent, for the water snakes are not fast swimmers and can catch only the misfits, the unwary, the sick, the old, the laggards—as is always the way with predators and their prey. Unchecked by predation, the misfits multiply. The total increase in numbers may bring catastrophe—a depleted food supply and slow starvation of hundreds or thousands, or stunting of growth so that more may survive on what little food is available or, frequently, epidemic diseases that decimate the population. Left alone, the predators will improve the breed of their prey animal—in this case producing larger, smarter, more desirable game fish for the sportsman.

Over much of its range the plain-bellied water snake *(Natrix erythrogaster)* is called "copperbelly," because its faintly spotted belly is often a dull, reddish color. A large snake reaching lengths of slightly over five and one-half feet, the plain-bellied water snake touches the American West only in the Pecos River Valley in extreme southeastern New Mexico. Otherwise it is found from sea level to 6,700 feet over much of Texas, ranges up to southern Michigan and southward into Zacatecas, Mexico.

Whatever its ancestral origins may have been, this snake has moved its habitat farther and farther into arid lands, always seeking water. The water it seeks need not be permanent. If a rancher scoops out a basin or builds a cattle tank, the copperbelly may soon move in. Irrigation ditches, canals, rain ponds—all provide a suitable habitat. During rainy weather, in fact, when many temporary ponds or puddles dot the countryside, the copperbelly is often found far from standing water or streams.

The plain-bellied water snake resembles the common water snake: it has a moderately heavy body, strongly keeled scales with apical pits, blotches on the back and sides, and (in males) knobs on the dorsal scale keels near the anus. However, the copperbelly most often has blotches all the way from head to tail; they are dark brown edged with black, against a lighter brown or gray background. Blotches on the back alternate with blotches along each side. Occasionally individuals have light crossbars, black-edged, instead of blotches. The belly, without half-moons, is normally a pale yellow, sometimes tinged with orange, except in those eastern portions of the range where it becomes reddish.

In most other ways the plain-bellied water snake resembles the common water snake. It eats crayfish, fish, salamanders, tadpoles, toads, and frogs and is live-bearing.

In the American West one subspecies, found in New Mexico, is the blotched water snake *(N. e. transversa)*.

The common water snake *(Natrix sipedon)* is found throughout most of the central and eastern United States, touching the American West only in eastern Colorado. This snake requires a watery environment, lives exclusively in swamps, marshes, rivers, ponds, lakes at altitudes from sea level to about 4,500 feet within its range.

A fairly heavy-bodied snake with head distinct from neck, adults vary in length from one and one-half feet to four and one-half feet. The scales of the common water snake are prominently keeled and bear apical pits—two small, round pits on either side of the keel on each dorsal scale. Sometimes these pits are no more than spots with no indentation; most often they are truly pitted. Male water snakes have knobbed keels on the scales above the anus. On the forward part of its body the common water snake has reddish brown or black crossbands. Starting about midbody these become blotches that continue, alternating with blotches on the sides, all the way down to the tail. These bands and blotches are set against brown or pale gray. Not infrequently the common water snake is dark, with the pattern of blotches partially or totally obscured. Along the belly is a regularly or irregularly arranged pattern of reddish or black half-moons. Frequently the belly is orange or yellow down the middle, graying near the sides.

Young water snakes, from six and one-half to ten inches long, normally show more contrast in their markings than adults do. Occasionally individuals with the more reddish blotches can be confused with the corn snake. The most notable difference between the two is in the scales: the water snake is keeled, the corn snake is smooth. Moreover, the corn snake has the spearhead pattern on the top of its head.

Frequent sun-baskers along the shores of their watery homes, the water snakes find easy refuge from intruders either by diving down below the surface to hide on the bottom or by moving into reeds or other watery plants. In diving to the bottom of pond, lake, or stream, the water snake can stay down for long periods of time, certainly over thirty minutes and probably longer. Obviously this ability in an air-breathing creature without gills gives a pronounced

Water Snakes and Garter Snakes

advantage in escaping from predators. The water snake shares this ability with seals, porpoises, manatees, beaver, and several other air-breathers that can remain underwater for long periods (Murdaugh and Jackson, 1962). All these animals experience bradycardia when they cease their normal breathing, as they must while diving. Bradycardia means their heartbeat slows, often quite markedly. Their stored oxygen supply is rationed, so to speak, by the slow beat of their heart. Moreover, the oxygen is used more sparingly. Less goes to muscle; more goes to the brain. Without breathing, the snake remains alert, perceptive, wholly capable of continuing action.

One survey of water snake habitats included everything from rivers to rain pools, but always found the common water snake near water. The common water snake's food is almost always aquatic—crayfish, fish, salamanders, tadpoles, toads, and frogs. Sometimes, though, it catches insects and small mammals. If a water snake is caught, it will almost invariably discharge excrement and musk that is sickeningly offensive to humans.

Common water snakes, active from late February to early November, mate during the spring. The mating behavior requires some study. From published but inconclusive descriptions, it would appear that great numbers of snakes partake in writhing orgies on branches, rocks, and logs near streams. One observer noted that a single female, apparently a charmer, was being courted by six males at once. No male combat has been reported.

However the mating is done, the young are produced generally during August and September, in broods of from nine to seventy young, born live. The young are fully equipped for predation, but now small and vulnerable, they are preyed upon by fish and large frogs that perhaps will eventually be eaten by one of the few young water snakes that will survive the first year of life.

The lone subspecies of the common water snake in the American West is the northern water snake *(N. s. sipedon)*. It is found only in eastern Colorado.

The red-bellied snake *(Storeria occipitomaculata)* is also called Storer's snake, brown snake, copper snake, ground snake, little brown snake, red-bellied garter snake, spot-necked snake, grass snake, and perhaps a few other names as well. (One can readily see the need for scientific names.)

The red-bellied snake is a natricine snake that has adapted to a terrestrial existence, or perhaps it is one that didn't adapt to an aquatic existence. In any event, this small snake—from eight to sixteen inches in length—is a frequent neighbor of urban man over much of its range. Primarily it is a snake of the eastern and southern United States and the southern portions of eastern Canada. Preferring wooded hills as habitat, it is not found over much of the Midwest and, in fact, has a spotty distribution everywhere.

One relictual population of red-bellied snakes is isolated in the Black Hills of South Dakota and a portion of extreme eastern Wyoming. This western subspecies, the Black Hills red-bellied snake *(S. o. pahasapae),* normally has running down its back four narrow dark stripes and a broader light-colored middle stripe. These are set against a brown or, occasionally, black background, since this snake is sometimes melanistic. Generally these snakes have light blotches at the back of their head, the top of which is black. The Black Hills subspecies sometimes has only small blotches or even no blotches at all. On most specimens the belly is bright red, but on some it may be orange or yellow. On melanistic individuals the belly is black. The dorsal scales are keeled.

An animal that may be quite common in a vicinity yet seldom seen, the red-bellied snake spends its days under boards, bark, logs, or stones, or inside rotten stumps. It is frequently found around houses. In the evening it leaves its hiding place to hunt earthworms, slugs, and soft-bodied insects. It makes a good pet for a terrarium and will even take earthworms from its owner's fingers. Young red-bellied snakes, born live in litters of one to twenty-one, are so small that one can coil on a dime. In the field, threatened, this little snake has been observed to lift an upper "lip" almost like a snarling dog.

Men encountering snakes in the American West probably most often encounter the ubiquitous garter snakes. Here, there are 24 separate species and subspecies of garter snakes. These snakes are generally, though not invariably, found near water—often where people go to swim, fish, picnic, take naps, or engage in water sports. Found in

Water Snakes and Garter Snakes

The Garter Snakes

almost every part of the American West, garter snakes are true live-bearers and produce many offspring each year. Some litters, in fact, may have fifty or more young. Their abundance and choice of habitat, therefore, increases the likelihood that they will be seen by man.

The term "garter snake" has an obvious origin. Most garter snakes have three distinct stripes down their backs that give them a pattern similar to that of an old-fashioned garter. Moreover, they are frequently slender, relatively small snakes, so that the fancied resemblance to a garter is not destroyed by size. In being slender, in usually lacking apical pits, in usually having single instead of divided anal plates, and in most cases being striped, the garter snakes differ from the true water snakes. They are similar in having keeled scales and heads wider than their necks.

Abundant, concentrated in their habitats, adaptable to captivity, the garter snakes have probably been more studied by herpetologists and other naturalists than any other group of snakes. Not only have they been the subject of study because of their confusing taxonomy, but also because they lend themselves to broader studies in physiology, behavior, and ecology.

The studies have shown, among other things, that garter snakes are truly viviparous. Not only are the young born live, but also there is a rudimentary placental relationship between mother and embryo. In a truly egg-laying snake the mother does not feed the embryo, for the food is carried in the egg. In an ovoviviparous snake the mother may simply act as a repository for the eggs until they are ready to hatch. In viviparous garter snakes the connection by placenta between mother and embryo marks an advanced stage in evolutionary development. The natricine snakes, in fact, show every stage of these various relationships between mother and embryo. All members of genus *Natrix* in the United States are live-bearing, but in Europe some are egg-layers.

Studies of garter snakes showed also that females of the various species have the capability of storing sperm—a capability that they share (it has now been shown) with several other unrelated species of snakes, such as the prairie rattlesnake *(Crotalus viridis viridis)*. After copulation the female snake stores the male's sperm in order to fertilize eggs she has not yet produced. Thus a female garter snake can perpetuate the species through stored sperm without relying

134

upon an encounter with a male before producing her next litter. As a practical matter this ability to store sperm is particularly valuable in colder climates. If, as frequently happens, the reproductive cycles of a mating male and female are out of synchrony, the female's capacity to store sperm bridges an otherwise unbridgeable gap. The normal synchronized mating results in egg and sperm coming together at exactly the right moment. But what happens when the female's cycle of egg production has not produced an egg at the time of mating? There being nothing to fertilize, the sperm is wasted. In a colder climate, where the time gap between production of garter snake litters is two years rather than one as in warmer climates, such waste of sperm could be disastrous to the species. The capacity to store sperm assures survival. (One cannot help but think here of the present-day efforts to [1] establish banks where human sperm is kept alive in subfreezing liquid nitrogen against future use, and [2] establish cell blanks with chromosomal keys stored that will theoretically allow future geneticists to reproduce a vanished species of animal.)

One should not conclude from this discussion that there is any sexual problem between male and female garter snakes. On the contrary, the aggressiveness of both spring and fall matings has been noted by observers for many years. Naturalist C. F. Seiss writing about the common garter snake in 1890 noted: "The males and females immediately seek each other, and may often be found in warm sunny spots, joined in copulation. At this season [spring] especially they emit a rank and disagreeable odor, particularly noticeable when captured, and I feel convinced that the sexes follow and find each other entirely by scent."

Although Seiss may have confused defensive discharges of musk with the sexually attractive odors, he had a valuable insight. For it is true that eager male garter snakes follow eager females by scent. The pheromone "perfume" is laid down through glands in the skin. In the male garter snake, it apparently causes a wild, irrational excitement that makes him disregard what he would otherwise deem dangerous. Several observers have noted that they could approach quite closely to a rutting garter snake where normally it would have slipped quietly away.

Among reeds or grasses that grow out of water, in places where frogs croak and dragonflies hover, along sunlighted rocks and sands in the beds of mountain streams—these are the haunts of the garter snakes.

At first glance most people would mistake the narrow-headed garter snake *(Thamnophis rufipunctatus)* for a water snake, for it is one of the few unstriped garter snakes, and in its checkered pattern of brown spots set against an olive or brown ground color it somewhat resembles the plain-bellied water snake. The resemblance is not superficial. There has, in fact, been a tug-of-war between herpetologists as to whether this snake should be in the genus *Natrix* or *Thamnophis,* and at one time or another it has been assigned to both. There is general agreement, however, that it does represent a bridging species between the two genera, for studies indicate that *Thamnophis* developed after *Natrix.*

The narrow-headed garter snake is much more slender than the plain-bellied water snake, and its long head that narrows down into a blunt wedge from rear to front distinguishes it not only from the water snakes but also from other garter snakes. On some specimens the shadowy vestiges of both back and side stripes may appear on the snake's neck. The pattern of brown spots fades on the tail. Adults are from slightly under two feet to nearly three feet in length.

The narrow-headed garter snake is a Mexican variety that has ranged northward to form an isolated population in the mountains of central and eastern Arizona and southwestern New Mexico. And it is found in the Sierra Madre Occidental of Mexico down to central Durango and eastward on the Mexican Plateau to Coahuila. This snake prefers well-lighted places in clear mountain streams that run over rocks in the pine-oak or piñon-juniper forests. Here, living in or near water, it hunts fish, salamanders, tadpoles, toads, and frogs. Its refuge is the water. Frightened, it dives down to find a crevice or sheltering rock.

The sorting out of garter snake species has been a challenging occupation of herpetologists for many years, often creating reputations for those scientists who succeed in getting their conclusions accepted. Many scholarly arguments have boiled up simply over separating and fixing the various subspecies of the common garter snake

(Thamnophis sirtalis). As far back as 1890, C. F. Seiss complained: "Naturalists from time to time have made about 26 distinct species out of this one *sirtalis,* and it is extremely perplexing, and enough to make the young scientist weary, to study these many long, dry, and useless descriptions, only to find in the end that they describe one common species of snake known to science since 1758."

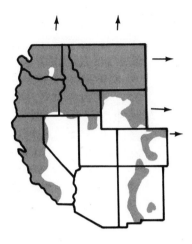

One common species, indeed, but what a species! This snake is the widest-ranging reptile in North America. From sea level to 8,000 feet it is found from the Atlantic to the Pacific and from southern Alaska (in which state it is the *only* snake) to Chihuahua in Mexico. It is absent only from the dry regions of the Southwest.

In all of its various subspecific guises, several characteristics remain constant. Adults are from a foot and a half to over four and a quarter feet long. Most often a common garter snake has three stripes—one down the center of its back and one down each side on the second and third scale rows up from the ventrals. Frequently it has red blotches on each side between the back and side stripes. Within the species there is great variation in the color of the top of the head—brown, red, gray, black. The color of the belly, pale bluish gray on the throat, darkens from throat to tail. Like most garter snakes, *T. sirtalis* has large eyes. Among garter snakes the count of labial (lip) scales is a particularly important means of separating one species from another. The common garter snake generally has seven upper labials and ten lower. Males, and males only, have knobs on the scale keels above the vent.

One cannot help but admire a creature with a knack for survival. So many animals that conservationists quite rightly want to preserve from extinction have adapted to restricted habitats or specific types of food. Deprived of those habitats or foods, they soon die out. If a disease or pesticide wiped out slugs, the sharp-tailed snake would not survive. Without muddy ponds, the mud turtle dies. One is tempted to say of the common garter snake that it has selected for survival under almost every condition except aridity. It is at home almost anywhere that water, which may mean only dampness, can be found. Swamp, damp forest meadow, marsh, pond, slough, stream, rain ditch, canal, puddle on a vacant city lot—all provide a suitable habitat. About anything a small snake can eat the common garter will eat—earthworms, slugs, leeches, fish, sala-

Water Snakes and Garter Snakes

manders, tadpoles, toads, frogs, birds, small mammals. Its voraciousness is legendary. James Oliver tells of a two-and-a-half-foot garter snake that caught and endeavored to swallow a full-grown bullfrog about eight inches long and as bulky as a bullfrog can get. There was no way the snake could swallow the frog, but the struggle continued for several moments until finally, reluctantly, the garter snake relinquished its hold. Even now the ten subspecies of the common garter snake, seven of which are scattered over the American West, are evolution's outriders for the main specific body. Whatever forces are now threatening the species, from pesticides to Ice Age, cannot, one thinks, threaten it all at once. Somewhere one outriding subspecies will survive, and from it new subspecies will spring in constant adaptation to whatever the future holds.

Of the seven subspecies of the common garter snake found in the American West, one is threatened with extinction, largely through encroachment by human beings. This one, considered by many herpetologists to be one of the most beautiful of snakes, is the San Francisco garter snake *(T. s. tetrataenia)*, found only on the peninsula south of San Francisco, California, which is a fast-growing residential area. The San Francisco garter snake, now fully protected by law, is quite distinctive. The greenish yellow stripe down the center of its back is edged in black. This combination is bordered by a broad red stripe on each side, then another black one. The top of its head is red, and its belly is greenish blue. This spectacular snake equals the mountain kingsnake in bizarre beauty.

The eager mating adventures of the common garter snake have led to some exaggerated tales concerning marital devotion. Active from March to as late as November before going into hibernation, this live-bearing species may mate at almost any time. During periods of intense activity several males may pursue one female until finally one succeeds in copulating with her, whereupon the others generally leave. However, there have been several observed instances where females have mated with several males in succession. The marital devotion stories may be based on the inability of male garter snakes to tell a live female from a dead one during mating periods. One early observer placed a dead female garter snake in a bucket and returned later to find a male copulating with the dead snake. When the male attempted defense, the observer interpreted it as a gallant stand over the dead mate.

In considering the next two species, the western terrestrial garter snake *(Thamnophis elegans)* and the western aquatic garter snake *(Thamnophis couchii)*, we run into a problem. The terrestrial garter snake is sometimes aquatic and the aquatic garter snake is sometimes found on land. The distinction between the two species is valid, though, for with some exceptions the terrestrial garter snake is primarily a land snake and is often found far from water. It is reasonably safe to say that one can distinguish between the two species when attempting to capture them. The terrestrial garter snake will normally seek shelter in brush, rocks, or other refuge on land; the aquatic will head for the nearest water.

In a classic study Douglas A. Rossman (1964) demonstrated that the skulls of the terrestrial group differed markedly from those of the aquatic group in overall shape and in the shape and proportions of individual bones. The problems of classifying these two groups of garter snakes have not been simple to solve. If they are separate species, one would expect that they would maintain their integrity during matings. Thus one would expect the subspecies of each species freely to interbreed with one another, but not with subspecies of the other species. And in fact this proved to be true for the western terrestrial and the western aquatic garter snakes—with one possible exception. The subspecies *T. e. biscutatus*, known as the Klamath garter snake of the terrestrial group, was for some time thought to interbreed freely with the Oregon garter snake *(T. c. hydrophila)* of the aquatic group. Confronted with this anomaly, scientists had to persevere patiently, as Rossman did, with studies that would show beyond doubt which snake belonged where. In the course of his studies Rossman captured a number of specimens where the interbreeding was supposed to take place. On the basis of external characteristics, none appeared to be hybrids.

With adults ranging in size from a foot and a half to three and a half feet, the western terrestrial garter snake normally carries the three typical "garter" stripes one down the middle of the back and the other two as side stripes on the second and third scale rows up from the ventrals. Between the stripes are dark checks set against a paler ground color. Sometimes, however, the area between the stripes is dark with whitish flecks.

Since telling one species of garter snake from another is difficult even for experts—unless only one or two species occur in a specific area—one must turn to such technicalities of herpetology as scale characteristics. The western terrestrial garter snake has nineteen scale rows at midbody, eight upper labial scales, and ten lower. The sixth and seventh upper labials are enlarged and are often higher than they are wide. The internasal scales are usually broader than they are long and are not pointed on their front ends.

Found often in brush, grass, and forest from sea level to 10,500 feet, the western terrestrial garter snake ranges widely over the American West and well into Canada. Like most garter snakes, it eats a wide variety of foods, in this case a somewhat wider variety than most: leeches, slugs, earthworms, fish, salamanders, tadpoles, toads, frogs, lizards, snakes, birds, and small mammals.

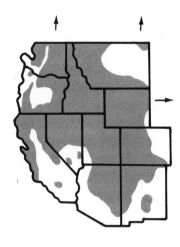

The range of the western terrestrial garter snake often overlaps that of the western aquatic garter snake. Sometimes, indeed, the common garter snake will also be found in the same range; thus three species of garter snakes, all voracious hunters, occupy the same general area. When this apparent conflict occurs, the principle of "competitive exclusion" applies. This principle holds that complete competitors for food cannot coexist. Limited competition among predators almost always exists, but seldom do two different species compete for the same food supply at the same time in the same place. Time, space, and differences in prey tend to separate predators hunting in the same area. Thus the western terrestrial garter snake prefers slugs, lizards, snakes, birds, and small mammals as food, while the western aquatic garter snake prefers creatures that live in or around the water, including fish eggs. In 1952, in a pioneering study of this principle, Charles C. Carpenter studied overlapped populations of the common garter snake, the eastern ribbon snake *(T. sauritus)* and Butler's garter snake *(T. butleri)*. The best example of competitive exclusion was found in comparing the diets of the three species. The common garter snake's diet was eighty percent earthworms, fifteen percent amphibians, and five percent miscellaneous; the ribbon snake's diet was ninety percent amphibians and ten percent leeches; and the diet of the Butler's garter snake was eighty-three percent earthworms, ten percent leeches, and seven percent miscellaneous.

In addition to differing in diet, the ribbon snake and Butler's garter snake tended to occupy different "spaces"—the former preferring shrubs and bushes, the latter grassy areas near water.

The most widespread of the six subspecies of the terrestrial garter snake is the wandering garter snake *(T. e. vagrans),* the name of which, both common and scientific, brings to mind a kind of amiable tramp that moves without seeming purpose across the land. In fact this subspecies does cover one of the largest ranges of any garter snake subspecies and often is found wandering far from water. It too is a snake of the far north, being found in western Canada. The presence of garter snakes this far north raises a question about their ability to function in colder climates. True, they do hibernate during the coldest weather, being most active during the warm months of summer. But at both ends of their functional year, in spring and in fall, they must occasionally encounter temperatures low enough to make them sluggish, barely able to move. In such conditions the natricine snakes have shown their great adaptability. They are capable of metabolically raising their body temperatures by $9°$ F. when they get cold. The survival value of this response is obvious: caught by an early autumn snow that might immobilize another snake, the garter snake can generate enough heat to keep moving. Hibernating garter snakes can also survive temperatures below freezing for fairly long periods of time. R. M. Bailey found that garter snakes could live up to twenty-eight days in subfreezing temperatures.

For a garter snake, the western aquatic garter snake *(Thamnophis couchii),* and particularly one of its subspecies, is quite large. Adults may reach a length of nearly four and three-quarter feet, although more normally they will be in the eighteen-inch to three-foot range. This snake, almost always associated with rivers, streams, swamps, lakes, or other bodies of water (including marshes where saltwater and freshwater mix), is known in a great variety of guises in both patterns and colors. As a species it lives at altitudes from sea level to 8,000 feet, from northern Baja California to southwestern Oregon. Its various subspecies have only a few features in common. The

THE WESTERN AQUATIC GARTER SNAKE
34

body is normally blotched whether or not a faint stripe is present, for on some of the subspecies the midstripe is weak or lacking entirely. Again scale examination must be used as a determining factor. The western aquatic has internasal scales that are narrower than they are long and point forward. Usually it has eight upper labials, the sixth and seventh of which are not larger than the others. Its chin shields are about equal in length.

Like most garter snakes the western aquatic hunts during the daytime. More than most it also hunts in the twilight and early evening—searching for leeches, earthworms, fish eggs, fish, salamanders, tadpoles, toads, and frogs.

Among the six subspecies of the western aquatic garter snake two are worth particular note. One of these, appropriately named the giant garter snake *(T. c. gigas)*, is the largest of the garter snakes. Some specimens reach a length of nearly four and three-quarter feet. The largest snakes are probably females, for among garter snakes females grow larger than males. The giant garter snake is found in California's San Joaquin valley, where in the days before the extensive farming of this vast central valley, there were many streams and ponds with the muddy bottoms and reed shores that this snake favors. The giant garter snake has always been noted for its wariness, perhaps because it often lives in open land without the overhanging branches of trees that could shelter it from hungry hawks. Even in olden days it was a hard snake to catch. Hunters could hear it in the reeds, hear it slither away, and hear a splash as it entered the water to seek shelter on the bottom. But they could seldom see the snake. Now as plows cut the land into long straight rows and ponds and streams are destroyed or lined with cement, this wary snake can find fewer and fewer places to live. It has become an endangered subspecies.

Another subspecies, the two-striped garter snake *(T. c. hammondii)*, is notable in having only two stripes; the normal garter snake midstripe is lacking. The snake's back is plain—dark olive, brown, or gray with spots along the sides. The two-striped garter snake is found along the coast of California from Monterey southward into northern Baja California. It is also found on Santa Catalina Island. At one point, the extreme northern end of its range, its range overlaps those of the coast garter snake *(T. e. terrestris)*, a subspecies of the western terrestrial garter snake, and the Santa Cruz garter snake *(T. c. atratus),* another subspecies of the western aquatic garter snake.

The strange fact is that these two subspecies of the same species do not interbreed. This failure to produce young that are the result of matings between representatives of each subspecies seems doubly strange when one considers that interbreeding does occur between all other subspecies of this garter snake. The explanation for this curious situation is found in an application of the *Rassenkreis* concept. This concept explains the role of impersonal nature—in this case climate and impassable barriers—in the evolution of a species. Changing weather conditions cause a species to migrate. At the beginning it is a single species with no subspecies. Forced by climate into continuing its migration, the species comes to an impassable barrier—a mountain range, a large lake, or as in the example provided by the western aquatic garter snake, an arid valley surrounded by mountains. Members of the species start around the barrier on both sides. Ages pass while evolution works, changing the original species into subspecies, which on either side of the barrier are different. More time passes, and a chain of subspecies evolves as the animal continues its differentiated development on each side of the barrier. The subspecies on one side interbreed freely with those on the same side and with the original. Then the day comes when the two subspecies in the vanguard of the advance around the barrier come into contact with one another at the nether end of the barrier. Each subspecies is the result of the separate and distinct evolutionary development that has taken place during the thousands of years that they and their progenitors have been separated. Actually related, members of the same species, they are now so different that they can no longer interbreed.

The probable original species of the western aquatic garter snake is the Sierra garter snake *(T. c. couchii).* Moving westward it came to the relatively arid San Joaquin valley of California and began an enveloping movement that saw subspecies develop along both the north and south flanks of the barrier. During this envelopment one subspecies, the giant garter snake, actually moved into the valley, occupying the lowland wet places. It remained separated by mountains from the subspecies to the west. As the envelopment proceeded, subspecies proliferated, particularly to the north, until finally the barrier was completely encircled. The two subspecies *T. c. atratus* and *T. c. hammondii* moved together into the area from Santa Barbara to Monterey. But unlike the other subspecies linked in the chain, they did not interbreed.

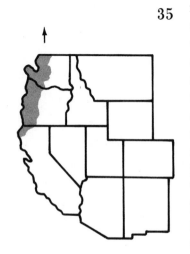

The northwestern garter snake *(Thamnophis ordinoides)* has adapted to life in the Great Northwest, starting at the very northwestern corner of California, thence ranging north well into British Columbia and on the southern half of Vancouver Island. A largely terrestrial garter snake itself, the northwestern garter snake lives at altitudes of sea level to 4,000 feet in the thickly forested regions, where in grassy clearings or meadows that have ground covering shrubs it may be seen sunning itself on warm days. It is an eater of slugs, earthworms, frogs, and salamanders. A small snake, fourteen to thirty-three and one-half inches long, it normally has a distinct red, orange, or yellow midstripe and indistinct stripes on the sides set against base color of black, dark brown, green, or occasionally blue. Sometimes the midstripe is not present. The belly, frequently blotched with red or black, is faint yellow, olive, or slate. To completely distinguish it from other garter snakes whose range it shares, one must use both coloration and scale counts. The common garter snake does not have red markings on the belly; the western terrestrial garter snake usually has eight upper labial scales to the northwestern garter snake's seven and has a higher count of back scales—nineteen scale rows just below the head, nineteen at midbody, seventeen just before the anal plate, compared to seventeen, seventeen, fifteen on the northwestern garter snake. The Oregon garter snake is duller in color and has eight upper labials.

The whitish or pale yellow midstripe is present in the black-necked garter snake *(Thamnophis cyrtopsis),* but here is one garter snake that can at a glance be distinguished from those we have discussed so far. Behind its head, separated by the midstripe, are two distinctive black blotches.

Adult black-necked garter snakes range from sixteen to thirty-seven inches in length. The black blotches are not the only bizarre feature of this snake's coloration. The stripes along its sides, generally on the second and third scale rows up from the ventrals, are sometimes irregular, even wavy, because of encroaching black spots. These black spots, in two alternating rows between the stripes, give a zigzag effect. Set against an olive brown ground color, they fade on the tail. The belly is greenish white.

Home for the black-necked garter snake is the Southwest. In southeastern Utah, southern Colorado, and a good part of Arizona and New Mexico, this snake lives near rock-strewn brooks, canals, rivers, even streams that do not run all year but leave some water holes during the summer months. During wet weather the black-necked garter snake sometimes moves away from the permanent streams. Its range, from sea level to 8,750 feet, runs also to central Texas and southward to Honduras. In the American West its distribution is uneven, since water is required, but it may be found in various habitats—pure desert, mesquite flats, grassland, and pine and fir forest. It eats toads, frogs, and tadpoles.

Only one subspecies, the western black-necked garter snake *(T. c. cyrtopsis)*, is found in the American West.

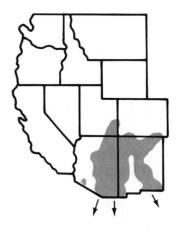

The Mexican garter snake *(Thamnophis eques)* is represented in the American West by one subspecies *(T. e. megalops)*, which ranges from Mexico into highland areas of Arizona and a tiny portion of western New Mexico. Adults are from a foot and a half to over three feet long. Three distinct yellow stripes stand out against an olive or brown base color that is checkered with black. The midstripe separates a pair of black blotches behind this snake's head, which may cause some confusion with the black-necked garter snake that is found in the same area. However, the Mexican garter snake is darker in color, has the side stripes on the third and fourth scale rows up from the ventrals, instead of the second and third, and has a crescent-shaped, greenish intrusion into the black blotch at the corner of the mouth.

The Mexican garter snake likes watery places in the higher mountains and highlands among firs and pines, ranging up to 8,500 feet. Some of these snakes live in the lowlands, however, around Douglas and Tucson, Arizona, probably demonstrating the distributional pattern of an essentially highland species that followed the course of streams until some individuals found them-

Water Snakes and Garter Snakes

selves living and breeding in the lowlands. Wherever it lives, this snake is primarily a frog eater. The other subspecies are found in the highlands of Mexico south to the state of Oaxaca. One Mexican subspecies, the beautiful *T. e. virgatenuis,* was not discovered and described until 1963. This fact should lend some small encouragement to those romantics who sometimes despair that all discoveries have been made.

THE CHECKERED
GARTER SNAKE

38

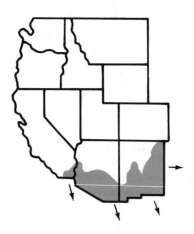

While the Mexican garter snake lives mainly in the highlands, the checkered garter snake *(Thamnophis marcianus)* favors the lowlands over much of the same range and additional areas. Found from southeastern Kansas through western Oklahoma and Texas, this snake in the American West ranges over southern New Mexico and Arizona and the extreme southeastern corner of California. It is also found south into northern Mexico and, after a puzzling gap, from the Isthmus of Tehuantepec to Costa Rica. Although primarily a snake of lowland ponds, springs, streams, and rivers in arid country, it does go as high as 6,000 feet.

A rather pale snake, *T. marcianus* grows larger than the black-necked garter snake, with which it might be confused. Adults are from eighteen to forty-seven inches long. They are distinctively checkered with large square checks set against a yellow, yellow brown, or olive background color. The yellow midstripe on this snake may look somewhat like a dotted line. Behind the head, separated by this midstripe, are two black blotches. The "crescent" is also present at the corner of the mouth—whitish, it intrudes into the black blotches. The side stripes are mostly on the third scale row, but toward the tail they may also be on the second.

In sharp contrast to the normal trend among snakes, the checkered garter snake has actually benefited from the works of man. Canals and ditches used to irrigate such arid regions as California's Imperial Valley have enabled this snake to extend its range and consequently improve its chances of survival. Now, whenever man builds new waterworks adjacent to its present range, new territory will be opened to this snake, just as the St. Lawrence Seaway opened the Great Lakes to the lamprey. Such extension of range, of course, does no good unless food is available. But the checkered garter snake's main prey—fish, toads, frogs, tadpoles—also extend their ranges along the grassland irrigation canals dug by men. Moreover, this garter snake is perfectly capable of living on lizards, slugs, earthworms, and other invertebrates.

In wet grass, in swamps, along streams, and near rivers and ponds in the prairie lands of the Great Plains from southern Canada to northeastern New Mexico and from central Montana to Ohio, the plains garter snake *(Thamnophis radix)* is one of our widest-ranging snakes. In the American West it is represented by one subspecies, the western plains garter snake *(T. r. haydenii)* which is found at altitudes from 500 to 6,500 feet in the eastern portions of Montana, Wyoming, and Colorado and in northeastern New Mexico.

THE PLAINS GARTER SNAKE

39

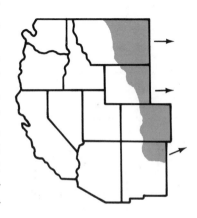

Adult plains garter snakes are from nearly two to three and one-half feet long. The well-defined midstripe may be orange or yellow near the head, shading into a paler yellow toward the tail. This and the two side stripes on the third and fourth scale rows up from the ventrals are set against a base color that may be reddish, brown, olive, or even green gray. Between the stripes are two rows of black squares; below the side stripes is a row of black spots set against brown. On most individuals these markings are distinct. Occasionally, however, individuals will be so dark that the markings are obscured.

The plains garter snake eats a wide variety of garter snake foods—the usual earthworms, fish, salamanders, tadpoles, toads, and frogs. In addition, it also eats mice, insects, and—unusual but not unknown in a few other species of snake—carrion. An abundant snake, it is sometimes found in large numbers within a particular vicinity. During six months in 1950 the herpetologist H. C. Seibert captured 298 plains garter snakes on one 320-acre tract near Chicago, Illinois. No comparable record exists in the American West.

This snake played a role in a discovery concerning the virus of western equine encephalitis (Gebhardt et al., 1966), the fatal sleeping sickness, which has been known to sweep through lands as it did Texas in 1971, infecting and killing thousands of horses. The disease is spread by mosquitoes. But in the intricate fabric of nature, ecological relationships may be extremely complex. Complexity shows

Water Snakes and Garter Snakes

147

here in the fact that garter snakes (and probably some other snakes as well) are reservoir hosts for western equine encephalitis. Over winter the virus lives in garter snakes (and apparently in their principal prey, frogs). The snake, innocent of what it is harboring, is not harmed. The virus lives, quiescent now, but ready in the spring to be picked up by mosquitos as they take blood from the snakes and through them once again to infect a population of horses.

THE WESTERN
RIBBON SNAKE

40

The highly adaptable western ribbon snake *(Thamnophis proximus)* barely makes it into the American West, being found only in southeastern and northeastern New Mexico and in southeastern Colorado. It ranges eastward to the Mississippi and southward along the Gulf Coast to Costa Rica. With all the beautiful snakes that live in the American West, it would be selfish to wish that this graceful, slender long-tailed snake were more common. Yet, one cannot help but wish so. The one subspecies that enters New Mexico and Colorado is the Pecos ribbon snake *(T. p. diabolicus).* Among garter snakes, the western ribbon snake is more like the racers. It has a slender body, ranging in length from a foot and a half to four and a quarter feet long, although most adults are from two to three and a half feet long. The western ribbon snake, three-striped like most garter snakes, is easily identified both by its slenderness and by the ivory-colored upper labial scales that stand out starkly against the much darker head. Seeing this snake, one can understand the subspecific name *diabolicus;* for it is not difficult to imagine these pale labial scales as the bare and grinning teeth of a death's-head. The paleness of these scales is carried toward the snake's tail by the two side stripes that fall on the third and fourth scale rows. The midstripe may be yellow, orange, reddish, greenish, or brown, although on *diabolicus* it is normally orange. The base color is brown, olive brown, black, or gray. The whipsnakelike tail is extremely long, representing one fourth to one third the length of the snake.

The western ribbon snake has to be given a high mark in adaptability. While it is seldom found far from water, to which it retreats when frightened, it lives in a great variety of habitats; forest and woodland, swamp and prairie, marshes and sloughs, from sea level to 8,000 feet. A good climber, it spends much time basking in shrubs and in trees bordering streams. Not a few fishermen or lazing vacationers have been startled to have a ribbon snake, either frightened or finished basking, fall from a tree branch and plop into the water near them, then swim gracefully off. This snake eats earthworms, insects, fish, and frogs.

The correct classification of the lined snake *(Tropidoclonion lineatum)* is disputed among herpetologists. Some believe this small snake, so similar in appearance and characteristics to the garter snakes, should in fact be assigned to the genus *Thamnophis.* Other scientists have pointed to the differences and have maintained that this colubrid snake must be kept in a distinct genus, *Tropidoclonion.* The principal difference in the lined snakes is the number of caudal scales (those on the underside of the tail). The lined snake has thirty-two to forty-five; the garter snakes always have forty-nine or more. Moreover, the lined snake has a head not much wider than its neck, whereas on true garter snakes the head is distinct. Altogether, the differences warrant a separate genus for the lined snake.

The Lined Snake

41

Back in the days when innocent optimism prevailed in America, and small boys in school had fun at the expense of small girls, the lined snake came to be known as the "schoolboy's snake." Its small size—nine to twenty-one inches—allows it to fit easily into pockets, and where it ranges it is abundant and fairly easily caught. So across much of the Midwest and parts of Colorado and New Mexico in the West, many boys carried lined snakes to school to frighten girls or, better yet, to demonstrate the boys' courage—hopefully to much "oohing" and "ahhing" and shy, admiring glances.

In the American West at altitudes from sea level to 6,400 feet, are found two subspecies of the northern lined snake. Three well-defined stripes run down the back. The midstripe may be orange, yellow, pale gray, or white. Bordering the stripes are spots set against the base color—either dark or light olive gray. The belly is distinctive, for against a white or yellow color are set two rows of black spots, one on either side of the midline.

The lined snake, while abundant, is seldom seen unless one looks for it. During the day it hides under rocks, boards, brush, old pieces of cardboard or tar paper, or whatever else it finds in its habitat in woods, prairies, city parks, and backyards. When evening comes, it leaves the hiding places and searches for earthworms and insects. Since rains bring earthworms to the surface of the ground, lined snakes are more active in wet weather.

Like the garter snakes, the lined snake has keeled scales and a single anal plate. Two to twelve young are born live during August.

Chapter 12

» » » » »

THE SAND
SWIMMERS

In the arid parts of the American West, where there are sand hummocks on prairies, dry and sandy river bottoms, or windswept desert dunes—in these places live small, secretive, burrowing snakes. They have been called the sand swimmers because several of them can travel effortlessly just below the surface of the sand. In fact some of these snakes spend most of their lives under the sand, sometimes pushing up to the surface at night, but only when air and ground temperatures are exactly right to venture forth to hunt for grubs, millipedes, spiders, insect larvae, crickets, and grasshoppers. People seldom see these hunters, for even when they lie exposed on the surface, their colors blend with their surroundings, and when they are threatened, if sand is beneath them, they disappear as though a hidden magician had waved his wand.

As they hunt, away from the security of their sand cover, these snakes fall prey to larger creatures—kingsnakes, coyotes, foxes, and owls. Yet, because they live in wild places, spend most of their lives hidden below the earth's surface, and hunt creatures like insects, their chances for survival are greater than those of most snakes.

As man crowds out or kills the more obvious snakes, the tiny, secretive snakes, secure in burrow or crevice, remain. In evolutionary terms perhaps they are the fittest to survive.

An extremely large adult western ground snake *(Sonora semiannulata)* is a foot and a half long; a small one is only eight inches long. Several color patterns are characteristic of the species. Frequently, the western ground snake has black crossbands against a ground color of buff, orange, or red. Or it may be striped lengthwise in orange, red, or buff, with one stripe down the center of its back. Sometimes it is a plain buff color, or greenish or bluish gray, or it may have a neckband of black. Or instead of crossbands it may have saddles. The belly may be plain or it may have dark crossbands. Moreover, all variations of patterns may be found on specimens taken from a single locality. In earlier days of herpetology this variable snake caused great confusion among taxonomists. Even now, in fact, the snakes of this genus need thorough taxonomic study and revision.

There are some points of similarity among all western ground snakes: each scale has a dark spot on its forward portion, a feature more noticeable on the snake's sides. The snake's short, blunt head is only slightly wider than its neck. The scales are smooth with a satiny luster. Females can be distinguished from males because the female has forty-five or more paired subcaudal scales while the male has fifty-three or more. The subcaudal scales serve also another purpose: they help the herpetologist distinguish this snake from the quite similar ground snake, which has fifty-two or fewer subcaudals in males and forty-four or fewer in females.

Small and nocturnal, able to conceal itself in tiny crevices or under sand, loose soil, or rocks, the western ground snake is seldom seen. But it is not rare and may even inhabit some localities in great numbers. Burrowing owls in Imperial County, California, include it as a regular food item. Largely it is found in dry country where there are many rocks and much sand. One associates it with willows in dry western riverbeds, with mesquite by sand dunes, with sagebrush across the wide plains of Nevada. It ranges as far north as a small portion of southeastern Oregon and southwestern Idaho, thence southward over much of Nevada, parts of eastern California,

The Western Ground Snake
42

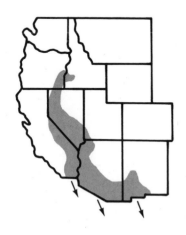

a large portion of southwestern Arizona, and a smaller portion of southwestern New Mexico and western Texas. Below the border it is found in Baja California and on the Mexican mainland in Sonora, Chihuahua, Coahuila, and Nuevo León. It may be found from sea level to 6,000 feet.

One rare cousin, the species *Sonora mosaueri,* occurs in southern Baja California and on San José Island in the Gulf of California. Few specimens exist in collections. One addition, however, was made through an ingenious collecting method devised by Mrs. Hope Warren Shaw. Mrs. Shaw, a radio and TV producer, while on a trip to La Paz near the tip of Baja California, promised that she would try to collect for the San Diego Zoo some rare (in collections) mole lizards. The method she used was simple and highly successful. She advertised for the lizards on the La Paz radio station XENT. Not only were many mole lizards brought in, but several snakes as well, including a *mosaueri.*

Hunting by night, the western ground snake looks for grubs, centipedes, spiders, crickets, and grasshoppers. It is an egg-layer.

Many characteristics of the western ground snake also apply to the ground snake *(Sonora episcopa),* only one subspecies of which, the Great Plains ground snake *(S. e. episcopa),* occurs in the American West, in the extreme southeastern portion of Colorado and eastern New Mexico. The principal range of this species is eastward across the Great Plains of Oklahoma and Texas. It extends south into Coahuila, Nuevo León, and Tamaulipas, Mexico.

The Ground Snake

43

Writing about the Great Plains ground snake, the herpetologist William H. Stickel (1938) noted: "The color is phenomenally variable: plain, streaked, striped, barred, collared; gray, brown, black, red. Combinations and intermediates of all these variations have been seen from one locality." In other words, one cannot identify this species of snake by color pattern alone. Like the western ground snake, the Great Plains species has a blunt head little wider than its neck. Adults are from nine to sixteen inches long. Each scale on the back has a dot or bar on it; in combination these marks often appear like a series of dashed lines. The scales are smooth.

A snake of dry areas, the Great Plains ground snake is associated with sand and rock in prairie country at altitudes from sea level to 5,200 feet. W. W. Milstead and his colleagues (1950) collected twenty-one specimens in the following associations: "Cedar savannah, 3; cedar-ocotillo, 9; persimmon-shinoak, 2; cedar-oak, 3; mesquite-creosote, 2; walnut-desert willow, 2."

As hunter the ground snake searches for spiders, centipedes, scorpions, ant eggs, and insects. Like the western ground snake, it is oviparous. The ground snake has been recently added to the growing list of snakes that have been observed in male combat during mating season (Kroll, 1971). Since most observed combat between males has involved larger snakes, the sight of two tiny ground snakes endeavoring to subdue one another has a particular fascination. The observed combat took place in the presence of the female—and the victorious male, left alone with the female by the departing loser, immediately went to her and began to copulate.

The Sonora Shovel-Nosed Snake

44

The Sonora shovel-nosed snake *(Chionactis palarostris)* is represented in the American West by one subspecies, the Organ Pipe shovel-nosed snake *(C. p. organica),* which barely extends its range into the United States. Mostly this ten- to sixteen-inch snake is found in Mexico, inhabiting the Sonoran Desert as far south as Hermosillo.

The smooth-scaled Sonora shovel-nose is a lovely snake. It is banded with red, black, and yellow bands which mimic the venomous western coral snake found in the same area. This mimicry is more evident on specimens from Mexico which normally have red bands much wider than the Organ Pipe subspecies. Starting with a black mask from eye to eye across the top of the head, the pattern runs black band, narrow yellow band, wider red band, narrow yellow band, black band for the length of the snake. The easiest way to distinguish the Sonora shovel-nosed snake from the coral snake, since the order of the bands is similar, is by the color of the snout—yellow on the shovel-nose, black on the coral snake.

The Sonora shovel-nosed snake is associated with the giant saguaro cactus growing out of rock-strewn desert hillocks. The Sonora shovel-nose is less of a sand swimmer than its cousin, the western shovel-nose, from which it can be distinguished by having a less-pointed snout, broad red bands, and fewer than twenty-one black bands. It, too, is oviparous.

Searchers for the desert snakes have noted a curious fact about the tiny (ten to seventeen inches) banded western shovel-nosed snake *(Chionactis occipitalis)*. Hunting by car at night on blacktopped roads or by lantern from shrub to shrub across sandy dunes, many a searcher has been puzzled by this phenomenon: under conditions that seem ideal, no snakes will be seen during much of the search. Then suddenly, in an area that has been previously covered, the snakes will appear in large numbers. What mysterious force produces shovel-nosed snakes so suddenly where there had been none before? The question is further complicated by the fact that this burrowing snake, classified as nocturnal, is sometimes taken on the surface in late afternoon and evening during the spring and fall, but only late at night during the summer. The herpetologists Kenneth S. Norris and J. Lee Kavanau (1966) studied this mysterious phenomenon. Assuming that changes in the environment would provide the answer, Norris and Kavanau studied the interrelated elements of air temperature and sand pressure. They found that both air temperature and the related subsurface sand pressure upon the dug-in shovel-nosed snakes influenced whether they moved toward the surface or remained below the sand. But movement of shovel-nosed snakes to the surface for brief four- to five-hour periods is also apparently related to the snakes' most recent period of activity. Responding to what biologists call a "circadian rhythm," the shovel-nosed snakes stay below the surface of the sand for roughly twenty-four hours after an activity period. Then, if sand pressure upon their bodies gives them the message that surface conditions are favorable, they move up, sometimes resting just below the surface until the final temperature-pressure signal comes. At that moment they emerge—many snakes simultaneously—and begin their search for food.

This temperature-regulated life accounts, of course, for the difference in time of emergence between spring, fall, and summer (during winter the snakes are hibernating). In spring and fall surface temperature becomes right earlier in the evening than during the days of unrelenting summer sun, when the surface sand temperatures remain too hot for the snakes during the early evening, finally cooling off late at night.

The results of Norris and Kavanau's studies suggest that other

The Western Shovel-Nosed Snake
45

desert snakes—and quite possibly all snakes—may respond to both circadian and temperature "messages." The general dependence of "cold-blooded" creatures upon temperature has been obvious since man first started studying them, but the study suggests that this temperature-circadian rhythm relationship is much more finely tuned than was previously suspected.

The beautiful western shovel-nosed snake is highly adapted to a life of sand swimming. Its head is indeed shaped somewhat like a shovel; from the top of its head to the snout there is a continuous slope. The snout itself is flattened top to bottom and rounded to the sides. The lower jaw is inset beneath the upper. The nasal passages are protected by a valve, which, Norris and Kavanau conjectured, is closed at least most of the time when the snake is burrowing. The two biologists determined, however, that these snakes do breathe underground, but at a different rate than on the surface, since their basal metabolic rate when buried is slower than it is above ground. They breathe underground into and from a tiny sand-free cavity produced by their downward bent heads and an overhanging rostral scale. Interestingly, as though they don't want to foul their under-sand environment, the shovel-nosed snakes defecate only on the surface.

As would be expected of a sand swimmer, the shovel-nosed snake is almost always found where sand is abundant and vegetation —sand-related species like creosote bush, mesquite, cactus—is scarce. In these sandy places, at altitudes from sea level to 4,700 feet, the western shovel-nosed snake is found in southeastern California, southwestern Nevada, and much of western Arizona. Thence it ranges southward into northeastern Baja California and northwestern Sonora, Mexico.

In coloration this is one of the most beautiful snakes in the American West. Alternating dark and light bands run the length of its body, starting on a head that is a little wider than the body. The black or dark brown bands, sometimes saddles, sometimes encircling the body, generally number twenty-one or more on the body. Frequently orange or red saddles appear between the dark bands, but separated from them by the yellow or whitish ground color. The scales are smooth.

This striking color combination in bands around the body seems almost too bright if one examines the live snake on a tabletop. The western shovel-nosed snake is not quite so ostentatious as a milk snake or a mountain kingsnake, but like them, it is conspicuous in its coloration, so conspicuous that one wonders how it can survive in a world full of predators. But bands, even on brightly colored snakes, serve to deceive the eye—certainly the human eye and probably predators' eyes as well. This deception takes two forms. Banded snakes often appear to be larger than they actually are, just as a man wearing a banded T-shirt will look larger. This illusion is sometimes strengthened by the behavior of some snakes that roll and thrash about so that bands are presented to the predator like rings on a barber pole in a constant shifting movement, with those the predator sees in the foreground looking larger than those in the background. Such apparently eccentric behavior may cause the predator to pause in its attack until it can comprehend what it is dealing with.

The second illusion presented by banded snakes is probably more often seen. In the shovel-nosed snakes this illusion is pronounced. It presents one of evolution's most fascinating examples of protective coloration in animals. Most people think of protective coloration as patterns and colors that simply melt into natural surroundings because they look like those surroundings—like leaves on the forest bed or rocks on a river bottom. But colors can also be protective when they are arranged in sequences, as in bands, that allow frequencies sent by particular colors to strike the onlooker's eye rhythmically. In total darkness the snake cannot be seen, but in moonlight or in automobile headlights it can hide behind the illusion produced by the flicker-fusion phenomenon. As the snake moves forward, seeking a hiding place, the bands on its back follow one another like the spokes on a wheel. Depending on the nearness of the predator, the width of the bands, and the intensity of the light on the snake, and perhaps the blinking of the predator's eye, the results may be startling. At the very least an astigmatic condition may be produced in the onlooker. Most often, however, the flicker-fusion phenomenon brings a fusing in the beholder's perception of the snake's bands, a graying of them, to the point where bands and the snake no longer exist. The beholder stares fixedly at the spot where he first saw the snake and misses the fact that the snake is passing from his view.

Students of evolution note that this flicker-fusion phenomenon is more effective against some predators and less against others. Consequently the size and arrangement of bands "selected for" on banded snakes must be effective on either the greatest number of predators or the principal predator in an area. These students will note, too, that the most successful predators will be those whose ancestors "selected for" vision that reduces the flicker-fusion effect. The evolutionary struggle to be a survivor never ends.

The western shovel-nosed snake eats insects and other invertebrates, including spiders, centipedes, chrysalises of moths, and—gingerly—scorpions (Glass, 1972). The snake approaches the task of subduing a scorpion with extreme care, seeking to avoid the lobster-like claws and venom-injecting stinger. The snake is seldom successful in completely avoiding the stinger, however, and may be stung between one and six times while subduing its prey. The western shovel-nosed snakes are egg-layers.

For a time two of the four subspecies of the western shovel-nosed snake provided a taxonomic mystery in the eastern part of San Diego County, California. There occurs a mixture and hybridization of one subspecies, the Mojave shovel-nose *(C. o. occipitalis)* with another, the Colorado Desert shovel-nose *(C. o. annulata)*. L. M. Klauber (1951) provided a fascinating possible reason for this hybridization that illustrates the effects of geological changes on existing species. Klauber pointed out that the Salton Sea of Imperial Valley had once been a vastly larger body of water, Lake LeConte, which probably provided a geographical barrier between the two subspecies. As the water receded, the Mojave shovel-nose moved south and the Colorado Desert shovel-nose moved north, thus causing the intermingling and eventual hybridization of the two subspecies.

If a sand-swimming meet were held for the burrowing snakes, the banded sand snake *(Chilomeniscus cinctus)* would win most of the events. This seldom encountered snake spends most of its life under the sand or gravel of the desert country in central and southwestern

Arizona, Baja California, and the west coast of Mexico through Sonora. It is also found on Cedros and Magdalena islands and, in the Gulf of California, on San Marcos, Monserrate, and San José islands. Beneath the surface of the sand, this stout but tiny snake (seven to ten inches) can move nearly as fast as it can above ground. The banded sand snake is highly adapted to its subterranean life. The lower jaw is so deeply countersunk that this snake has been called the "Andy Gump" snake after the chinless cartoon hero. The head, no wider than the body, appears blunt when viewed from above but shows a chisellike taper when seen from the side. Its small eyes are directed upward, and nasal valves can be closed to keep sand from nostrils.

The Banded Sand Snake

46

The skin of this species is so bright and smooth that it appears to be varnished. On its back the banded sand snake has from fourteen to thirty-nine black crossbands set against a background of pale yellow, orange, or yellowish white. On some snakes orange saddles appear between the black bands.

As its description perhaps indicates, the banded sand snake is probably a close relative of the shovel-nosed snakes. This probability has been made greater by studies of karyotypes of these snakes (Bury, Gress, and Gorman, 1970). The karyotype of the western shovel-nosed snake is identical to that of a Mexican species of sand snake *(C. stramineus)*. And while both have a diploid number of thirty-six like most other North American colubrids, they are unlike others in the detailed arrangement of their chromosomes.

Coming to the earth's surface only briefly, and then at night, the banded sand snake lives at altitudes from sea level to 3,000 feet among creosote bushes of open desert, or in rock-strewn, sand-pocketed uplands where paloverde and saguaro grow. Not infrequently in outlying desert residential areas specimens turn up in swimming pools or other man-made sinks into which snakes can fall but not escape. Searchers for the snake look for its "track," formed when the snake's tunnel through the sand collapses behind it, leaving a tiny furrow that, until wind once more smooths the sand, points directly to the concealed burrower. So fast, however, can the tunneler move that one herpetologist, attempting to block a banded sand snake with a spade, miscalculated and inadvertently cut the poor creature in two.

The banded sand snake, an egg-layer, eats centipedes, sand cockroaches, and probably ant larvae and other insects.

The Western Hook-Nosed Snake
47

Although it is only seven to fourteen inches long, the western hook-nosed snake *(Gyalopion canum)* with its upturned snout might be mistaken for a western hognose snake. The hook-nose is rather stout of body and has crossbands of brown or yellow brown edged with black, set against a yellow gray or gray brown ground color. Moreover, the rarely encountered western hook-nose has a dramatic defensive act. Writing in 1931, the herpetologist E. H. Taylor described it well: "immediately on being touched [the snake] began to writhe and to throw its body in strange contortions, as if in agony, sometimes almost throwing itself off the ground. It would continue these actions for several seconds and at the same time it would extrude and retract the cloaca rather rapidly, for a distance of half an inch or more, which resulted in a popping sound."

This cloacal popping, as we shall see, is done also by the venomous Arizona coral snake found in much of the same area. It is difficult to guess at the significance, in evolution, of such an act. Patently it serves some purpose—just as does the loud hiss of a gopher snake or the rattling of a rattler. As the latter "signals" are obviously threatening, so may be the popping. Even a trained herpetologist, let alone a hungry predator, might be repelled momentarily by the popping sound, so strange and unexpected, so alien to anything in experience. And in its being alien may lie its purpose. The creature, otherwise small and inoffensive, is about to be caught. It needs time—one second, two seconds—to find a sandy spot or crevice. Throwing itself into convulsions it suddenly goes— pop! One considers now the reflexive action of the predator, confronted with a strange sound and possible danger to itself. A drawing back. A pause. A second or two to assess the changed situation before renewing the pursuit. For the hunted, escape may thus be made possible.

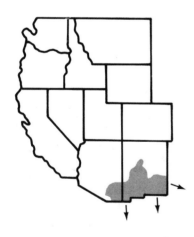

The quickest way to tell a hook-nosed snake from a hognose snake is to compare the scales. The hognose has keeled scales; the hook-nose is smooth. Moreover, the nocturnal western hook-nosed snake is primarily a burrower, encountered by people most often on warm summer nights after rains. In the American West it is found

160

only across southern New Mexico and southeastern Arizona. To the east it ranges to central Texas. Primarily a Mexican snake, it is found over a large portion of mainland Mexico as far south as Querétaro. Its habitats are semiarid or arid at altitudes from 1,000 to 6,500 feet. Frequently, it is associated with grassy desert plains, piñon or juniper woodlands, or brushy areas. An egg-laying snake, it feeds principally on spiders. Trying to feed the first specimen to be exhibited in a zoo, C. F. Kauffeld (1948) of the Staten Island Zoo, New York, found that in addition to spiders the captive would eat centipedes, but it steadfastly refused millipedes, lizards, smaller snakes, frogs, and newborn mice.

The Mexican West Coast hook-nosed snake *(Gyalopion quadrangularis)* is found just over the border in Santa Cruz County, Arizona. In its length of six to thirteen inches, and in its stout size and upturned rostral scale, this snake resembles its generic cousin the western hook-nosed snake. However, the Mexican West Coast hook-nose has black saddles set over a broad rust red stripe that runs the length of the snake's body on each side. Both saddles and stripes are set against an ash white ground color. The consequence is that from above the snake has a series of ash white rectangles running down its back. Added to this already fascinating combination is a plain belly of pale yellow with a slight green tinge.

One finds this presumably burrowing snake at altitudes from sea level to 4,400 feet in the alluvial fans formed where streams emerge from the mountains. Mostly it lives along the western slope of the Sierra Madre Occidental in Mexico. The Arizona representatives of this species live in mesquite grassland of the Gila River drainage area, where like the western hook-nose, they go abroad on the surface on warm nights after rains.

Little is actually known of the habits of this species. Presumably, like the western hook-nose, it favors spiders. It is an egg-layer.

The Mexican West Coast Hook-Nosed Snake 48

Chapter 13

» » » » »

THE REAR-FANGED SNAKES

A mouse being constricted by a kingsnake can struggle and bite, but a mouse struck by a rattlesnake shivers, has convulsions, and dies. The kingsnake thus runs a somewhat greater risk of being injured by its prey, as does a garter snake that uses the grab, hold, and gobble down technique in capturing a frog. In snakedom the safest and most efficient way of subduing prey is to numb or kill it with venom. Then the prey animal cannot injure its attacker. Numbed or dead, the creature can be leisurely swallowed.

Among the hundreds of species of colubrid snakes, a small number have evolved means of producing and using venom to subdue prey. In the American West there are a few of these venom-using colubrids. Unlike the dreaded boomslang, a venomous African colubrid that is dangerous to man, none of the venomous colubrids in the American West has ever harmed a human. They are all small snakes with poorly developed venom-introducing apparatus, in which venom glands dispense venom down grooves in enlarged teeth at the back of the upper jaw. To use its venom, the snake must chew until these rear fangs can be embedded, a process which is next to impossible for a small snake to accomplish on a human being. In fact, unlike the highly venomous snakes, these small creatures have to hold on to prey or enemy, thus risking retaliation. They represent a stage in the development of venom-dispensing apparatus—and a risky stage at that. Finally, though little is known on the subject, the venom itself of those rear-fanged colubrids in the American West is probably not powerful enough in small quantities to harm a man. In fact, even if a lyre snake, for example, could work the venom into the tissues of a human, the effect probably would be no more serious than that of a weak beesting. People, then, should consider these snakes harmless. Evolution has provided them with instruments—venom glands and rear fangs—that enhance their chances for survival, but these instruments threaten prey animals, not people.

The rear-fanged colubrids in the American West fit no pattern. They include snakes that are vastly different in size, appearance, food habits, and habitat. The wonder is that these diverse creatures have all separately evolved venom systems and the capacity to use them.

Averaging only seven to eighteen inches as adults, secretive, and seldom seen by people, the black-headed snakes, often called tantillas, are widespread over the American West, particularly in the Southwest. Their common distinguishing mark is, of course, the black color of their heads. In some individuals the black is little more than a cap; in others it covers the whole head and is stopped on the neck by a collar.

The Black-Headed Snakes

Telling one species of *Tantilla* from another is not difficult once a person has seen snakes from the various species. However, in identifying subspecies, even experts are sometimes confounded. Most often the chore entails counting scales and noting their arrangements. This problem of distinguishing one subspecies from another is sometimes made more difficult because of intergrades at the edges of subspecific ranges. In these geographical areas two or more subspecies mix and interbreed, producing variants that are different from the subspecies involved. Intergradation occurs in other snakes too, but seldom does it add as markedly to the difficulties of identifying one snake from another. It is safe to say that in those places where ranges overlap and intergrades occur, about all the amateur herpetologist can hope to do is identify the species of black-headed snake involved. The job of pinning down the subspecies may require an examination in the laboratory. Fortunately, there are many areas where only one subspecies of black-headed snake occurs.

In common, then, these glistening little snakes with their black caps and smooth scales are equipped to use venom through grooved rear teeth, but are totally harmless to man. In the evolutionary development of the venom-using capacity, they stand as primitives. In the evolutionary hierarchy of the colubrids, however, they are well advanced, in spite of the fact that they share with the primitive slender blind snakes a common anatomical characteristic—the loss of the left oviduct in females. This loss probably occurred because these secretive snakes selected for slenderness, since a slender snake can hide more readily than a bulkier one.

The sharing of characteristics between primitive animals and more advanced forms points to one of the pitfalls of natural science, the tendency to assume that creatures alike in one characteristic are alike in others. For a long period some herpetologists assumed blind snakes and slender blind snakes shared a common ancestor simply because female snakes of both genera had only one oviduct. Quite obviously, however, there can be no common ancestor for the blind snakes and the much more highly evolved tantillas. It follows then that anatomical similarities alone are not sufficient evidence to place animals into the same family, subfamily, or genus.

All tantillas are oviparous. There are four species in the American West.

THE PLAINS
BLACK-HEADED
SNAKE

49

The plains black-headed snake *(Tantilla nigriceps)* is on the average larger than the western black-headed snake; it ranges from seven to eighteen inches in length. The chief clue to distinguishing these species, however, is that the black or dark brown cap of the plains black-headed snake extends three to five scale rows behind the parietals and is pointed toward the rear. This pointed cap is quite different from its western cousin's squared-off cap. Normally, moreover, the plains species has no collar.

Smooth-scaled like all tantillas, the plains black-headed snake has a brown body, often with a yellowish tone. Its underside is white, but with a light orange or pink stripe up the center.

Living mainly on the Great Plains at altitudes up to 6,100 feet, the plains black-headed snake is found in eastern Colorado, over much of New Mexico, and in a small part of eastern Arizona. To the east it ranges over plains states and southward through Texas into Durango and Tamaulipas, Mexico. It is another "secretive" snake about which little is known. Specimens have been taken in sometimes curious places—eight inches below the surface of the soil on top of a bluff, on high school grounds, in a basement. Most often tantillas are found by turning over rocks, flat boards, torn pieces of cardboard, and the like. One should not neglect flats of desiccated cattle dung, under which several specimens have been found; after all, bison supplied this kind of shelter for small snakes long before man provided boards and cardboard.

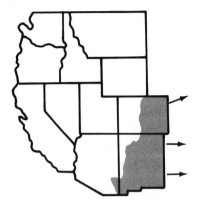

Of the two subspecies of the plains black-headed snake the one in the American West is *T. n. nigriceps.*

Widespread through southwestern California from Alameda County southward, the western black-headed snake *(Tantilla planiceps)* is found also in isolated populations in eastern California, Nevada, Utah, Colorado, Arizona, southern New Mexico, and the Texas Panhandle. It is found southward to the tip of Baja California and on mainland Mexico to San Luis Potosí. Over much of its range it is probably fairly common, since it is able to survive in cities. One was captured not long ago in a sand trap at the La Jolla Country Club in La Jolla, California.

THE WESTERN
BLACK-HEADED
SNAKE

50

The black cap of the western black-headed snake covers the top of its head and extends as many as two-and-one-half scale rows behind the parietal scales (the two large scales that cover the rear top of the snake's head). Sometimes at this point a white collar bordered by black dots may stop the black. Sometimes, however, no collar appears or one is found without black dots. (We wish we could make this easy, but nature has been capricious in this aspect of coloring black-headed snakes.) The black cap may extend down the sides of the head to or below the corner of the snake's mouth, or it may not reach the mouth. One point to note, because it may help distinguish the western black-headed snake from other tantillas, is the

The Rear-Fanged Snakes

fact that the black cap does not normally *point* to the rear but is, rather, squared off.

Black-headed snakes as a genus have no visible necks, their heads being but extensions of the body. Body color on the smooth-scaled western black-headed snake ranges from gray to brown. A stripe, barely visible, runs down the center of the back on most specimens. Along the middle of the white belly runs a fairly broad, orange to red stripe.

Perhaps because the name "tantilla" sounds vaguely ominous, or perhaps because of the implications of black head in the association between black and death, all the black-headed snakes have in some localities been given an undeserved reputation as dangerous snakes. They are in fact harmless to man. Little else, however, is known about them.

The western black-headed snake seems to have no particular favorite association with vegetation, having been taken in chaparral, woodlands, and grasslands near various kinds of trees and shrubs. It does appear to favor rocky places—most often it is taken on snake hunts where many rocks are overturned. The snake seldom appears above ground and then only on warm evenings. Much of its life is spent, apparently, in crevices and cracks, under rocks, or in the burrows of small mammals. From what little is known, it appears to prey on millipedes and earthworms.

There are five subspecies of the western black-headed snake. The subspecies in desert habitats are lighter-colored and have smaller black caps. Often, in fact, instead of being brown, the desert subspecies are a cream color lightly punctated with brown.

THE YAQUI
BLACK-HEADED
SNAKE

51

In 1907 Dr. C. L. Edmondson of Bisbee, Arizona, captured a black-headed snake that established a northern record for the species, the Yaqui black-headed snake *(Tantilla yaquia)*. This single specimen was somehow overlooked in a museum jar, so it was not until 1964 that the Yaqui black-headed snake was officially reported in the United States by Clarence J. McCoy, Jr. (1964).

Ranging from southeastern Arizona to Nayarít, Mexico, the Yaqui black-headed snake is found mainly through the Mexican states of Sonora, western Chihuahua, and Sinaloa. Adults are from seven to twelve and three-quarters inches long.

HARMLESS SNAKES

Sometimes called the Arizona tantilla, the Huachuca black-headed snake *(Tantilla wilcoxi)* is primarily a Mexican form that ranges northward from Zacatecas and San Luis Potosí to the area around Fort Huachuca in Arizona's Apache country. This rare snake lives mainly at altitudes of from 3,000 to 6,800 feet on cactus-covered rocky hills, in grasslands, and in pine-oak forests. It differs from all other tantillas in having a broad white collar that, crossing the rear tips of the parietals, borders its black cap. The collar, in turn, is bordered with black.

The Huachuca black-headed snake is a small (seven to fourteen inches), smooth-scaled snake that feeds principally on spiders.

Anyone looking at a three- to five-foot vine snake *(Oxybelis aeneus)* would know it was a snake, but unless he was familiar with tropical snakes he would be startled at how unlike most snakes the vine snake is. More than slender, the vine snake is so thin it seems drawn out, as though a smaller, thicker snake had been stretched from both ends. Yet so muscular is this vine-colored snake that it can hang down and out from a tree limb for long periods, seeming like part of the natural greenery, a simple extension of the tree itself. Its head, too, is strange, shaped like a spear, extremely long and narrowing down rapidly from the thickest part, which is itself not much thicker than the thin body. The spear-shaped head, in fact, has given this snake another name, "pike-head tree snake."

The vine snake is in fact a tropical form, ranging through forest or jungle habitats as far south as Brazil. Normally associated with tropical jungles, it has ranged into the southwestern United States. Arizona, mostly desert country, does have its leafy parts, like the canyons in the Pajarito Mountains where oak, wild grape, and sycamore grow. It is here on the tree-covered hillsides or thickly grown stream bottoms, barely five miles from the Mexican border, that the vine snake exists—one of the snakes in the American West.

One wishes that the vine snake were more common, for it is one of our most interesting snakes. Pencil-thin, variable in color, but mostly with a mottled brown that blends perfectly with vegetation, it seems alert and intelligent. Not so fast as a racer on the ground, it can move with great deception in eluding any pursuer. It is more at home in the trees, however, moving gracefully from branch to

The Vine Snake
53

branch or tree to tree. Defensively, if it cannot escape, it opens its mouth wide and like a cottonmouth shows a white gape.

The evolutionary process that brings this defensive response can, of course, only be guessed at. In the complex web of relationships that bring about evolutionary change, what strands come together to designate white—rather than orange or yellow, for example—as a warning sign? Perhaps all that is required is sudden, startling contrast, a flash of pure white against green and brown, the strangeness of which brings pause to the predator. And pause, the momentary stopping of action, the ticking of a few seconds while the predator is off guard, may be all that the threatened creature needs to make its escape.

The vine snake is most commonly found in the Calabasas, Walker, and Peña Blanca canyons at altitudes between 3,000 and 5,000 feet. There, living mostly in the trees, it stalks, or lies waiting for fast arboreal lizards—its chief prey—while they are basking during the morning or late afternoon. Its eyes, interestingly, in relation to the line-of-sight theory discussed in chapter 8, have both a black stripe and a grooved channel extending forward from eye to nose. Moreover, this snake sometimes waves gently from a branch for moments, mouth closed and tongue extended almost as though the tongue itself were an additional sighting device. An earlier herpetologist advanced the theory that the vine snake protrudes its tongue to "fascinate" prey. This theory partakes of the familiar legend that snakes hypnotize small mammals, birds, and, in this case at least, lizards so that they will remain still, placidly awaiting capture by the snake. The theory gained some supporters because it is true that prey animals often remain motionless as a snake approaches, sometimes waiting too long. Where early flight would save them, they often are caught in a final swift lunge by the snake. Studying this phenomenon in vine snakes, the herpetologist Edmond D. Keiser, Jr. (1967), observed one vine snake stalking anoles 112 times over a three-month period. In only thirty-seven cases, Keiser was convinced, were the lizards remotely aware that nemesis was approaching. Of the thirty-seven that were aware, twelve attempted to escape. Only nine of the remainder remotely appeared fascinated, not by the snake's tongue but by its entire head. The difference between fascination in the hypnotic sense and mere fatal curiosity—often the result of inexperience—is, of course, a small one if being eaten is the final result.

In extending its tongue, the vine snake may be simply making a more prolonged sensory survey of its surroundings, thrusting the tongue out to pick up particles that can be "tasted" and classified through Jacobson's organ.

The vine snake eats insects, frogs, lizards, and birds. It captures prey either in trees or on the ground, grasping the creature and chewing to embed the rear fangs. The venom acts rapidly to paralyze, then kill. Normally, the vine snake does not bite people. In several recorded cases when people were bitten, itching, redness, slight swelling, numbness, and a large blister occurred in the region of the bite within ten minutes.

The oviparous vine snake would perhaps be more numerous in Arizona were it not for its chief predator, the pugnacious, bristly jabalina, or collared peccary, which views the vine snake as a tasty morsel.

There exists in the American West a species of rear-fanged snake that is unusual in being cat-eyed and bizarrely marked. This is the lyre snake *(Trimorphodon biscutatus),* so named because on top of its head is a distinctive marking shaped like the lyre used by an ancient Greek poet to accompany the chanting of his verse. This V-shaped marking has the closed end forward, coming to a point between the eyes. The arms of the lyre extend back, each ending just behind the widest part of the head on each side at a point where head and neck join. In the American West, the adult lyre snake ranges from two to three and one-half feet in length. It is a nocturnal snake, whose elliptical pupils, like those of a cat, contract or expand to take advantage of full moon or the merest glimmer of starlight.

The Lyre Snake

54

L. M. Klauber (1940) discovered early that lyre snakes prefer the massive granite boulders that cover so many Southwestern hillsides. Here, where earth movements and temperature changes cause fissures to appear in monolithic rocks, where the inexorable wear of wind and rain help to flake the mightiest boulder, the lyre snakes live, secure under flakes or in fissures during daylight, prowling in search of food at night. Klauber found that unlike the granite night lizard *(Xantusia henshawi)* and the night snake *(Hypsiglena torquata),* the lyre snake does not hide out under the granite chips, but prefers larger flakes and deeper crevices. It has been found from sea level to 7,400 feet—often where trees and shrubs grow among rocks. It is a good climber.

Aside from catlike eyes and the broad distinctive head with its lyre marking, the lyre snake can be identified by a series of brown blotches on its back. Each of these hexagonal markings is divided by a lighter-colored crossbar. They are set against a pale gray or light brown ground color. On the pale yellow or cream belly brown dots frequently occur.

The lyre snake specializes in a kind of prey that has not heretofore been mentioned—namely, bats. The granite night lizard, granite spiny lizard *(Sceloporus orcutti),* and mice are all commonly eaten, too, but the lyre snake actively searches out bats, going to their roosts in crevice and cave. Like the other rear-fanged snakes, the lyre snake injects its venom through a chewing motion. The venom, which apparently causes hemorrhaging in the prey, appears to be more effective on lizards than on mice or bats. However, even in death a prey lizard can sometimes triumph. Preserved in the museum at Grand Canyon is a lyre snake that was collected in the park. Preserved with it is its partially swallowed killer, a large spiny lizard, which in its death throes had ruptured the lyre snake's esophagus.

Several observers have reported that the lyre snake has a peculiar habit when frightened or seeking to escape. It raises the forward portion of its body off the ground not unlike a hunting whipsnake. Cornered, it may strike and attempt a chewing bite. Its strike, however, is more accurate at night than during the day.

The lyre snake frequently vibrates its tail when it is in a defensive coil. In dry grass or leaves this vibration can sound much like a rattlesnake's rattle. This noise combined with the somewhat triangular, or spade-shaped, head of the lyre snake might cause confusion in the mind of a hiker or camper with little knowledge of snakes. However, the rattlesnakes all have much thicker bodies; the lyre snake is relatively slender.

The oviparous lyre snake is one of two wide-ranging members of its genus. The other species, *T. tau,* is entirely confined to Mexico. The lyre snake has six subspecies whose ranges run from southwestern Utah to Costa Rica. Only three of these subspecies are found in the American West.

The night snake *(Hypsiglena torquata)* is small; adults measure twelve to twenty-six inches in length, but like many snakes in search of prey, it is willing to take on target animals of almost any size. Adult night snakes, it is known, favor lizards and frogs as prey, but juveniles are more likely to eat insects. However, the herpetologist John D. Goodman recounts in a classic article (1953) the struggle between a small night snake, which measured only seven inches long, and a sagebrush lizard *(Sceloporus graciosus),* itself a juvenile of about two inches in length. The night snake, grabbing the lizard by the base of its tail, began chewing vigorously to embed its venom-injecting rear fangs. Within a few seconds the lizard was paralyzed, first in the hind quarters, and soon after, completely. Death came in one hour. The most fascinating aspect was the paralyzing effect of the venom and the rapidity with which it acted—an illustration of the evolution of venom and venom-injecting apparatus providing snakes with a quick means of subduing prey at less risk to the hunter.

Night snakes are actually quite common in the American West, but because they are nocturnal they are seldom encountered unless one is actively looking for them. Small, with a distinct head that is barred in black or dark brown through the eye, they are beige or gray with brown or dark gray spots down their backs. Their belly is yellow or white. Two features distinguish them: like the lyre snake, they have elliptical pupils, and just behind the head they usually have two large dark brown blotches. The blotches vary greatly in size, which helps to distinguish the various subspecies. The total effect of small size and blotched body might cause a casual observer to confuse a night snake with a young racer, which is blotched in a not dissimilar fashion. Racers, however, have round pupils. More often the night snake is mistaken for a young rattler, a mistake made more understandable not only because of a similarity in general appearance—somewhat spade-shaped head, a dark streak through the eyes, blotches on the back—but particularly because of the elliptical eyes, like those of a rattler.

Found from sea level to around 8,750 feet, the oviparous night

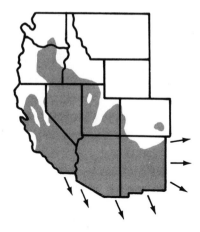

snake appears to favor rocky habitats within its extensive range. Starting from south central Washington, the range spreads inland through much of eastern Oregon and southern Idaho, over most of Nevada, much of California to the coast (including Santa Cruz Island off the coast), much of Utah, a tiny pocket of Colorado, Arizona, and most of New Mexico. Thence it ranges southward through Baja California and much of the Mexican mainland down to Guerrero and eastward into Texas, Oklahoma, and southwestern Kansas. Although it prefers rocks, the night snake does not care what type of country the rocks are in—grassy plains, sagebrush flats, deserts, forests, or chaparral. Most often snake hunters find the snake under boards, rocks, and fallen branches of trees. A nocturnal snake, it is often taken crossing blacktopped desert roads at night.

The night snake has a peculiar form of symbiotic relationship with the desert tortoise *(Gopherus agassizii)*. The night snake frequently hibernates in the dens dug by desert tortoises. (Sidewinders and Great Basin rattlesnakes also enjoy this relationship.) This type of association is an example of inquiline commensalism. Commensalism is a jawbreaking name for symbiosis in which one of the animals involved derives an advantage from the relationship, while the other is unaffected. Inquilinism refers to a situation in which one animal uses a shelter made by another.

A relative of the night snake provides one of the most fascinating illustrations of zoological detective work in existence. The first specimen of this snake was originally caught in 1921 by Joseph R. Slevin at Puerto Escondido in southern Baja California. Slevin, one of herpetology's foremost collectors, took the specimen to the California Academy of Sciences. It was not until 1943 that Wilmer W. Tanner (1946) published the original description of this one specimen, placing it with the night snake and giving it the name *Hypsiglena slevini.* So it essentially remained until 1960.

Meanwhile, working on an entirely different subject, the cat-eyed snakes *(Leptodeira)* found in the American tropics, William E. Duellman published a monograph in 1958. Duellman had no knowledge of *H. slevini.* In his monograph he postulated that the closely related genera of the night snake *(Hypsiglena)* and the cat-eyed snakes *(Leptodeira)* must have sprung from a common ancestor. Working backward from both genera, Duellman postulated what

HARMLESS SNAKES

the common ancestor must have looked like. He included the hypothesized description of this ancestor in his monograph.

We turn now to 1959. Alan E. Leviton and Hugh B. Leech collected the second specimen of what was then *H. slevini* near La Paz, Baja California. This was an adult female 16¾ inches long, in contrast with the original 1921 specimen—a juvenile 8⅜ inches long. Now the two stories converge. Working with the second specimen of *H. slevini*, it dawned on Leviton and Tanner (1960) that it almost exactly fit the hypothesized description given by Duellman for the common ancestor of the genera *Hypsiglena* and *Leptodeira*. What they were dealing with, they realized, was not just another species of night snake. It was a snake from a relict population existing only in the cul-de-sac that is the southern end of Baja California—and as it later turned out on one of the offshore islands. It was, in fact, the common ancestor of the night snake and the cat-eyed snakes. Leviton and Tanner concluded that it had to be given its own genus. So what was once *H. slevini* is now *Eridiphas slevini*. Other specimens captured since the first two have confirmed both Duellman's perceptive hypothesis and the correctness of placing this relictual snake in its own genus.

PART THREE

》 》 》 》 》 》

VENOMOUS SNAKES

Chapter 14

»»»»»»

ENCOUNTERING VENOMOUS SNAKES

Venomous snakes bite men not out of an aggressive desire to kill, but because they react to what their instincts interpret as an attack. They bite people who are ignorant, careless, foolish, or sometimes just plain unlucky. They usually bite people who either don't know the habits of venomous snakes or who ignore safety precautions. Not infrequently they bite people who, while handling them, suffer a momentary lapse of concentration, a fateful distraction.

Whatever the reason, snakebite still takes its annual toll in the United States. Each year some people die. Many others, bitten not fatally, suffer prolonged, often painful medical treatment before they recover.

Snakebite statistics were greatly neglected in the United States until a decade ago when the first annual count was made. It showed that venomous snakes bite many more people than anyone had guessed—doctors treat about 7,000 people every year. Of these, however, only fourteen or fifteen die. (Twice as many people die from bee and wasp stings.) The state of Texas, where the rattlesnake population includes many of the large, touchy western diamondback rattlesnakes, leads in number of snakebites, accounting for about a thousand a year. The greatest number of fatalities, ninety to ninety-five percent of which are from rattlesnake bite, occur in Arizona, Texas, Georgia, and Florida.

As one might expect, the innocently ignorant and the venture-some account for the greatest number of victims. Children playing within short distances of their homes crawl under porches, jump into bushes, pull boards of wood from a pile, and are bitten. Teen-age boys, showing off their courage, tease or pick up a rattlesnake, and are bitten. Actually about one out of three venomous snakebites happen to people who are handling snakes, not only in the field but also in their own homes, garages, basements, on stages, or at religious festivals. There are now no wild venomous snakes in the Bronx, New York, but about ten bites are recorded there each year.

As we have seen, most snakes, including rattlesnakes and coral snakes, are not usually abroad during daylight, preferring early morning, evening, or nighttime. During the day most snakes, again including venomous snakes, stay in crevices, under rocks, beneath shady shrubs. Moreover, snakes are active only during a limited number of months of the year—late spring through early fall for snakes in colder climates; early spring through late fall in warmer climes. Most of the time, in other words, snakes are abroad when people aren't and live in places where relatively few people dwell. These facts minimize the chance of what some have called "legitimate" snakebite—that is bites administered upon people who just happened to be passing by (as opposed to "illegitimate" snakebite, administered upon people who are handling snakes).

Where do most encounters with venomous snakes take place? A statistical study by Dr. Henry M. Parrish (1957) shows that by far the greatest number of bites are inflicted upon fingers and hands. This statistic indicates that people get bitten while handling snakes (true) and that people in wild country sometimes put their hands in the wrong places (also true). The next largest number of bites occur on the ankles, when people jump or step into places where they haven't looked. Mostly, unless they are handling snakes, people are bitten by surprise, the bite being the first indication that a snake is near.

The comforting thought that rattlesnakes always forewarn their victims by rattling is more fiction than fact. If the snake is awake, or if the victim-to-be approaches it fairly noisily, the snake may very well rattle. Many times, however, the snake is as surprised as the victim. Lethargic, inactive, asleep under a bush or in the shade of a boulder, the snake is suddenly stepped on or brushed against and reacts instinctively, striking or simply biting if it can't strike. Even when lying in the open, perhaps stretched out across a path, the snake may be invisible to even the most experienced hikers because of its protective coloration.

Thus the way to keep from being a victim of a venomous snake is to avoid handling such snakes and to proceed warily in venomous snake country. Since most venomous snakes move about during the dawn, dusk, or night, one may expect more encounters during the early morning or late afternoon, fewer during the middle of the day. Most encounters in broad daylight are with snakes that are sleeping or are otherwise inactive. One practically never encounters snakes in late fall or winter, except occasionally in the semi-desert regions. The probability of encountering a snake while hiking at noontime on a winter day is practically nil. Indeed the odds are against seeing any snake, let alone a venomous one, at any time unless one deliberately goes to those few spots where snake population is greatest, near streams in garter snake country, for example. Actually, many snake encounters, whatever the species, occur near streams, ponds, or lakes, since snakes like other animals, come there to drink.

Comforted by the knowledge of the general habits of snakes, the traveler in wild country can further assure his safety by taking a few precautions. No North American rattlesnake's fangs can effectively penetrate a good pair of hiking boots. Since a high proportion of snake bites occur around ankle level, boots will considerably reduce the odds of being bitten. The sensible hiker (or gardener) will look before he places hands or feet in strange places. Before stepping into thick brush, he will poke it with a stick. Given a chance, the rattlesnake that may lurk there will rattle. When climbing, the hiker will carefully look before placing his hands on a ledge. Snakebites on fingers or hands, and occasionally on head or shoulders, have been administered to climbers who placed hands where they couldn't see what they were gripping or who raised head

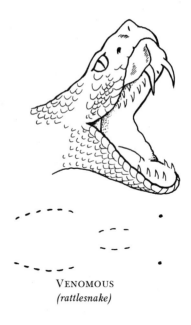

VENOMOUS
(rattlesnake)

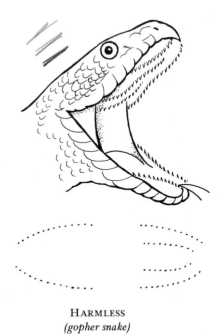

HARMLESS
(gopher snake)

BITE PATTERNS

and shoulders above a ledge on which a snake was coiled. Not a few snakebite victims have been gardeners who, working in their own gardens in suburban outskirts, have reached into flower bed or decorative brush and been struck by a rattlesnake. In rural and suburban areas of rattlesnake country, the gardener should carefully inspect bushes or flower beds before thrusting his hands in. One recorded rattlesnake bite, probably by a sidewinder, happened to a woman gardener in the resort town of Palm Springs, California.

Of all the many snake legends, the one about snakes not dying until the sunset after they are killed comes closest to truth. Snakes die, of course, when they are killed, no matter what the time of day, but their nerve and muscle reflexes continue for some time after death. In fact, a rattlesnake can administer a fatal bite *after* it has died. If a person carelessly handles a dead snake, he may well trigger reflexes that enable the snake to bite. Dr. Findlay E. Russell has shown rattlesnake venom not exposed to air retains its virulence for more than twenty years. Therefore the venom of a recently dead snake is every bit as poisonous as that from the bite of a live one. The moral of this story, of course, is that a dead rattlesnake should not be handled as though it were an old piece of rubber hose. If a person wants to skin the snake, he should first carefully decapitate it—with shovel, ax, or some other tool that keeps one from being in close proximity—and bury the head.

Snake venoms are chemically complex, and there is wide variance in the composition and virulence of venoms from one species of venomous snake to another. Some venoms may have their greatest effect on a victim's respiration or heart action; others may severely damage or destroy tissue and blood cells. Still others may do both. There is no way in which venoms can be superficially grouped, as they too often have been in books on herpetology. One must respect the separate evolutionary development of each venomous species. This evolution has imparted to the venom of each species a unique chemistry which makes it in some respects unlike any other venom. For example, the venom of the Mojave rattlesnake is quite unlike the venom of any other rattlesnake. For this reason polyvalent antivenin, used as a standard therapeutic measure in cases of snakebite, will not work in all cases; sometimes antivenins have to be developed for individual species.

The evolution of venoms and venom-producing snakes is a fascinating, though largely hypothesized, subject. The most likely hypothesis holds that venom glands evolved from specialized salivary glands, which are present in any snake's mouth. The salivary fluids produced by these specialized glands enter the prey through tooth punctures, and protein (chiefly enzyme) action begins the process of digestion even as the prey is being swallowed (just as saliva in a human mouth begins to break down the cell structure of food being chewed). Over a period of years, it is hypothesized, certain snake species, through natural selection, "improved" on this process by producing more powerful enzymes, enlarging glands for storage of fluids, or developing grooved teeth as an aid to administering the fluids. The venom itself evolved through the process of natural selection; it retained and emphasized the qualities that made it useful in killing or subduing prey. Today we can find representative snake species at various stages in this hypothesized development. There are rear-fanged snakes with weak venoms that barely help to subdue prey. There are front-fanged snakes with permanently erect fangs that carry small supplies of venom. And there are the highly efficient envenoming machines—like the rattlesnakes—that have large-capacity venom storage, hollow fangs that swing into position immediately before the snake bites, and spare fangs ready to replace those damaged or lost.

The defensive use of the venom and fang system is at best secondary to its predatory uses, and may in fact be totally unrelated to the evolutionary development of the system. As Sherman and Madge Minton point out in *Venomous Reptiles* (1969), the venomous snake is often guilty of "overkill" when it defends itself by injecting a venom that brings death to its victim. Nature more usually employs a defense that drives off intruders or frightens them—the skunk with its scent, the porcupine with its quills. Warned once, the threatening creature tends to leave skunk or porcupine alone in the future—an ideal arrangement since both threatener and threatened survive the encounter. Moreover, if the attacker belongs to an animal species with a way of passing on knowledge, the future generations are taught to avoid skunk or porcupine. But the victim of a venomous snake cannot use its new knowledge that the snake is dangerous—much less pass it on—for the victim frequently dies.

Evolution of Venom

Michael S. Loop studied this aspect of venom-injecting systems and found evidences that evolution is providing a decrease in toxicity of snake venoms. The evolutionary trend, Loop believes, may be toward an optimum situation in which the prey-killing capability remains constant (and effective) while the defensive use of venom normally provides a sublethal dose, thus allowing bitten predators to "learn" from a painful bite to avoid the venomous snake, its relatives, and possibly its mimics in the future.

Many variables are present when a venomous snake uses its venom in defense. Virulence of venom varies greatly from one species to another even among closely related snakes. The tiger rattlesnake of Arizona has a venom that is normally much more virulent drop for drop than the venom of the red diamond rattlesnake. But the adult tiger rattlesnake is much smaller than the adult red diamond, which therefore might inject much more venom while biting an enemy.

The phrase "might inject" is used advisedly. There is considerable evidence to show that venomous snakes regulate the amount of venom they use in subduing prey or in defending themselves. It was once thought that venom was injected through largely involuntary muscular contraction of the venom sacs behind the fangs in the snake's head. It now appears that the snake has complete control of this system. This control may be another example of the efficiency brought about by natural selection. A snake that used all its venom in one bite would be helpless during the period when it was manufacturing new venom, helpless both in hunting and in defense. Maintenance of reserves is an aid in assuring survival; therefore, in the process of natural selection, those snakes that maintain venom reserves survive longer, breed more often, and in their genes pass on the capacity. Perhaps also, in an instinctive effort to avoid "overkill," the snake in defense seeks only to discourage an attacker, to drive the attacker off so that the snake itself can escape. Unfortunately for the snake, it has no way of gauging another important variable in the envenoming process—that is, the general state of health of its victim. Moreover, it has no control over weather, yet temperature definitely affects the production of venom. In warmer weather more is usually produced; in colder weather less.

To the person bitten by a venomous snake these variables become an academic consideration. His chances of surviving rattlesnake bite are good even if he doesn't get medical treatment. But statistical evidence that he will probably survive is one thing; the emotional shock and pain of a rattlesnake bite are two others. And with so many variables present—size of snake, virulence of venom, interrelation of venom with the bitten person's general health, amount administered, and so on—the bitten individual would find it difficult to be relaxed about assessing his chances for survival. Medical attention is called for, and as soon as possible. If the victim is a child, the statistical odds are not quite so good.

Arguments persist over the best method of giving immediate treatment for rattlesnake bite. Years ago the best treatment was thought to be whiskey, preferably taken internally as a preventative measure, but certainly taken in copious quantities after a bite. One doctor, in fact, thought that the snakebite victim should drink a quart of brandy and a gallon of whiskey within thirty-six hours after being bitten. A persistent story tells of a bitten man who was given this treatment. Several days later, recovered from both bite and whiskey, he was seen looking for another rattlesnake to bite him. (There is also the story of an overworked small-town rattler who had a waiting list of twenty people.) Certainly this role of whiskey has passed into the language. Instead of offering whiskey to his guests, many a modern rancher, particularly if he is an old-timer, will ask, "Care for some snakebite medicine?"

Unfortunately, like other homespun snakebite cures, whiskey and other alcoholic beverages are of no real value in overcoming the effects of venom. In fact, most experts believe alcohol to be actually harmful, arguing that it speeds up heart action, increases circulation, and thus hastens the spread of venom. At best it could do no more than calm a person and help overcome the effects of shock. Liquor is not to be relied on as a cure.

One of the problems in discussing cures for snakebite springs from the fact that most victims recover *without* treatment. Consequently people who have applied perfectly worthless "cures"— snake stones, witchcraft chants, herb teas—can argue that their "cure" helped save a victim. The logic is inescapable: victim is bitten; cure is applied; victim lives; therefore cure works. One finds it difficult to convince either the victim or his benefactor that the victim would have lived anyway. It might appear, then, that no harm is done by the continued use of potions and nostrums to cure snakebite. But of course real harm is done when people think a cure is efficacious and it isn't; for then comes the one victim who is given the ineffective treatment and dies.

The long list of folk cures for snakebite has been compiled by Findlay E. Russell, M.D. (1961), one of the world's foremost authorities on treatment of snakebite. Over the years Dr. Russell has received thousands of suggested remedies from people; some out of the goodness of the sender's heart, others from self-appointed experts who wanted to split fees. "Cures" have ranged widely. Sometimes they are magical chants: "Sprinkle cold water on the face of the victim and shout in a commanding tone thrice: 'Get up. It is the command of T. C. Ramachauder Rao.'" Sometimes they involve remedies to draw off the venom: "The first cure and remedy for Snake-Bite . . . is the warm body of a Bird, chicken, or other fowl. Slit the bite, put the warm body of the inside of bird on the Bitten part. When Bird turns black from poison, have another ready, and so on until Bird does not turn black." This particular letter, Dr. Russell noted, was followed by a fascinating P.S.: "The bird must be of the fowl family."

The list of curative agents goes on—kerosene and cornmeal, animal excrement, toad urine, roots, leaves, or bark from various plants, milk, mud, cauterization, amputation, magical stones, and many others.

Even truly "medical" treatments for snakebite may turn out to be worthless. For years snakebite kits contained potassium permanganate with directions that it be injected or applied in crystal form to the wound and the area around it. Unfortunately the medicine in this case did not neutralize the venom, and in sufficient quantities it destroyed tissue, thus worsening the victim's condition.

For some twenty years now cryotherapy, the application of cold by ice pack or other means, to the wounded limb has been advocated by some authorities. The objective here is to retard absorption of venom into the bloodstream—to localize, as it were, the effects of venom. The method has always been controversial and in the past few years most experts have opposed it as a worthless and dangerous method which has caused a large number of amputations.

How can a snakebite victim best be helped? The process involves three steps:

» One. *Immediate* first-aid treatment.

» Two. Injection of antivenin, preferably by a physician, after a test for sensitivity to horse serum.

» Three. Supportive therapy by a physician or in a hospital.

The immediate first-aid therapy includes some procedures that are controversial and some about which there exists general agreement. The controversial first-aid measures involve making small cuts through each fang puncture and applying a constriction band.

Making cuts involves some slight risk. The idea is to create access to the site of the wound in order to facilitate sucking venom from the area. If the method is used, it should be used very carefully. The cutting instrument—knife, razor, sharp piece of glass, should be sterilized to minimize the danger of infection. The idea of a tourniquet, of course, is to prevent spread of the venom from the injured area. Venom is spread rapidly, both because of the normal rapid rate at which the blood supply is completely recycled and because elements in the venom are quickly absorbed. If a tourniquet or constriction band *is* used as a first-aid measure, it should be loosened every fifteen to twenty minutes.

The immediate application of suction to a bite puncture proves to be the best of all immediate first-aid measures. Working with dogs, Dr. Joseph F. Gennaro and associates (1961) demonstrated that slightly more than half the venom can be removed from a snakebite wound if suction is started within three minutes after the bite. Even if started within two hours after the bite, the treatment removes enough venom to make its use worthwhile. Suction works effectively, however, only when venom has been injected into skin. Venom injected into muscle cannot so readily be removed. Fortunately, most snake fangs do not penetrate deeply enough to hit muscle.

Modern snakebite kits, available at most drugstores, generally include a mechanical suction device. Such a kit should be part of the standard gear for anyone hiking or camping in rattlesnake country. However, without a mechanical suction cup, the giver of aid can use the widespread primitive method of sucking by mouth. The method brings some additional risk to the victim, since mouth-borne bacteria may cause secondary infection. It provides no risk to the person giving the aid if he does not have open wounds in his mouth or bad teeth. The first-aid administrator must suck and spit, suck and spit. As he does so he can take comfort in knowing that rattlesnake venom won't harm him if swallowed.

To review, then, the full on-the-spot first aid is:

» Apply constriction band.

» Make *small* incisions through each fang puncture.

» Apply suction to the wound.

In addition, the patient should be treated as a victim of shock and kept warm.

Some authorities believe that if the victim can be rapidly moved to a doctor or hospital it is better to get professional treatment immediately rather than wait for first aid to be administered. In any event, right after first aid, professional medical treatment should be sought.

Antivenins

The most common form of treatment administered by doctors is the injection of an antivenin. Antivenins should only be injected by a physician or a person who is properly qualified. The principle of antivenin was first reported in 1887 by Henry Sewall, a professor of physiology at the University of Michigan, who had successfully built up immunity to snake venom in pigeons, proving that successful antitoxins can be developed. More work was done in Europe, which resulted in antitoxins for diphtheria and tetanus. By 1895 in France horses had been successfully immunized against cobra venom by Sebert Calmett, a French bacteriologist. A modification of the method he used is still being used today to make antivenin. A great step forward in antivenin development came with the founding by Dr. Vital Brazil, near São Paulo, Brazil, of the Butantan Institute which even today continues research on venomous animals. But it was not until 1927 in this country that a commercial antivenin against rattlesnake venom became available.

Everywhere the production of antivenin follows the same basic procedure. First, a horse (or in some cases a rabbit or goat) is injected with a less-than-lethal dose of venom. The dose is increased until, within a few months, the animal suffers no harm when given what would ordinarily be far more than a lethal dose. Then the animal is bled and from its blood a serum containing antibodies is separated. With further refinement the serum becomes antivenin.

An antivenin for a single species of snake is called a monovalent antivenin. Fortunately there are some polyvalent antivenins, which can be used against the venoms of several related venomous snakes. Polyvalent antivenins are generally made by mixing representative venoms of a family of snakes—several rattlesnake venoms and a *fer-de-lance* venom, for example. The object, of course, is to achieve a treatment effective for any of the venoms of the family.

Because horse serum proteins are foreign to the human body, antivenins sometimes produce unpleasant side effects, ranging from hives to death from shock. People allergic to horses, or for that matter, to snake venoms, may suffer side effects—generally fever, itching, hives, and sore joints six to ten days after the bite.

Because of these allergic reactions to horse-produced serums, toxinologists have sought other possible means of producing either immunity to snakebite or a neutralizing serum that doesn't produce side effects. Some attempts are being made to produce antivenins in humans, and Japanese scientists have been studying the use of toxoids, chemically treated poisons that are themselves nontoxic and produce antibodies to counter specific venoms. Some antivenins for rattlesnake venoms are now being prepared from goat serum. These have been successfully used on snakebite victims who are sensitive to horse serum.

Properly administered antivenins seldom fail to neutralize venom already in the human patient. Before antivenins came into extensive use, about 200 people died of snakebite each year in the United States. So efficient are the antivenins that the best-equipped reptile houses, with many venomous snakes in their collections, keep antivenins for each venomous species under refrigeration.

(The San Diego Zoo went one step further by installing a "snake alarm" in its reptile houses. A bitten keeper can immediately summon aid by pressing a button that sounds an alarm in the constantly manned zoo security office.)

In those rare cases when a snakebite victim, with or without antivenin, continues to show a worsening condition, hospitalization can bring him the complete support system of modern medicine, including machines that can take over the functions of lung, kidneys, and heart. Unless he is backpacking in the wilderness, it is difficult to conceive of a situation in the American West where a snakebite victim would be more than a few hours away from a hospital. Even in rugged Baja California, much of it roadless, a radio or telephone could probably be reached within a few hours, and immediate help by helicopter would be forthcoming. Yet a traveler in sparsely settled country would be well advised to include a snakebite kit in his supplies.

Let us end with a word for the snakes. No rattlesnake will aggressively pursue a person. Its defensive bite is reserved for those who appear to threaten it. The person who steps on it or next to it or who ignorantly or foolishly picks it up is obviously a threat and may get bitten. But if the person retreats, the snake will not deliberately follow; instead it will seek sanctuary. Hopefully, in what little wild country remains to us, rattlesnakes, a distinctive and valuable part of the ecology, will be allowed to seek sanctuary when they are not actually around permanent dwellings. Rattlesnakes are characteristic of the American West, and from the beginning, when they were chosen as the symbol of defensive readiness for our first flag, they have played a role in our legend and history.

Chapter 15

» » » » »

THE CORAL SNAKE

Among snake families one of the most interesting is the Elapidae, the large group of snakes that includes the cobras, kraits, and coral snakes. Of these the most familiar example is the spectacled cobra of India, so much used by snake charmers. But the cobra family, which has branches in Asia, Australia, Africa, and the Americas, includes many smaller snakes that lack the ability to flatten their necks into "hoods," but carry in their venom sacs the same deadly nerve-attacking venom that is one of the distinguishing features of the family. Often these smaller snakes are inoffensive in appearance, for most of the Elapidae—certainly the smaller members of the family—belie the myth that venomous snakes have triangular heads, like the heads of arrows. Among the smaller members of the cobra family are the coral snakes, almost all of them beautifully marked with rings of bright colors—black, red, and white or yellow.

Wherever they are found, the coral snakes have generated local legends—mostly about incredible feats of poisoning. To the coral snakes, for example, has been attached the story of the "minute" snake. Wherever this widespread legend has sprung up, the coral snake is described as being so poisonous that any creature—bear, elephant, or man—will die within a minute after being bitten by the snake. This legend is also often applied to the mamba or the krait, and occasionally the "minute" snake described resembles no species on earth but is entirely an imaginary creature.

This is not to say that the coral snakes should be regarded as benign, harmless creatures. Most of them are quite deadly; a few have caused human deaths. But fortunately they are relatively small snakes, secretive, often burrowers; so they are infrequently encountered by man, and when they are encountered, they are seldom large enough to administer an effective bite. Of the two species found in the United States only one, the eastern coral snake, has ever killed a human.

The coral snakes are found only in the New World. They number approximately fifty species, belonging to three genera. Two of these species are found in the United States. The eastern coral snake *(Micrurus fulvius)* is found throughout Florida, northward into the Carolinas, and westward into Texas and Mexico. Other species of the genus *Micrurus* are found southward through Mexico and Central America into Uruguay and northern Argentina. Another genus of coral snakes *(Leptomicrurus)* occurs only in northern South America. The only coral snake found in the American West, the Arizona coral snake *(Micruroides euryxanthus euryxanthus),* represents the third genus.

Coral snakes, like other members of the family Elapidae, have short, permanently erect fangs in the front of the upper jaw. When they bite, the neurotoxic venom is released through a tube that runs down the center of the fang. This type of fang, found also in the sea snakes (family Hydrophiidae), characterizes what scientists call the proteroglyph snakes.

Brightly colored, as though painted with enamels, the Arizona coral snake has few rivals in beauty. Along its body are alternating rings of red, white (sometimes cream), and black. It is primarily a Mexican snake, barely extending its range into the United States in Arizona and New Mexico. Farther south in Mexico two additional subspecies occur in Sonora and Sinaloa. The Arizona coral snake lives in the moist parts of the semiarid desert areas bordering the foot of the southern plateau from Mohave County, Arizona, in the northwest to Grant County, New Mexico, in the southeast. It is also found on Tiburón Island in the Gulf of California.

Arizona coral snake

Several snakes in the Southwest can be, and sometimes are, confused with the coral snake. Chief among these are the shovel-nosed snake, the long-nosed snake, the California mountain kingsnake, and the Sonora mountain kingsnake. In order to avoid confusing these harmless snakes with the venomous coral snake, the observer can keep two differences in mind: the coral snake has rings of color that *completely* encircle its body; the "imitators" do not have complete rings. On the coral snake the red rings are bordered on either side by yellow or whitish rings. Yellow borders red, a sequence found on only one of the American look-alikes, the Organ Pipe shovel-nosed snake. The Sonora mountain kingsnake, which perhaps most closely resembles the coral snake, not only has a different sequence of colored rings—black borders red—but also has a white snout instead of the black snout found on the coral snake. A verse serves as an aid to remembering the difference between the coral snake and the harmless "imitator": Red and yellow, Kill a fellow./ Red and black, Venom lack.

The presence of look-alike snakes in the same general area as the Arizona coral snake provides one of the many controversies one finds in zoology. Some theorize that the harmless look-alikes are truly "mimics" of the coral snake, in effect taking shelter under the umbrella provided by their resemblance to a venomous species. This theory holds that this "imitation" increases their chances of confusing and thereby escaping enemies who mistake them, if even momentarily, as a potential threat to be avoided.

Mimicry

The whole subject of mimicry in animals is fraught with controversy. Without question mimicry does exist. The problem is determining when it applies and when it doesn't. Ever since the English naturalist Henry W. Bates first propounded his theory of mimicry in 1862, an enormous amount of ink has been spilled by scientists affirming and denying specific examples, including the numerous species of coral snakes and their look-alikes in the New World. Bates's idea, incorporated in what is now called Batesian mimicry, was fairly simple. Some animals, the models, are either venomous or inedible to the point where most predators avoid them. Other animals in the same area, entirely different species, perfectly edible and nonlethal, take shelter under this umbrella of protection from predators by mimicking the models—that is by looking like them, exuding similar scents, or sounding like them.

To another naturalist, the German Fritz Müller, this explanation was not sufficient. In 1878 he published his theories which helped to explain one great discrepancy in Bates's idea. Bates had noted but failed to explain why several inedible or venomous animals closely resemble one another. Why should one animal that predators avoid resemble another that predators avoid? What did the creature gain by such mimicry? The answer, embodied in Müllerian mimicry, is that the animals are involved in a numbers game. There is no absolute protection from predators. Some members of the prey group will be lost. Chances for survival of the species are greater if fewer members are taken by predators. If out of a hundred in the species, ninety-five are eaten, the chances for survival of the species are considerably less than they would be if only fifty are eaten. There is benefit, therefore, in developing standard signals that warn predators to avoid individuals of several species. For example, if a honeybee developed a pink and blue plaid pattern on its abdomen while a wasp developed black and yellow bands, then many more individuals of each species would be lost before predators learned to avoid them, since predators would have to go through two "learning" processes. But, if honeybees, wasps, and hornets, all with venomous stingers, develop a standard signal of black and yellow rings, the predators may take the same absolute number of individuals before they learn to avoid such creatures, but greater numbers of each species will survive. Not only that, but many non-stinging, edible flies and moths can mimic through black and yellow rings and find themselves less in demand by predators.

When we apply the concepts of either Batesian or Müllerian mimicry to the coral snakes and their imitators in the New World, we run into a major problem. Coral snake venom frequently kills the predator, giving the predator little opportunity to "learn" from the experience or to pass on its learning. Other species of coral snakes, let alone mimics, cannot benefit since virtually the only predators that have "learned" to avoid brightly-colored banded snakes are dead. Robert Mertens (see Wickler, 1968) provided a solution to this dilemma. The models being imitated, he suggested, were not the deadly coral snakes but some look-alikes, the bites of which on most predators produced pain and discomfort but not death. These were the snakes that the predators learned from—and both the venomous coral snakes and harmless mimics benefited from this learning. The numbers of mildly venomous species in South America, where Mertens gathered his data, tend to bear out his theory. The mildly venomous "coral" snakes actually outnumber both the true coral snakes and harmless "coral" snakes. Unfortunately the theory has little application to the southwestern United States, where there are no mildly venomous snakes that look like coral snakes. If one accepts the concept of mimicry, one has either to assume that the Arizona coral snake itself is the model, since it is not so deadly as many coral snakes, or to assume that the origin of this mimicry took place during a period long passed when there were mildly venomous snakes that participated. Perhaps, indeed, all latter-day coral snake mimicry developed during a much earlier period when coral snakes themselves were at a different, less deadly stage in the development of venom.

Many biologists do not believe that coral snakes and their look-alikes are involved in mimicry. They argue that these snakes, remarkably similar in the color, size, and number of their bands are examples of convergent evolution that saw them develop the same patterns of protective coloration.

We favor the theory of mimicry. Anyone who has seen some of the South American models and mimics would recognize that more is involved than convergent evolution. Some nonvenomous mimics look so much like their venomous models that even a trained herpetologist would think twice before capturing one by hand. Moreover, it is difficult to explain some facts without holding to the theory of mimicry. For example, the ranges of the Arizona coral snake and the Organ Pipe shovel-nosed snake overlap. The Organ Pipe shovel-nosed snake is a much more pronounced mimic of the coral snake than its close cousin, the western shovel-nosed snake, which has a different range from that of the coral snake. But the western shovel-nosed snake and the California mountain kingsnake are "mimics" that exist where the coral snake does not—a point made by the critics of mimicry. This argument, however, takes into account only the now of evolution, not the past when the ranges of the progenitors of the coral snake and all its imitators may have been the same.

The Arizona coral snake is a small snake, adults generally being about fifteen to eighteen inches long. The largest individual known measured only twenty-two inches. The coral snake's body is nearly cylindrical, with a diameter not much greater than that of an ordinary lead pencil. The neck is not distinct, and the head is small and blunt.

Like many another with an exaggerated western reputation, the Arizona coral snake is a gunman with no notches on his gun. There have been no authenticated cases of human death resulting from the bite of this snake. Indeed there are remarkably few bites recorded.

Perhaps there would be more danger if the snake were larger, but the snake is small and its fangs are short. These fangs, like those of all the elapids, are permanently erect. They must be short, therefore, to be accommodated when the snake's mouth is closed. Otherwise the snake would have fangs extending below its lower jaw like those seen in prints of Chinese dragons. The coral snake's fangs are so short that as a rule they are not long enough to pierce the skin of an average adult human.

The snake is further handicapped by another feature of its fangs; the opening through which venom is injected into prey is not at the extreme tip of the fang, but above it on the front face of the fang. Consequently the snake must embed its fangs at least to the point where the opening is beneath the skin surface, or no venom can be injected into the bloodstream.

The unlikelihood of such a small snake effectively biting a grown man is well illustrated by the first recorded bite of an Arizona coral snake. James Oliver, director of the New York Aquarium, was holding a coral snake as he prepared to pose it for a photographer. Momentarily diverted by the photographer's instructions, Oliver looked away from the snake. An instant later one of the bystanders called his attention to the fact that he was being bitten. The coral snake, employing the chewing motion typical of elapid snakes, was busily but ineffectually trying to embed its fangs in Oliver's little finger. Examination proved that the snake's short fangs had not penetrated the skin. No venom had been injected; no symptoms or aftereffects were noted.

In the three recorded instances when an Arizona coral snake has successfully injected venom into a human victim, the symptoms, none of them severe, have been rapid and alike in all three cases. The victim felt pain at the immediate point of the bite, pain which continued from fifteen minutes to a few hours. Some hours after the bite each victim experienced drowsiness, nausea, and weakness. All felt a tingling or prickling sensation, in one instance limited to the finger bitten, but in the other two cases spreading to the hand and wrist. In two of the cases symptoms disappeared within seven to twenty-four hours after the bite. In the third and most severe case symptoms persisted for four days—and no wonder, for the twenty-two-inch attacking coral snake was the largest ever recorded. Not only were its fangs correspondingly longer, but presumably its supply of venom was correspondingly greater.

This most severe case was experienced by an Arizona physician whose avocation was herpetology. As both doctor and herpetologist, he elected to record in meticulous detail the most complete available account of a coral snake bite and its aftereffects. In addition to the symptoms described above, he recorded several others. Six hours after the bite his handwriting had deteriorated to the point where it looked like that of a five-year-old child. He had difficulty in focusing his eyes, and on several different occasions he walked into doors. He noted also that he experienced some sensitivity to light. The normal flow from his tear ducts greatly increased. Afterward, trying to recall the four days, he could remember very little about them.

It is fortunate that the Arizona coral snake is relatively small and inoffensive, since no specific antivenin for its venom is yet available. There is an antivenin available for use in case of bites by the eastern coral snake, but it doesn't work against the venom of the Arizona coral snake. Because bites by this secretive snake are uncommon and there have been no recorded deaths, the recommended first aid has been limited to a thorough scrubbing with soap and water of both the bite and the area around it. So shallow is the depth to which these small snakes can bite that in many cases, even if envenomation has taken place, at least some of the venom may be removed by scrubbing. However, since the bite of any venomous snake must be taken seriously, the victim should place himself or be placed under a doctor's care. A child in particular could be seriously affected, with treatment besides scrubbing required.

Although the Arizona coral snake was discovered around 1860, next to nothing is known of its life history and habits. Secretive and concealed most often during daylight hours, it lives in rocky desert areas with sandy soil at altitudes of from sea level to 5,800 feet. The loose sandy soil permits burrowing; rocky areas provide cover and concealment beneath the rocks or in rock fissures. From either sand burrow or rock cover the snake can venture abroad at night to hunt its prey. A few coral snakes have been observed in daylight hours, but usually only on overcast days or immediately after a rain.

The coral snake probably preys on any small lizard or snake that it can subdue with its venom. The slender blind snakes appear to be a favored food, although scanty field observations indicate that other small snakes may be equally sought. Ronald McConnaughey, a herpetologist from La Jolla, California, found an adult coral snake in Organ Pipe Cactus National Monument that regurgitated a recently swallowed Organ Pipe shovel-nosed snake. The prey (one of the coral snake's "imitators") was nearly as long as the predator. A coral snake has also been observed attempting to eat a juvenile whiptail lizard. One observer witnessed an hour-long battle between a coral snake and its intended prey, a black-headed snake. The coral snake won the fight and rewarded itself by eating the prey snake. Charles Lowe of the University of Arizona, on a trip to Tiburón Island in the Gulf of California, observed a coral snake subdue and eat a banded sand snake.

The coral snake, a poor pet under any circumstances, does not as a rule do well in captivity. The San Diego Zoo's longevity record for a coral snake is three years and eight months. This snake ate five different species of lizard and five species of snakes, most of which were not native to its own range. Such variety tends to support the contention that a coral snake will eat almost any lizard or snake small enough for it to subdue and swallow.

Herpetologists assume that the Arizona coral snake lays eggs, although this aspect of its life history is not known with certainty.

Maturing probably takes place during the spring months, with egg-laying occurring in late spring or early summer. No hatchings have been observed, although, presumably, they would take place in the fall.

The Arizona coral snake has achieved a measure of fame from one peculiar habit. It produces from its cloacal vent a kind of Bronx cheer. The snake most often makes this sharp popping sound when it is molested or annoyed, so it is perhaps not unrelated to the warning rattle of a rattlesnake. As we have already mentioned, a perfectly harmless snake, the western hook-nosed snake, gives a similar performance.

Chapter 16

» » » » »

LEGENDS ABOUT RATTLESNAKES

Their family is known scientifically as Crotalidae, but to the common man in the American West they are known simply as rattlesnakes or rattlers, and they have played an important part in the region's lore. Their single most important distinguishing mark is the rattle, a peculiar appendage unmatched in nature, carried by no other snake. Made of keratin, the same basic substance as human fingernails, the rattle starts as a single "button" at the end of a newborn snake's tail and grows through the addition of a segment with each shedding of skin; in a large, mature snake there may be as many as twenty-four segments. Since a segment is added each time the snake sheds, and since the snake may shed several times a year, there is nothing to the theory that a rattlesnake's age is the same as the number of rattles it bears. In addition, snakes lose rattles through natural wear that comes when the snake crawls between two rough rocks, or hooks a segment on a protruding twig, or simply shakes a segment off while rattling.

Hearing a large rattlesnake rattle in the wild when one is unable at first to locate the snake can be a most frightening experience.

Why the sound is so sinister it is difficult to say. Even when isolated from the snake and mixed into songs on a record, the sinister quality comes through. And there is nothing else like it. On a warm day in the mesquite the hiker hears a cicada and wonders if he is hearing a rattlesnake; but were he actually to hear a rattlesnake there would be no doubt in his mind. He would immediately become alert and start cautiously looking around to locate the source of the sound.

The sound is clearly a warning. But it is a meaningful warning, being given by a creature that can deliver a lethal dose of venom, striking hard and fast and with great efficiency. Various attempts have been made to describe the rattle's sound, none of them quite successful. Commonly it is likened to the sound of wind in dry leaves, or a breeze rattling the dry stalks of reeds, or the rapid clicking together of light castanets. Yet it is no more these than it is the cicada's song. It starts like the clicking of dried bones, grows in intensity and volume until the individual clicks are a strident blur, runs together and up and down the scale with a sound like escaping steam, yet with that dried-bones effect still present, and finally subsides into a series of individual clicks.

In one of the earliest accounts written about rattlesnakes, Captain Thomas Walduck, delivering a paper before the Royal Society of London on January 7, 1714, described the terrifying effect of the rattle: "They never bite but first make a rattling with their tayls, & they may be heard 20 yards off. Those men yt use ye woods say they never come near a Rattle Snake but they are aprised of it before they either hear or see them, & they are in a fright as tho' a Spectre was near them, & that their breath inflames ye Air & before they either hear or see them they are seized with sorrow."

On the small rattlesnake species, the massasaugas and rock rattlesnakes, for example, the rattle is so tiny that it does not produce a terrifying effect on human beings. Often, in fact, one cannot hear the little creature rattling more than a few feet away.

If human beings could hear higher frequency ranges, however, they might be terrified. For much of the "noise" produced by a massasaugas or the rock rattlesnakes is to man ultrasonic. The sound is there, but man can't hear it. In his egocentric way man assumes that animal warnings are intended primarily for him. Small rattlesnakes, however, have other enemies—deer, foxes, coyotes, whose acute hearing can pick up sounds at frequencies beyond the ability of man to hear. Over evolution's eons the warning rattles of the smaller rattlesnakes developed through natural selection more to warn enemies that in years past were more frequently found and more deadly than man.

In our history the rattle has served as more than a terrifying warning device at the end of the rattlesnake's tail. Probably influenced by Indian lore, Americans early came to believe in the use of rattlesnake rattles in medicine, particularly as a means of hastening childbirth. When on February 11, 1805, the Lewis and Clark expedition was at Fort Mandan, Captain Lewis wrote: "About five o'clock this evening one of the wives of Charbono was delivered a fine boy . . . her labour was tedious and the pain violent: M. Jessome informed me that he had frequently administered a small portion of the rattle of a rattlesnake which he assured me had never failed to produce the desired effect, that of hastening the birth of a child." After describing exactly how to administer the rattle—crumbled into water—and noting that no more than ten minutes after taking the "medicine" the woman had delivered, the scientific-minded Lewis added: "Perhaps this remedy may be worthy of future experiments, but I must confess that I want faith in its efficacy."

The first picture of a rattlesnake, which appeared in the 1628 Latin edition of a book by Spanish explorer, Hernandez, showed the rattles incorrectly, the broad face vertical to the ground instead of horizontal, as rattles in fact are. Ever since then men have misunderstood the function of the rattles. Some have thought the rattle itself dispensed poison in the form of a powdery dust shaken into the air. Others have seen it as a signal to other rattlesnakes—a warning, a call to joint action against the enemy, a call to join in hibernation, a mating call, a call for help. Still others have thought it was a lure for prey. And some, curiously, have thought the rattle to be a warning not only to enemies but also to prey animals, as though the rattlesnake, totally unlike any other predator in nature, would forego the advantage of surprise out of some gallant scruple that required it to warn its prey before striking.

Most of these ideas about the rattle are not even remotely true. The rattle is not poisonous; it is not a lure for prey animals, nor does it warn them. It may be used to signal other rattlesnakes, although probably not in any highly sophisticated manner—without, in other words, a rattlesnake equivalent of the Morse code. C. B. Perkins several times saw captive rattlesnakes apparently shake their rattles at other rattlesnakes once they had subdued prey and started to eat it. This rattling could have been reflexive, but it could also have been the equivalent of the growl a dog gives when it settles down to a bone with other dogs around. Several observers have noted the tendency of rattlesnakes in groups to start a kind of rattling chorus apparently spurred by a single snake's warning rattle. In light of the evidence that snakes "hear" airborne sound, such choruses might be seen as rattlesnakes warning one another. However, in a new, as yet unpublished study, Joseph M. Pylka, James A. Simmons, and E. Glen Wever come to the conclusion that rattlesnakes cannot hear their own rattles because the sound is not within the frequency range to which they are sensitive.

The most likely reason rattlesnakes rattle is to warn an enemy, not from an altruistic desire to preserve the enemy but to give the rattlesnake itself time to escape.

How and why the rattle evolved remains a mystery, the only solution to which may come through the gathering of fossil evidence. Some biologists believe that the dangers from hooves of bison, pronghorn, or similar plain dwellers made the rattle into a useful tool with a clear role in aiding the survival of the snake. Perhaps hundreds of thousands of years ago a snake that normally vibrated its tail defensively developed a rudimentary rattle, which was passed on in the genetic code and evolved into the sophisticated rattle of today. But many snakes—gopher snakes and kingsnakes among others—vibrate their tails just as vigorously as rattlesnakes, yet none of these has developed rattles. Moreover, on the vast reaches of the African savanna with its great aggregations of wildebeest, zebra, and antelope, no snakes have developed rattles.

One is tempted to believe that some hundreds of thousands of years back in the dim antiquity of rattlesnakes, there occurred a mutation and that from this beginning, probably somewhere on the

Mexican plateau, evolved the complex mechanism known as the rattle. It is complex, a real feat of natural engineering. Extended at each shedding by a new segment, each segment must loosely but securely grip the segments on either side of it along an axis that tapers from broad base attached to the tail to narrow tip at the end. If the segments were too firmly joined, no rattle would occur. If they were too loose, they would readily fall apart.

We would be remiss in not pointing out that in one instance the evolution of the rattle has worked in reverse. On the small island of Santa Catalina in the Gulf of California there exists a strange species of rattlesnake *(Crotalus catalinensis)* similar in all respects to the other crotalids except that this rattlesnake has no rattles. Apparently an inheritable defect in the matrix upon which the rattle is formed has doomed this species to retain only the keratin surrounding the matrix and nothing else. As new segments are grown they are cast off when the snake sheds. All that remains is a single button that by itself can produce no sound.

Early Stories

It is hard to say which is more marvelous—the rattlesnake of legend or the rattlesnake of fact. Dramatic in their often bizarre markings, ominous in appearance, massive in girth, and above all possessed of the terrifying rattle, rattlesnakes have generated more legend and myth than any other group of snakes.

Captain Walduck set the tone by reciting as fact a number of the legends that had developed. Now looking back over 250 years at Walduck's tendency to accept fanciful stories as fact, we could easily laugh at his errors, but we shouldn't. Knowledge comes to us through the serious efforts of people like Walduck to gather material and present it. In the transmission of knowledge about any new discovery—even today—much error is included; but solid fact is also passed on. Over the ensuing years the errors are corrected. When Walduck wrote, no one knew much about rattlesnakes, and he had to stumble to his own conclusions in trying to separate fact from legend.

Walduck told as fact, for example, the story of the deadly boots —a story that even today is occasionally retold as fact, whether the object is a boot or some other article of clothing. A man wearing boots, the story goes, is bitten by a rattlesnake. He comes home to his wife and dies. The boots are hung up in a closet. The woman remarries. The new husband uses the boots on a short journey, complains of a pain in his leg, and dies. The boots are hung up again. Sure enough the woman remarries again and the third husband uses the boots, complains of a pain in his leg, and dies. Since the finger of suspicion now points at the boots, the surgeon who had attended the third husband dissects them and finds "ye tooth of ye Rattle Snake that bitt ye first husband & did all ye Execution since as small as a hair." The surgeon takes this "tooth small as a hair" and experimentally pricks a dog with it. The dog dies. Keeping the "tooth" locked up, the surgeon many days later brings it out and pricks another dog. This dog lives, and "it was supposed that ye Snake was dead."

Here we have two common legends combined. One deals with the viability of even small amounts of venom; the second deals with the idea that snakes, even badly mangled ones, live on at least until sunset of the day they are killed, and sometimes even longer. This last chilling idea is, of course, pure nonsense. But the idea that venom retains toxicity has a basis in fact. Dried rattlesnake venom will keep its strength and death-dealing potential for many years—at least fifty and probably more. However, the story of the deadly boots stretches this truth a bit in asserting that a fang the size of a hair could kill three grown men and a dog. Nevertheless, this story persists, being told today as fact about boots left behind by an old prospector in his mountain cabin, or by a cowboy in a bunkhouse. There is even a modernized version that holds that rattlesnakes can puncture automobile tires by biting them and that mechanics or service station attendants have been killed by fangs left in such punctures. One can imagine what Captain Walduck would write about this: "And ye Rattle Snake bit ye automobile tyre, thereby bringing it to deflate so that it became necessary for ye owner to take it to a garage where ye mechanik put his hand upon the hole in ye tyre and right after died."

Captain Walduck also cited as fact in his treatise the idea that rattlesnakes have the power to exert a "wonderful fascination" on squirrels and birds, even to charm them out of trees fifty feet high with a charm so compelling that it brings the hypnotized animal right into the snake's mouth. This method of getting prey is necessary, Walduck goes on, because rattlesnakes "are a Slothfull heavy Creature . . . otherways they could not gett their prey. . . ." Of course no snake has the ability to charm and hypnotize. The idea that rattlesnakes are too large and slow-moving, too slothful, as Walduck put it, to run down fast-moving rabbits or squirrels is echoed in a newspaper article in the *San Diego Union,* October 10, 1878: "The question occurred to me that it would be impossible for so (apparently) clumsy an animal to run down, or jump upon, either rat, rabbit, or any other active animal. They must seize their prey asleep or use some strategym to get it within their coil."

What, of course, neither writer was aware of is the ability of a rattlesnake to trail prey or wait in ambush for it by using its sensing equipment—the nostrils and Jacobson's organ for trailing and the heat-sensing pits to detect warm-blooded prey and give it the equivalent of stereoptic vision for accuracy in striking. And the strike, itself, as we shall see, is not exactly the action of a "slothful" creature.

Captain Walduck accepted from the stories passed to him another false notion about rattlesnakes—that they stand in danger of poisoning themselves when they eat the prey they have killed. To avoid this danger, Walduck notes, "They apply themselves to a certain Root which they eat & in an Antidote to their own poyson. . . ." Many people even today confuse venom, which is hypodermically injected and spread through the bloodstream, with the kind of poison that one takes internally by swallowing. One can swallow rattlesnake venom without harm, although it is not advisable to do so, since there could conceivably be ulcers or other open internal sores through which venom might reach the bloodstream. Certainly a rattlesnake is not harmed by swallowing its own venom. It is doubtful, in fact, that it can be killed through injections of its own venom or venom from other rattlesnakes. Having no need of an antidote after eating, rattlesnakes obviously do not have to partake of Walduck's mysterious "Root." The idea that a root or a stone or other natural objects can be used as a cure for rattlesnake bite, however, still remains part of our lore. As we pointed out in chapter 14, reliance on such folk remedies is not advisable.

The idea that rattlesnakes must be coiled to strike is another fable that Walduck passes on, along with the fascinating idea that rattlesnakes have navels: "The Rattle Snake cannot bite running, he must be quoiled round with his head in ye middle & then he will rise as high as his navel, & no higher. . . ." As some people have learned to their sorrow, a rattlesnake can bite from any position. It is true that a rattlesnake will coil defensively when it knows an enemy is present from which it cannot escape. Its first inclination is to lie still and use its ability to adapt its color and pattern somewhat to blend with its surroundings. In this ability they are not so successful as chameleons and some other lizards, but they nonetheless can vary their color enough to achieve some concealment. If the enemy appears to be moving toward or away from it the rattlesnake may attempt escape, sometimes, unfortunately, giving itself away by rattling. But when escape is impossible, it assumes the defensive coil, half of the body coiled against the ground to give a secure base, half raised with head drawn back into an S. From this stance they face the enemy, ready to catapult the head forward with great force and accuracy. Most often rattling the tail, slowly flicking the tongue, giving prolonged violent hisses, the coiled rattler presents a most formidable appearance—an appearance that often achieves its objective of driving off the enemy.

But the same rattlesnake stretched out full-length across the trail need not wait to coil. It can turn and bite with alacrity any enemy, animal or man, that steps on it.

From a coiled position a rattlesnake generally strikes one-third to one-half its own length. One should not be misled, however, into believing that the strike has to be horizontal with a slight upward incline in its trajectory. If necessary, the rattlesnake can strike almost straight up. The mechanics of the strike are interesting. It is swift from start to finish; no sloth shows here. The snake's head moves nearly as fast as a good boxer's short right to the chin, and with somewhat similar force. High-speed photography shows that the snake's jaws are open from the instant the head starts forward. The fangs, positioned forward and normally retracted against the upper jaw, spring into place. These fangs curve slightly back toward the rear of the snake's mouth. At the moment of impact the snake's mouth is fully open, which means that upper and lower jaws are on

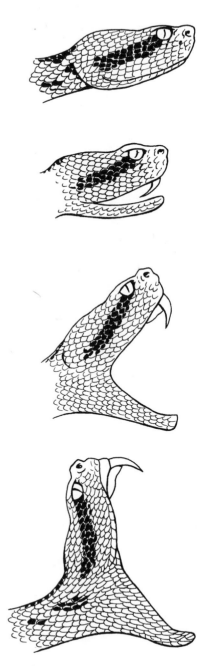

Fangs are hinged permitting them to swing back when mouth is closed.

Fang of rattlesnake

**RATTLESNAKE
FANGS**

the same vertical plane. The fangs hit, sink, and are quickly retracted as the snake withdraws again into the S, once more ready to strike. The whole deadly movement has taken no more than the blink of a man's eye.

Underneath the functional fangs of a rattlesnake are several reserve fangs, those on top being in a position to spring into place if a functional fang is lost. Interestingly on a newborn rattlesnake the first reserve fangs are actually longer than the functional fangs. Growth is rapid, and the reserve fangs are sized for a larger snake.

The entire fang and venom mechanism of the rattlesnakes marks an advanced stage in the evolution of the use of venom. The fangs themselves are curved hypodermic needles, hollow from venom duct to a point near the sharp end. By comparison, cobras are less advanced. Their fangs are hollow, and they can replace them. But cobra's fangs are permanently erect, lacking the hinging mechanism that enables the rattlesnake to have longer fangs since they can be laid back against the upper jaws. The difference between permanently erect and retractable fangs is pronounced. The cobra must take longer in biting or chewing on prey to embed the shorter fangs and inject venom. As a result the cobra is more exposed to immediate counterattack. The rattlesnake strikes and withdraws. Counterattack by the shocked or surprised target animal is less likely.

Snake fanciers who think they can protect themselves by removing a pet rattlesnake's fangs may find themselves in for an unpleasant surprise. If a person insists on keeping a pet rattlesnake, he should either avoid handling it altogether or have its venom glands surgically removed.

Size

In describing rattlesnakes, Captain Walduck accepted as gospel the tale told to him that back in the woods some monsters grow to be twelve feet long. This exaggeration foreshadows the often repeated myth of the giant rattlesnake, a myth one may occasionally hear today. Repeated as fact by solemn-faced tale-tellers, the story goes that a giant rattlesnake, generally around fifteen feet long, has been found dead, killed by train, truck, or automobile. The enormous rattles are unfortunately destroyed when the giant creature is run over. The destruction of the rattles is necessary to this story because the storyteller sometimes offers to show the giant's skin. Invariably, a herpetologist will find that it is the skin of a boa constrictor or python. The seeming need of men to elaborate on nature is what one finds most fascinating here. As though a good-sized rattlesnake were not big enough nor venomous enough, the storyteller must elaborate, making the snake even larger and more venomous. Almost invariably estimates of rattlesnake size are wrong, with the error on the large side. Partly such misjudgment results from the thickness of the rattlesnake's body, for the rate of girth to length increases greatly in the larger rattlesnakes. Thus a western diamondback rattlesnake, three times the length of a sidewinder, will weigh thirty-seven times as much. This enlargement in girth makes a four- or five-foot rattlesnake appear much larger. Commonly people estimate length at six or seven feet. The report, "I saw a six-foot rattler," probably means the observer actually saw one three to five feet long. Partially this tendency to exaggerate is caused by the snake's girth; partially, no doubt, it is another manifestation of the human tendency to enlarge upon danger as a means of attracting more attention to oneself. Suffice it to say that only one species of rattlesnake in the American West attains lengths of over six feet. That is the western diamondback rattlesnake, seven-foot specimens of which have been caught and measured. Occasionally the red diamond rattlesnake reaches lengths of approximately six feet. However, the average range of length is two and one-half to four feet.

Not all the folklore and legends about rattlesnakes had their origin with Walduck and his contemporaries. As the westward movement in the United States took place, new legends were bred, some by old-timers who couldn't resist spoofing a tenderfoot—that same tenderfoot who would wait patiently for three or four hours in the wilderness to bag a "snipe" on an elaborately set up but completely phony "snipe hunt."

Other Legends

Whatever their origin, many snake stories were retold so many times as fact that they became deeply ingrained in western history, some being taken as fact even today. Many people, for example, believe that young rattlesnakes when threatened will run to their mother, who, to preserve them, will swallow them until the danger has passed. Even in official documents this type of lore will turn up.

In *Reports of Exploration and Surveys to Ascertain the Most Practicable and Economic Route for a Railroad from the Mississippi to the Pacific Ocean* (Washington, D.C., 1860), Dr. J. D. Cooper mentions a rattlesnake seen near the Columbia River in Washington: "One specimen was killed, from the mouth of which three young ones were said to have escaped." Young rattlesnakes, it should be noted, are completely independent from the moment of their ovoviviparous birth. They and their mother have no more association unless by pure chance.

Dr. Cooper also referred to the use by Indians of the rattlesnake's rattle to produce abortion. Then, in discussing one western rattlesnake, he mentions another of the most familiar legends: "In July and August they are found very common. . . . They are sluggish and stupid, being, according to popular belief, 'blind,' and are said to be at that season exceedingly venomous. . . . Hunters have told me that the serpents are 'blind' because they are at that time about shedding the cuticle, and that as evidence of loss of vision the snake, when provoked, will 'strike wildly.'" This concept that rattlesnakes are blind and consequently more dangerous one or two times a year, particularly in July and August, is widely held. It is true that with eyes opaque as the old skin begins to loosen before shedding, rattlesnakes cannot see as well, nor are they ordinarily found abroad at such times, since before shedding they seek cover. But they can never see particularly well much over fifteen feet anyway. Nor do they particularly have to. Their other sensory equipment—nostrils, tongue and Jacobson's organ, and heat-sensing pits—provides them with the intelligence they require to operate. They never have to strike wildly; in tested fact, rattlesnakes can strike accurately when blindfolded—although only at objects that have a temperature above or below the immediate environmental temperature.

There may be seasonal influences on production of snake venom, but if there are they are not sufficient to cause any great differences in toxicity. Many variables influence the effect of snake bite on human beings. But all other factors being equal, it is doubtful that a July-August bite will be any more or less dangerous than an April-May bite.

Old survey reports likewise turn up some fine snake stories. In a report on the survey of the United States and Mexican boundary (Washington, D.C., 1857), Major William H. Emory notes two legends, one still widely believed, the other so fanciful that it must take its place as a delightful classic in the annals of false natural history. Major Emory recounts how he and his companions have set up camp on a mountain where "suwwarrow" (saguaro) grows in southern Arizona. The glare of fires, he says,

> attracted a large number of rattlesnakes . . . a new species from the tiger-colored skins. . . . When you lie down in your blanket, stretched on the ground, you know not what strange bedfellow you may have when you awake in the morning. My servant insisted upon encircling my bed with a reata of horsehair to protect me from their intrusions. Snakes are said to have a perfect repugnance to being pricked by the extremities of the hair. The paisano, or chapparal cock, surrounds his antagonist, while asleep, with a chain of cactus thorns; when the preparations are all made the bird flutters over the head of the snake to arouse it to action; the latter, in its vain efforts to escape, is irritated to such a degree, by running against the barrier encompassing it, that it ends its existence by burying its fangs in its own body.

It is possible that some campers in rattlesnake country still encircle their beds with rough rope to ward off the snakes. This preventative, one of the most persistent erroneous notions in the continuing confrontation of man and rattlesnake in the United States, seems to be more widespread in the American West, where it most often is associated with cowboys sleeping on the range. Fortunately, unlike many legends that persist, this one can bring its believers to no harm. Rope, however, will not ward off a rattlesnake, whose coat of keratin with large keeled scales is not at all troubled by hair or other rough textures. But rattlesnakes, like most other wild creatures, *are* inclined to move away from camps and other places where man is found.

The "chapparal cock" to which Major Emory refers, is now commonly called the roadrunner. Roadrunners include rattlesnakes, generally young ones, among the items of their varied diet. From this fact has sprung the legend that roadrunners build cactus corrals around rattlesnakes, which in frustration engendered by their efforts to escape, bite themselves to death. How such a story got its start no one knows—perhaps from an Indian myth, perhaps from misinterpreting an actual observation of a snake coming out of a cactus clump with a roadrunner nearby, perhaps from the ramblings of a peyote chewer having hallucinations, or perhaps from the imagination of a twinkly-eyed storyteller.

Other legends abound. L. M. Klauber, an authority on rattlesnakes, completed a lengthy collection. He found, for example, a widely held belief that rattlesnakes actually hate people (particularly people dressed in blue) and will go out of their way to attack them. This hatred, the belief goes, becomes particularly acute if one member of a rattlesnake couple is killed. The surviving snake, we are told, will like relentless doom never cease hunting until it finds and destroys the person who killed its mate. We should pause here to comment that rattlesnakes do not as a rule travel in pairs. During mating season or denning they may be found together, but stories about "marital" devotion are false. Nor, of course, are rattlesnakes deliberately vindictive or aggressive toward man. Their striking coil is used to provide them with the base for what our Department of Defense calls "protective reaction."

Among the false stories about rattlesnakes' venom, some of which we have already included, is one particularly fascinating bit of folklore: a hornet that finds a dead rattlesnake will deliberately drink some of the venom in order to increase the potency of its sting. The story does not elaborate on how hornets discovered this path to supertoxicity.

The confusion of venom with poison causes many tall tales that originate in the false idea that a rattlesnake must avoid swallowing its own venom. Captain Walduck passed on the story that rattlesnakes swallow prey whole to avoid poisoning themselves. Related to this are stories that rattlers take out their venom glands (we are not told how) before drinking water to avoid floating venom down their throats. Another legend has it that courting rattlesnakes remove their fangs to avoid the possibility of "poisoning" each other during the ecstasies of lovemaking.

Typically western in flavor is a story about rattlesnakes and bullets. In firing at a rattler, the story goes, the gun handler need not take careful aim; the rattlesnake, seeing the bullet approach, will strike at it and so be killed when head and bullet meet.

Other myths deal with rattlesnakes as medicine. In addition to using the powdered rattle to bring abortion or hasten childbirth, men have at one time or another believed that venom, taken internally in small doses, can cure epilepsy and various other diseases; that the snake's skin worn around the throat will cure a cold or one worn around the head will cure a headache or toothache; that rattlesnake flesh, if eaten, will cure tuberculosis; that rattlesnake oil applied externally will cure rheumatism. None of these beliefs is born out by medical research.

The roadrunner story is not by any means the only bit of false natural history involving rattlesnakes and other animals. There exists also the belief that rattlers employ other snakes to lead them to their prey. (Such a story could have its origin perhaps in seeing a rattlesnake close to another snake as both move toward a major hibernaculum.) Most farfetched of all is the story that rattlesnakes sometimes mate with gopher snakes. It is believed that the offspring of this unnatural union are extremely dangerous, for they inherit the venom of the rattlesnake and the rattleless tail of the gopher snake.

It would be impossible here to cover all of the myths and legends about rattlesnakes. No doubt many of them will persist until the final rattle is shaken by the last rattlesnake. Fortunately, few of the false stories do harm and many of them, like all myths and legends, add much to the richness of life. Yet the *facts* about rattlesnakes are as absorbing as the legends. We turn now to the real rattlesnakes of the American West.

Chapter 17

» » » » » »

THE RATTLESNAKES

Nearly every man despises them, for though they are unique and beautiful, to men they seem malignant and deserving of destruction. These much maligned animals are the rattlesnakes, found only in the Americas, where their species number among the approximately one hundred species of pit vipers that exist in the New World. In the Old World, in Asia only, a few other pit vipers are known. All pit vipers are characterized by the heat-sensing facial pits that give them a three-dimensional infrared "profile" of heat-emanating objects and add immeasurably to their efficient operation as predators. Pit vipers include, in addition to the rattlesnakes, two of the best known snakes of the New World—the *fer-de-lance (Bothrops atrox)* and the bushmaster *(Lachesis muta)*, the scientific name of which means "silent fate." In the American East and Southeast occur two pit vipers that have no rattles—the copperhead *(Agkistrodon contortrix)* and the cottonmouth *(Agkistrodon piscivorus);* otherwise all the pit vipers in the United States, including all twelve species found in the West, are rattlesnakes.

The rattlesnakes have in common rattles, heat-sensing pits, elliptical pupils, highly evolved venom and fang systems, keeled scales, bulkiness, relatively thin necks, and massive spade-shaped heads. They differ, often markedly, in size, coloration, temperament, and type and potency of their venom. One does not with impunity fool with any rattlesnake, but some are much more dangerous to man than others.

The most dangerous snake in the American West is the western diamondback rattlesnake. Widespread, common in many parts of its range, large, aggressive, testy in temperament, the western diamondback probably accounts for more bites and fatalities than any other rattlesnake. Almost as dangerous, and somewhat similar in appearance is the Mojave rattlesnake, a moderately large, wide-ranging snake with a particularly potent venom that contains elements not unlike those in some of the cobra venoms.

Most rattlesnake species are found in the American Southwest, Arizona being the state with the greatest number—eleven species to New Mexico's seven and California's six. The month of greatest rattlesnake activity in the Southwest is not August, as many people think, but May. In May the snakes emerge from their winter dens, hungry for food and mates. Then they are most likely to be on the prowl, particularly in late afternoon and on warm nights. The hibernaculums, or dens, are used by successive generations of rattlesnakes. Each season as many as five hundred snakes use the same den in colder places; smaller numbers den together in warmer climates, and in the tropics the snakes are active the year around.

Normally one thinks of rattlesnakes as terrestrial creatures, crawling, often with rectilinear motion, on the ground or coiled beneath rock ledge or bush. In spite of their bulk, however, rattlesnakes can climb trees. It is not uncommon to find even large snakes four or five feet off the ground in mesquite, manzanita, or other shrubs. More than likely, they climb to such places to seek a basking spot where, in early morning particularly, before the sun grows too hot, they can warm their bodies to the temperature needed for efficient movement.

Rattlesnakes are likewise good swimmers. A stream, brook, river, lake, even the ocean does not hamper their movement. Western diamondback rattlesnakes, for example, have been taken at sea twenty miles from the land in the Gulf of Mexico, where they populate many islands off the shore of Texas. And in the warm-watered Gulf of California every island is populated by rattlesnakes, many of which are descendants of nearby mainland forms.

Great numbers of gophers or ground squirrels in an area is a good indication that not many rattlesnakes are to be found there. For in the balanced western ecosystem, rattlesnakes—in concert with other predators—help keep the rodent population under control. By doing so, of course, they perform a valuable service to man. Rodents—rats, mice, gophers, squirrels, chipmunks, rabbits—are the principal food of rattlesnakes, but by no means the only food. Sometimes birds are caught and rattlers that live near streams or lakes include frogs and toads in their diet. Small rattlesnakes, both juveniles and small adults like the sidewinder, eat lizards. The narrow-bodied lizards are normally easier to swallow than chunkier rodents of roughly the same body weight. Of course horned lizards and a few other spiny types do occasionally create problems for any snake that tries to swallow them.

Contrary to earlier ideas about their bulkiness and sloth, rattlesnakes are efficient hunters. They probably eat once every week or ten days—more often in the spring after emerging hungry from the winter's den, and more often in the fall when they build up fat for the dangerous hibernation to follow. The hunting rattlesnake seeks prey concentrations, often setting up an ambush along a well-traveled rodent trail. When the doomed squirrel or rabbit comes along, the snake strikes, using eyesight or heat-sensing pits to guide it. Then, venom injected, the snake withdraws and waits while the prey kicks futilely in its death throes. A few seconds tick away, for in a small rodent the venom spreads rapidly; then the snake, using chemical cues picked up by its tongue, nostrils, and Jacobson's organ, trails the rodent, finds it, and swallows it. Sometimes, particularly during the smothering heat of summer, the rattlesnake goes underground, living and hunting in rodent burrows, following the prey literally right into its bedroom.

Though they eat less often than most animals, rattlesnakes, like other snakes, ingest at each meal a far higher proportion of their body weight. This proportion will run from five to more than one hundred percent of body weight. The average, L. M. Klauber estimates, is around forty percent. With high intake at one meal a rattlesnake could theoretically live as long as a year between meals. Water, however, would be required, for in the arid Southwest snakes obtain water from the animals they swallow.

On their native ranges rattlesnakes have many enemies besides their principal enemy, man. Mostly these enemies will destroy only the juveniles or naturally small rattlesnakes. Adults of the larger species have increased their chances for survival simply by reaching adulthood. Kingsnakes, racers, and whipsnakes regularly eat rattlesnakes, and in wild country many other animals view rattlesnakes— if a bit cautiously—as tasty morsels. Coyotes, foxes, wildcats, and badgers all will eat rattlesnakes. So will dogs, cats, and pigs. Where hogs run, rattlesnakes are few. Rattler venom could kill a hog, but the chances are that the hog would be bitten in a layer of fat where the venom would do little harm. Hawks and eagles also regularly prey on rattlers (and other snakes), swooping down to secure the creature in the clamplike grip of sharp talons, carrying it aloft, thrashing but helpless, and eating it finally in a treetop or aerie by tearing off chunks of the still-living snake. Red-tailed hawks have been observed to sever the heads of rattlesnakes before eating them, an act they don't perform on other snakes. Man, too, occasionally eats rattlesnake, though it cannot be considered a gourmet treat.

Many hoofed animals attack rattlesnakes defensively. Deer, pronghorn, sheep, goats, horses, and cattle will often try to stamp on rattlesnakes unwary enough to be caught in the open on their ranges. Why this often successful action is taken no one can say. One can only hazard the guess that it is a manifestation of collective defense against a creature which, if it were to remain alive, would continue to threaten the herd, particularly young and inexperienced members.

Rattlesnakes are ovoviviparous. As in all ovoviviparous snakes the female retains her eggs in her body instead of laying them. When birth time comes, she deposits the now thin sacs, like so many cellophane-wrapped packages, and the young snakes, using their egg teeth, break out of their encasements. They emerge fully equipped with fangs, venom, and the pre-button beginning of a rattle. From that moment they and their mother have no further relationship, except by accident.

The Rattlesnakes

Since rattlesnakes usually mate in the spring, most young are born in August. Their most pressing immediate problem, like that of many newborn snakes, is to find the food that will sustain them through the upcoming period of hibernation. They have only a short interval—perhaps two months—between their entry into the world and the long winter's sleep. Young snakes that do not put on some fat before denning will not see their first spring.

Female rattlesnakes can store sperm. Consequently if a female and her mates are out of synchrony in their fertile cycles, no harm is done. Through sperm storage one brood of young rattlers may actually be the product of several matings.

A female rattlesnake generally produces its first brood in the third year of its life and a new brood every year thereafter until the end of its life. An exception to this annual cycle occurs in rattlesnakes in the northern United States and southern Canada, where females produce young once every two years. In the American West the only rattlesnakes that range far enough north to be affected are subspecies of the wide-ranging western rattlesnake, notably the northern Pacific rattlesnake, which ranges into British Columbia, and the prairie rattlesnake, which ranges into Alberta and Saskatchewan.

Among male rattlesnakes the combat dance is one of the most interesting in snakedom. Unlike the twisting contest of the gopher snakes and other colubrids, combat between male rattlesnakes finds the contestants rearing up so that perhaps a third of their length is off the ground. Heads elevated at a 45° angle, the snakes engage in what might be called intense pushing. Scute to scute they lock themselves, muscles rippling, tongues occasionally flicking. Here, like two grotesque candlesticks, they stay until one slips or is pushed off by the other and clumsily falls away. At its height the combat takes a side-by-side form with the more aggressive snake draped over his opponent's body. Again rearing up, both push sideways, endeavoring to entwine their necks as male giraffes do in combat. Here the battle takes its most violent form. If one snake succeeds in getting its neck twice around its opponent, it has taken a judo hold. With a sharp, undulatory, whiplike motion so rapid that observers can't follow it, it throws the opponent violently to the ground. The throw is powerful, and on occasions is audible as a sharp "thwack" to observers standing five or six feet away. The whole male combat dance may last for thirty minutes or more. At the end the loser is simply the one most tired of being thwacked against the ground. As in all successful battles the winner is left alone on the field. On it or near it may be a female rattlesnake, but the combat is often fought with no females around. In one caged combat three pairs of western diamond-back rattlesnakes squared off. All were males, and the immediate stimulus seemed to be a struggle for territory.

While the rattlesnakes share many common characteristics, as individual species they vary greatly from one another. One of the most notable points of difference is in squamation, the size and arrangement of scales, particularly on the heads. Head scales, in fact, account for the principal difference between the two genera of rattlesnake, *Sistrurus* and *Crotalus*. In *Sistrurus* the prefrontal and frontal scales form nine plates; in *Crotalus* there are many more.

In the East the massasauga *(Sistrurus catenatus)* is called the swamp rattlesnake or sometimes the little gray rattlesnake. The more commonly used name "massasauga" is derived from two Chippewa words which literally mean "great river mouth." The term probably was used because these small snakes are frequently found in the vicinity of streams, ponds, or swamps. Adult massasaugas generally measure around two feet long, although they may be as small as eighteen inches and as long as forty inches.

The subspecies in the American West is the southwestern or desert massasauga *(S. c. edwardsii)* found in southeastern Colorado, the southeastern three-fourths of New Mexico, and extreme southeastern Arizona. Thence it ranges eastward into Oklahoma and Texas and just across the border into Mexico. This snake is fairly easy to recognize because it has large prefrontal and frontal scales and distinctive head markings—long, dark brown streaks that extend back onto the neck and sometimes form a lyre on top of the head. Each has a streak running through it. Down the middle of the snake's back runs a row of thirty dark brown rounded spots, alternating with three rows of smaller spots, often fainter in color. The brown markings are set against gray or light gray-brown. The belly

The Southwestern Massasauga

57

is pale. In the six- to ten-inch young snakes all colors stand out more conspicuously than in adults and the tail is yellowish white. Melanistic specimens, almost entirely black, are not unusual.

The massasauga is most often found around water—river bottoms, grassy hummocks in swamps, or marshy areas near lakes or ponds. However, particularly during the summer, the desert massasauga may move into drier grassy plains or heavy brush with mesquite or yucca. It is found at altitudes from sea level to 5,000 feet.

Considered mild-mannered and sluggish, this rattlesnake poses no great threat to human beings unless they deliberately provoke it or accidentally step upon it—an easy thing to do since the snake will most often use protective coloration to achieve an uncanny blend with the natural ground cover. One should not depend upon its rattle as a warning. Like other rattlesnakes, it may not rattle at all, and the rattle itself, though unusually well formed, is quite small in proportion to the snake's size.

Its cicadalike buzz does not produce the same fright in man that is often caused by the sound of large rattlers. Man, however, is hearing only the lower end of the frequency range of sound produced by the massasauga's rattle.

In diet the desert massasauga differs quite markedly from most rattlesnakes in that it often eats frogs, other amphibians, and smaller snakes. It also eats mice and lizards. Apparently to accomodate toad eating, its adrenal glands are more enlarged than those in most snakes. However, these glands are not proportionately as large as those in a hognose snake.

Massasauga litters average eight or nine young, although litters of up to eighteen offspring have been recorded.

The Western Diamondback Rattlesnake

58

The king of snakes in the American West—the western diamondback rattlesnake *(Crotalus atrox)*—is large, malevolently beautiful, active, alert, and not inclined to give ground when confronted. Found in much of New Mexico, the southern half of Arizona, and southeastern California, the western diamondback also has been reported in southern Colorado and the extreme southern tip of Nevada. It ranges eastward over much of Texas and Oklahoma and southwest over much of Mexico.

Adults range in length from two and a half to slightly over

seven feet for the largest recorded specimen. Most adults are between four and a half and five feet long. Needless to say, such a large snake can administer a large amount of venom in its bite. On a potency scale its venom is not as powerful drop for drop as that of the small rock rattlesnake, but it is extremely potent, and to a person bitten by a large snake academic distinctions in the potency would not seem important.

Sometimes called "coontail" rattlesnake, the western diamondback is characterized by an easily identifiable tail barred in black and white like a raccoon's. The snake's ground color may be gray, light brown, or pink. Against this color are set the diamonds, or sometimes hexagons, of a darker brown in a row down the center of the back. Smaller blotches appear on the sides. The whole is often peppered with small specks that blur the clarity of the other markings — but no doubt help the snake in blending with its surroundings. From the eyes on both sides a stripe runs diagonally toward the rear of the mouth, intersecting the mouth well ahead of the corner. On the nine- to fourteen-inch young western diamondback rattlesnakes all markings are more clearly defined. The term "western" is applied to distinguish this snake from the even larger "eastern" diamondback rattlesnake *(Crotalus adamanteus)* found in the Southeast.

Within its range, from sea level to 7,000 feet, the western diamondback may live in a variety of different settings. Mostly associated with arid habitats — rocky cactus-covered hillsides, dry grass-covered prairie, flats of mesquite or sagebrush — this snake is also found in moist brush-covered river bottoms, along rocky streams, and in wooded areas. Some estimate of its numbers can be obtained from the count made by one Texas rancher. In clearing 10,000 acres of cactus and brush, he killed 1,200 rattlesnakes. In short, where it ranges, the hiker or camper cannot count himself safe in any particular habitat from this most dangerous of North American snakes. In fact, although it will most often be found abroad in the evening or at night, it frequently roams about in broad daylight.

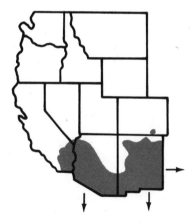

Like most large rattlesnakes, *C. atrox* often uses the rectilinear or caterpillar crawl method of locomotion, shuffling along so to speak on its scutes, making on sand or loose soil a straight track that looks like the track of a dragged log. Primarily an eater of rodents, *C. atrox* will not hesitate to take birds also. The naturalist Grace

Olive Wiley, probably the first person to breed *C. atrox* in captivity (December 29, 1924), fed the eleven young snakes quite successfully for three weeks on small bits of raw beef and liver.

The western diamondback is one of the few snakes whose mating habits in the wild have been thoroughly observed. Males of the species engage in the same type of combat dance described earlier in this chapter. Because of this snake's large size, these battles are quite spectacular, for in rearing up the combatants raise their heads quite high off the ground. In pursuing its chosen mate, the male is single-minded and aggressive. The herpetologists R. M. Perkins and M. J. R. Lentz noted this single-mindedness in the field during April of a mating season that runs from March through May. The two observers, visiting the site of a den from which the snakes had only recently emerged, found that the remaining rattlers "seemed to be running in pairs." They found one of these pairs in which the male was fairly small and paid absolutely no attention to the proximity of human observers. The herpetologists somewhat ungallantly lifted the female clear of the male and deposited her some fifteen feet away. Immediately the male showed signs of agitation and excitement and began crawling toward the female. Before he reached her the observers tantalizingly moved her to another place. The male scarcely paused; merely changing direction, he crawled rapidly toward her. The female was moved several times. Each time the male turned and crawled toward the female. The presence of Perkins and Lentz didn't faze him "for he would crawl toward us, or even between our legs, without rattling or assuming an aggressive attitude." When finally this frustrated male was once again allowed to catch up with his inamorata, he immediately resumed the courtship actions, which had been disturbed.

Young western diamondbacks, born live, are from nine to fourteen inches long.

Except for its redness the red diamond rattlesnake *(Crotalus ruber)* looks very much like the western diamondback, but it differs in temperament and is less venomous. A close relative of *C. atrox* and quite large—adults are two and a half to five and a half feet long—the red diamond seems by comparison a gentle snake. Often in the wild it does not rattle, and it is readily tamed in captivity. In fact it may become deceptively tame, encouraging its owner to take chances by picking it up fully loaded with fangs and venom. Yet it is a wild creature and can, like other "tamed" wild creatures, suddenly and without apparent motivation, attack the foolhardy person who handles it. Its venom is mild for a rattlesnake, but fangs on the adult snake are long and its venom is plentiful. It can kill a man.

In the American West the red diamond is found only in extreme southwestern California, mostly in San Diego County, but as far north as San Bernardino County. Actually it is a Mexican snake with a range covering all of Baja California and extending to many of the offshore islands in the Gulf of California. It is a snake of brush-covered hillsides on both sides of the mountains. A favored habitat is the reddish sandstone mesas covered with brush that have many small caves and clefts in which the snakes, often in groups, spend much of their time. L. M. Klauber observed that "beginning in February and during the Spring months until June, they are readily found in the warm sunshiny ravines, with slopes facing south, that have an abundance of cacti, sumac, and brush . . . protected from the west winds."

On such a slope a strange combat took place. In the San Diego Zoo's Wild Animal Park the animals roam within large enclosures over ancient rattlesnake territory, which until only recently was perfectly wild. In the African lion enclosure one day a young male lion came upon a red diamond rattlesnake. The vivid picture remains of the native American snake, coiled and threatening the uncomprehending lion that was ready for a romp. The lion moved, paw upraised to bat the snake; the snake struck, sinking its fangs by the lion's eye. Quickly the lion retreated. It was a classic ending. Even in a meeting of Old and New Worlds the efficient equipment of the rattlesnake triumphed. Later the rattler was captured. The lion, face greatly swollen, was extremely sick for several days.

The habit of some people in keeping this snake as a pet provides some fascinating anecdotes. One young lady of our acquaintance let her pet red diamond, venom sacs surgically removed, roam freely around the city house she shared with her parents. One day when she was absent a visiting nurse came to see her father, then recuperating from a heart attack. The nurse, chattering pleasantly, was getting portable electrocardiogram equipment ready when out

The Rattlesnakes

from under the very couch on which the father lay crawled five feet of red diamond rattlesnake. During the next few moments no one could have told who was the more seriously ill, nurse or patient. Both eventually recovered.

This pet rattlesnake was named John because it had been captured near a rural outhouse. John died an ironic death. When not roaming loose, he was kept in a large covered aquarium. One day his owner brought home a freshly captured sidewinder rattlesnake and, having no place else to put it, temporarily housed it with John in the aquarium. Angry, the sidewinder struck the venomless John, who by next morning was dead—the victim of rattlesnake bite.

The Speckled Rattlesnake
60

Many of the hillsides in Southern California, Nevada, and western Arizona are covered with boulders, some huge, mostly granite, flaking, chipping, cracking, tumbled in huge heaps by ancient volcanic action. Often indeed the land is so sun-drenched and barren that it has given rise to the kind of story that forms the mainstream of American western humor. One early traveler across such a rock-strewn landscape wrote, "The country is too barren to support any higher life than rattlesnakes and crows, and I believe the crows make their living principally by eating rattlesnakes that have died of starvation. . . ."

The rattlesnakes in this observation may well have been one of the two subspecies of the speckled rattlesnake *(Crotalus mitchellii),* a frequenter of rocky habitats mostly on the slopes of mountains, but also extending all the way to the seacoast in Baja California. The speckled rattlesnake ranges from southern Nevada, where it is called the Panamint rattlesnake *(Crotalus mitchellii stephensi),* to the tip of Baja California and from southern California into central Arizona. In the southern part of its range it is called the southwestern speckled rattlesnake *(C. m. pyrrhus).*

A moderately large snake—from two to slightly over four feet in adults—the speckled rattlesnake is colored much like the rocks among which it most frequently lives. The last statement suggests that the snake is dull in color, but in fact it is probably one of the most handsome of rattlesnakes, and certainly the most variable in color and pattern. Its ground color, always light, may be white, gray, salmon, brown, tan, yellow, or orange, the whole appearing

222

as if it had been fairly heavily speckled with salt and pepper. On the back are about thirty markings; sometimes vague, other times well defined, they often take the form of crossbars (this is why the Panamint rattlesnake is sometimes erroneously called tiger rattle-snake), but other times they are clearly defined geometric shapes—diamonds, hexagons, hourglasses. These markings vary in color from snake to snake—red, gray, brown, black, yellow—but are always darker than the ground color. The tails have alternating black and light rings. Normally the snakes within a specific rock setting will have a kind of community coloration. The whole effect—quite beautiful when an individual snake is examined, as one might examine a work of art, against a contrasting background—is to make the snake look as though it had been formed from granite, an appearance that allows it to use its protective coloration with great effect.

Living at altitudes from sea level to 8,000 feet, but mostly at about 2,500 feet, the nocturnal speckled rattlesnake may be found in sand or brushland as well as among boulders. Like the western diamondback, it will defend itself vigorously, being disinclined to give up territory if it is come upon suddenly or openly attacked. It eats rats, mice, squirrels, and occasionally birds. The young are eight to twelve inches long.

One of the smaller rattlesnakes, an adult rock rattlesnake *(Crotalus lepidus)* is from fifteen to thirty inches long. This snake ranges from southeastern Arizona through southern New Mexico into western Texas and thence southward to Jalisco, Mexico. As its name suggests, it is found mostly in rocky habitats, among boulder piles, or on rock ledges, chiefly in the mountains at elevations from 1,000 to 9,600 feet. The rock rattlesnake is most likely to be seen where streams run part or all of the year. Sometimes it lives in the pine belt, normally in the lower part where it is sometimes seen basking in rocky clearings.

The rock rattlesnake has a distinct pattern. Its ground color varies greatly, most often in relation to the color of earth and rocks where it dwells. In the Chisos Mountains, near the Big Bend of Texas, where a reddish igneous rock is found, the rock rattlesnake is known locally as the "pink rattler" because its ground color is pink-

The Rock Rattlesnake

61

ish. In timbered regions, on the other hand, specimens tend to be much darker, better able to use protective coloration in a woodsy setting.

A common name for this snake is "green rattlesnake," because it is often green in base color. But the base may also be bluish gray, tan, or plain gray and may be clear in color or flecked with dark spots that give a mottled effect.

The rock rattlesnake is distinguished by the widely spaced dark brown or black crossbars set against the ground color. Though regularly spaced, they are irregular in shape almost to the point of being jagged. Around each is a light-colored border. The tail is likely to be salmon or yellow brown with dark crossbands. On one of the four subspecies, the banded rock rattlesnake *(C. l. klauberi),* the tip of the tail is bright yellow.

Only two of the four subspecies are found in the American West; the others are Mexican species. In addition to the banded rock rattlesnake, the mottled rock rattlesnake *(C. l. lepidus)* is found in the extreme southeastern New Mexico, thence into southwestern Texas and Mexico.

Fortunately the rock rattlesnake is both small and nonaggressive, for its venom is probably drop for drop the most potent of any rattlesnake. This snake seldom bites, however, and there have been no recorded deaths from its bite. It preys on small frogs, lizards, and mice. Young are from seven to nine inches long.

The sidewinder *(Crotalus cerastes)* probably is one of the best-known snakes of the American West, even though not everybody realizes that it is in fact a rattlesnake. Its fame has been garnered chiefly by its unusual method of moving across the desert: in effect it walks on its chin and a loop of its body. When it moves, it looks as though it is going one way while it is actually going another. Or, to put it another way: if it actually went in the direction it appeared to be going, it would never get where it was going.

The sidewinder is known too from its "horns," the supraoculars that stick out like devil's horns over its eyes, giving it in some areas the name "horned rattler." Its scientific name, in fact, refers to these horns, for *cerastes* comes from the Greek *kerastes,* meaning horn. In western mythology these "horns" (found also on the look-alike

The Sidewinder
62

North African horned viper) were seen as a kind of lure that, protruding above the desert sand, somehow attracted birds and beasts.

The probable evolutionary basis for these horns is nearly as interesting as the myth. For a while it was thought that the horns shaded the snake's eyes from the hot desert sun. But L. M. Klauber pointed out that the snakes are nocturnal and remained buried in sand or secure in rodent burrows during the day. A second theory held that the horns protected the snake's eyes while it was buried, but this possible function was ruled out when Klauber pointed out that the buried snake is barely below the surface. Then, recently, using sidewinders in an unrelated experiment on water balance in snakes, Allen C. Cohen and Brian C. Myres (1970) made a fascinating discovery. When pressure is applied against a sidewinder's horns, they fold down, covering each eye like a tough eyelid. The horns, attached to the head by extremely subtle hinges, fit perfectly into the indentation of scales around the snake's eyes. Only pressure on top of the horns will cause them to fold down. The conclusion is fairly obvious. Moving through a rodent burrow where eyesight is no asset, the snake strikes the top of its horns against the roof of the burrow or exposed rocks or roots; the horns fold down over the eyes and protect them. In studying other snakes with similar horns, including the speckled rattlesnake, which has shorter horns than the sidewinder, the two experimenters found additional confirmation for their theory. Almost without exception in horned snakes—including such North African snakes as the horned viper, the desert puff adder, and the Iranian desert viper—the horns, subtly hinged, closed over the eyes when pressure was applied to them.

Fairly common in desert regions of the American West, the sidewinder is found in southeastern California, southern Nevada, and barely in southwestern Utah, thence southward through western and south central Arizona into northeastern Baja California and western Sonora, Mexico. In many parts of the desert, sand piles up in hummocks around mesquite, ocotillo, and creosote bush, or in some places simply forms barren, wind-sculptured dunes. These are the places sidewinders most often choose to live. In his famous sixteen-year census L. M. Klauber captured or recorded sidewinders in the following associations: "cultivated field 1, rocky desert 2, brushy desert 16, sandy desert 15, barren desert 26. Total, 60."

The Rattlesnakes

In these habitats, hunting mostly at night and often at times when winds bring air temperatures down and keep most snakes in hiding, the sidewinder scoots about, one of the fastest and least fatigue-prone of the desert snakes. Its agility, in fact, is bewildering and to the observer whose head is high above the moving snake, the sidewinding may momentarily become confusing, a factor that often helps the snake to make its escape.

Sidewinders are small snakes; adults range from a foot and a half to two and a half feet long. Females are normally larger than males (the reverse of the size relationship in other rattlesnakes). The young are from six and a half to eight inches long. In color sidewinders are pale—gray, tan, ivory, pink. They have a pattern of twenty-eight to forty-one indistinct blotches, but often they appear simply mottled with darker colors—yellow, olive, brown—against the light background.

Mainly an eater of lizards, small mammals, and insects, the sidewinder represents no great threat to man. In one study embracing the continental United States it was found that of eight species involved in snakebite reports, sidewinders were in seventh place, and there was some uncertainty about this, since other snakes are sometimes called sidewinders. The venom is of moderate potency, not so great as that of the rock rattlesnake nor so mild as that of the red diamond; but it must be treated with respect, for any rattlesnake venom has the capacity to kill.

In at least one instance of combat between sidewinder males, the dance was much the same as that reported for other rattlesnake species, but with a notable exception. At the end of the dance each snake struck at the other's neck—struck, fangs ready, with the apparent intent of killing. Neither, however, died, since they are immune to the venom of their own species.

One of the most bizarrely marked of the western rattlesnakes, the black-tailed rattlesnake *(Crotalus molossus)* always has a black tail and often has a black snout as well. In fact this fairly large snake is generally patterned in black and sulphur yellow, its normal ground color, although it sometimes is olive, green, or gray. Against the base color are set black or brown blotches, crossbands, or "diamonds," mostly irregular, sometimes markedly so. These markings are white-edged and centered with scales of the base color.

For reasons hard to guess at, this two-and-a-quarter- to four-and-a-quarter-foot serpent is sometimes called the dog-faced rattlesnake. Possibly this slightly ridiculous name was given originally by someone who saw one with a black tip on its nose—in appearance like the snout of a dog.

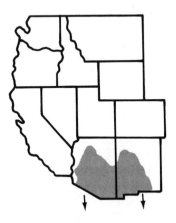

Basically a Mexican form, the subspecies of the American West, the northern black-tailed rattlesnake *(C. m. molossus)* is found from sea level to 9,500 feet over much of Arizona and New Mexico, thence eastward into Texas and southward over most of the Mexican plateau. It is a snake of saguaro-covered foothills and pine forests, having what appears to be an interesting accommodation with the rock rattlesnake and the twin-spotted rattlesnake. Inhabiting the same general region, the three species, all mountain snakes, quite obviously are in competition for the available food supply. The two smaller snakes, however, tend to stay on the rocky talus slopes where they can rapidly move to shelter when enemies threaten. The black-tailed rattlesnake occasionally ventures into rock rattlesnake and twin-spotted rattlesnake territory, but more often is found in the forested areas in between such slopes. It is frequently present around old dwellings in the mountains—a weatherworn cabin, deserted, boards falling in disarray; the broken-windowed building of an old saw mill; an abandoned mine shaft with supporting timbers rotting. Occasionally it is found at lower elevations on the desert plain, where it probably ventures unwillingly because it has been flushed from the mountains on the crest of a flash flood.

In its rocky haunts the black-tailed rattlesnake, eating mostly lizards and small rodents, displays one unfortunate habit. If, while hunting or searching for a mate, it wanders onto the shoulder of a road, it is quite likely to rattle loudly at passing automobiles. The result: when its presence would otherwise go unnoticed, it calls attention to itself.

A fairly large snake, the black-tailed rattlesnake could be dangerous to man. Fortunately it is not often involved in snakebite incidents, because it is relatively unaggressive. Moreover its venom is one of the least potent of any rattlesnake's, having only a small amount of the chemical substances that cause destruction of tissues around the bite.

Young black-tailed rattlesnakes are from ten to twelve inches long.

The Tiger Rattlesnake

64

Several features distinguish the tiger rattlesnake *(Crotalus tigris)*. Most obvious are the thirty-seven to fifty-two dark gray brown tiger stripes that cross its back from head to tail, stripes normally more distinct than those of any other rattlesnake. Second is the head, spade-shaped like all rattlesnakes', but smaller proportionately than heads of others. Third is the large rattle, again disproportionately large for the snake, adults of which grow from one and a half to three feet long. Fourth are the shorter fangs (which inject one of the most potent rattlesnake venoms). Altogether one would not think that the tiger rattlesnake could be confused with any other. Surprisingly, though, it is—notably with the speckled rattlesnake and with subspecies of the western rattlesnake that overlap its range.

The tiger rattlesnake differs from the speckled rattlesnake in its more distinct crossbands and, decidedly, in its head scalation. The speckled species has small scales between its nostrils and prenasal scales. The tiger does not. The subspecies of the western rattlesnake in the same range may appear striped but especially toward the head it has blotches rather than bands.

Ranging up from southern Sonora, Mexico, the tiger rattlesnake extends as far north as central Arizona, the only western state in which it is found. Over part of its range it has been displaced by the western diamondback, the western rattlesnake, or the sidewinder. The result is that tiger populations tend to be isolated from one another in foothills of the mountains within this snake's major range. It is found from sea level to 4,800 feet. Most often, however, it lives in rocky foothills among the cactus, creosote, and mesquite of the canyons. It may go as high as the oak forests.

In ground color the tiger rattlesnake may be buff, lavender, bluish gray, pink, or gray on the back, with the sides tending toward ivory or orange. While it has tail rings, they tend to be indistinct because the ground color is darker. Young tiger rattlesnakes are around nine inches long.

Frequently the Mojave rattlesnake *(Crotalus scutulatus)* is called "diamondback," "desert diamond," or "Mojave diamond" rattlesnake, and just as frequently it is confused with the western diamondback rattlesnake where the ranges overlap in southern Nevada, eastern California, much of Arizona, and the extreme southwest of New Mexico. Thence, the Mojave rattlesnake ranges southward to Puebla near the southern end of the Mexican plateau. It is not wise to confuse these two snakes, however, for a bite from the Mojave has to be treated differently from that of the western diamondback. The Mojave has a unique venom containing neurotoxic elements for which there has been developed no specific antitoxin. The bite of a Mojave, therefore, is potentially much more serious than that of a western diamondback. Difference in symptoms would, of course, show up sooner or later—greater tissue destruction around the wound delivered by a western diamondback and greater evidence of nerve involvement for the Mojave victim—but such symptoms might appear too late for effective treatment. It is always better to identify positively the snake that administered the bite. In fact, a person accompanying the person bitten might well try to kill the offending snake, if it is a rattlesnake, and bring it in for identification —but not to the neglect of the injured person, who will require immediate first aid. If alone, the victim should not make a strenuous effort to kill the snake, as exertion will only speed the distribution of the venom.

The Mojave Rattlesnake

65

Adult Mojave rattlesnakes are large, ranging from two to over four feet. The Mojave rattlesnake has sharply outlined diamonds or hexagons on its back. These are its hallmarks. Where the western diamondback's markings tend to be flecked and obscure, the Mojave's dark brown diamonds or hexagons are outlined by a border of lighter, uniformly colored scales that clearly set the diamonds or hexagons off from the olive green (occasionally brown or yellowish) ground color. On the Mojave's tail are alternating dark and light rings, with the light rings wider than the dark ones. Slanting backward from the snake's eye toward the corner of the mouth is a dark streak bordered by light scales. Distinguishing also are the enlarged scales on the snake's nose and between the supraocular scales.

Many rattlesnake species, as we have noted, prefer rocky habitats. Not so the Mojave. It is more often found in open country in the high desert where sparse growths of mesquite and creosote bush are common. Nor does it favor dense thickets or heavy chaparral: more often it occurs in scrub growth and grassland from near sea level—around the mouth of the Colorado River—to 8,000 feet in Mexico's Sierra Madre Occidental. Most often, though, the Mojave is found at lower elevations.

Many hybrids between the Mojave and other species of rattlesnakes have been noted. One of the first instances occurred at the San Diego Zoo, where in a cage of mixed rattlesnakes a male Mojave found happiness with a female Central American rattlesnake. As a result of the mating four young were born; three were males, one a female; all were marked unlike either parent. The offspring were not sterile, as are some other animal hybrids, such as mules. This fact was demonstrated when one of the male offspring mated with his sister; five young were born, none of them marked like either parents or grandparents.

Young Mojave rattlesnakes are from nine to eleven inches long. The subspecies in the American West is *C. s. scutulatus.*

The Twin-Spotted Rattlesnake

66

Sometimes called "mountain sidewinder," the twin-spotted rattlesnake *(Crotalus pricei)* is truly a snake of the high mountains, being found most often in habitats between 6,300 and 10,000 feet above sea level.

Limited to southern Arizona in the American West, the twin-spotted ranges southward in the Sierra Madre Occidental to southern Durango. The Arizona mountains in which it lives ring with names associated with the Apache Wars—Huachuca, Dos Cabezas, Santa Rita, Chiricahua. In the Chiricahuas in fact, it may be the most common—but most elusive—rattlesnake.

The two rows of brown spots that run along both sides of its backbone give this snake its common name. On some individuals these spots touch at the backbone to form markings like exercise dumbbells. Smaller spots dot the sides and the whole is flecked with brown. The base color is lighter brown or gray; sometimes the throat is salmon-colored. The tail has clearly delineated brown bands.

Amid the mountain rocks where it lives—often among the oaks and firs of the high forests—this small snake may rattle furiously at passing humans yet never be heard, at least not as a rattlesnake. The rattle is small and its sound is faint. Obscured by a mountain breeze, it may sound like a june bug and be simply one of the little noises one hears but does not separate from the totality of natural sounds—birds, insects, rustling leaves.

The nights are often cold where the twin-spotted rattlesnake lives; its activity may be curtailed by low temperatures, so that on the warm days even during mountain rains it may be abroad, driven by hunger. Mostly it lives on rocky slopes and there searches for small rodents and lizards. In the gentle sun of a summer's morn it may sometimes be seen basking. In spite of what may sound like a bizarre pattern, its protective coloration blends well with the light and shadow of tumbled rocks.

Little is known of the twin-spotted rattlesnake's venom, although it has been conjectured that it has a venom of high potency. There are no recorded bites to humans from this snake. It appears to be mild-tempered. Its young are from six and a half to seven inches long. The subspecies in Arizona—often called the Arizona twin-spotted rattlesnake—is designated *C. p. pricei.*

The ridge-nosed rattlesnake *(Crotalus willardi)* has the distinction of being the last rattlesnake of the American West to be discovered and named as a new species (1905). Strangely, the ridge-nose inhabits the same Arizona mountains inhabited by the twin-spotted and the rock rattlesnake, among others, all of which were discovered earlier. Such an oversight is particularly odd in this case, because the ridge-nose has a most unusual countenance. There is no mistaking the clear-cut ridge that follows the contour of its snout, a ridge formed by the bending up of the scales on the end of its nose.

The Ridge-Nosed Rattlesnake
67

Brown, gray, or reddish in ground color, the ridge-nose is a small rattlesnake, adults being fifteen to twenty-four inches long. Against the base color are set unusual white crossbars bordered forward and rear with dark brown or black, but simply fading into the ground color on either side. They look almost as though someone had made a series of chalk marks down the snake's back. Tail rings are present on the forward part of the tail. The snout may or may not have a vertical white stripe along each side.

The range of the ridge-nosed rattlesnake is relatively small.

It intrudes into the American West only in the extreme southern part of Arizona, where the subspecies is called the Arizona ridge-nosed rattlesnake *(C. w. willardi)*, and into the extreme southwest of New Mexico, and then only in Indian Creek Canyon of the Animas Mountains. Here the subspecies is the Chihuahua ridge-nose *(C. w. silus)*. Thence the species ranges southward over a small portion of the Mexican mountains. A new outlying subspecies *(C. w. amabilis)* has recently been discovered in Chihuahua, Mexico.

Apparently the ridge-nose occupies an ecological niche that differs slightly from those of the other mountain rattlesnakes in the same area. Like the twin-spotted rattlesnake, it ranges high, being found between 5,600 and 9,000 feet above sea level. However, instead of the sun-warmed talus slopes, it appears to favor the moist wooded country of fir, oak, and cedar. Often it lives in canyon bottoms where maple, oak, box elder, and other deciduous trees grow. Many specimens of this relatively rare snake have been taken in Carr Canyon of the Huachuca Mountains in Arizona.

The ridge-nose eats lizards and small rodents. The young are from six and a half to seven inches long.

The Western Rattlesnake
68, 69, & 70

If one rattlesnake were to be chosen as representative of the American West, it would have to be the western rattlesnake *(Crotalus viridis)*. For here, in its many guises, is the widest-ranging western rattlesnake, unquestionably the first rattlesnake to be encountered by the Lewis and Clark expedition and by countless wagon trains of pioneers, grinding through their own dust across prairies, mountains, and deserts on the long trek west. As one of these pioneers, P. J. De Smet, wrote: ". . . thanks to God by whose Providence we have been delivered from all such as are venomous, chiefly from the rattlesnake. Neither men nor beasts belonging to our caravan have suffered from them, though they were so numerous in places that our waggoners killed as many as 12 in one day."

Here, too, is the snake that appeared to many early observers to have a kind of unspoken understanding with the prairie dogs, in whose colonies, along with the burrowing owl, it frequently lived—even as it does today, in the rapidly dwindling towns of that highly organized prairie rodent. Naturalists, of course, soon disproved that sentimental theory, for the prairie rattlesnake *(C. v. viridis)* in a prairie dog town is simply interested either in shelter or food.

The subspecies called the Hopi rattlesnake *(C. v. nuntius)* plays an important role in the ancient snake dance of the Hopi Indians—a dance first observed and recorded in 1866 by R. B. Marcy and H. R. Schoolcraft, and definitively studied by L. M. Klauber in 1932. Ritualized from start to finish, the sacred dance actually culminates nine days of preparation, all of it part of the total ceremony. First comes the snake hunt. Snakes are sought in the open or dug from holes with consecrated tools. Any snakes are taken, notably bullsnakes, striped whipsnakes, and glossy snakes, but rattlesnakes are most used in the ceremony and of course to observers, and possibly participants, lend the greatest drama to the dance itself. The captured snakes are stored in sacred clay jars in the underground rooms, called *kivas,* of the men in charge, called the snake priests. For several days various ceremonies and preparations take place, with the snakes relatively undisturbed. Throughout, to manipulate or calm the snakes, the priests use a "snake wand," a "wooden shaft about eight inches long to which is attached a pair of eagle feathers." Eagle feathers are used because eagles, the Hopi believe, are masters of snakes.

On the morning of the ninth day the snakes are washed in a sacred liquid and allowed to crawl around the kivas until they dry. Finally at sundown on the ninth day the dance itself takes place. The snakes have been taken from the kiva in cloth bags, which are placed in a tepee-shaped bower called the *kisi.* At the height of the dance the participants, the snake priests, take snakes from the kisi and place them in their mouths. Sometimes the priests are bitten. The dance culminates when the priests, having previously dumped the snakes in a circle outlined in cornmeal, rush into the circle to grab up snakes by the handfuls and run with them in the four cardinal directions. At shrines located on the plain around the village the snakes are deposited, their mission now to be messengers for the Hopi to the rain gods. This role as messenger, incidentally, was the reason L. M. Klauber named the Hopi rattlesnake *nuntius,* which means messenger.

For years herpetologists and other critical observers wondered whether or not the Hopi rattlesnakes, or Hopi messengers, as they are sometimes called, had fangs intact and venom sacs full for the ceremony. That the snakes bit the dancers no one doubted; they could see it. Yet there were no apparent deaths, a fact not conclusive, but notable. Various theories were promulgated: The snakes were gentled during the days before the ceremony; they were allowed to strike leather or cloth objects to reduce venom content; the Hopi had a mysterious concoction that made them immune to rattlesnake bite (the mysterious root again); and others. One earlier herpetologist managed in 1883 to obtain some snakes from a kiva and found them to be fully equipped with fangs and venom. Then came Charles M. Bogert (1933). With great care and stealth, the herpetologist watched through a telescope as the snake priests released snakes at the shrine. Casually Bogert approached the shrine; unobserved, he captured a rattlesnake "messenger," placed it in a bag, and placed the bag in his hat so he wouldn't arouse suspicion. The snake, examined thoroughly by L. M. Klauber, was found to have *all* ready and reserve fangs removed. Klauber reported to Bogert, ". . . on the whole it was rather well done, if you forget the snake's feeling in the matter."

In short, this Hopi messenger was completely harmless. One instance doesn't make a scientific conclusion, however, so herpetologists sought confirmation. But not until many years later did a student who had watched another ceremony, capture another "messenger" just after it had been released. It, too, with near surgical precision, had had all fangs removed. The most plausible theory, in deference to the Hopi, is that fang removal, if it is practiced by both clans of dancers and in all five Hopi villages, is a modern development. As a result only the snakes suffer. Deprived of fangs, the released messengers, far from carrying the pleas of the Hopi to the rain gods, die relatively quickly of infection or slowly of starvation.

Of the subspecies of western rattlesnake, the Hopi is reddish; its near neighbor the Grand Canyon rattlesnake *(C. v. abyssus)*, the snake of the abysses, is pink or salmon; and the Northern Pacific rattlesnake *(C. v. oreganus)* is dark, tending toward black, with dark "diamond" blotches on its back. *C. v. oreganus* is the only rattlesnake of the Great Northwest ranging as a subspecies well up into British Columbia, Canada. A Northern Pacific rattlesnake was involved in one of the most fascinating true accounts of strange animal battles.

In October 1962, Douglas Duff came upon a Northern Pacific rattle-snake that had crawled between two large rocks on the bank of the Grande Ronde River in Oregon. What particularly attracted Duff's attention were several porcupine quills protruding from the side of the snake's head. The snake was sluggish and listless, perhaps because of the cold weather, but more than likely because of the quills. The snake neither rattled nor struggled when it was captured. Later, sick, the snake was killed and dissected. From this dissection a reasonable reconstruction of the battle was possible. Obviously the snake had struck at the porcupine's head. Several quills, those found only on a porcupine's head, had penetrated from inside the snake's mouth. A question remains. Did the snake strike to defend itself, or, late in the year at a time for hibernation, did it desperately seek for a last meal, perhaps the one that would see it through the winter?

The western rattlesnake grows quite large, although some of the subspecies are smaller than the norm for their cousins. The midget faded rattlesnake *(C. v. concolor)*, found in eastern Utah, western Colorado, and the extreme southwest of Wyoming seldom grows longer than two feet. Larger adult members of the species, such as the prairie rattler or the Great Basin rattlesnake *(C. v. lutosus)*, range from two and a half to over five feet long. During the gold rush in California, when miners came into frequent contact with the Northern Pacific rattlesnake, the usual exaggerations took place and numerous reports of "six-foot" rattlers appeared. None this length has been captured, however, by herpetologists.

Characteristically, the western rattlesnake has a pattern of brown or black blotches, although on some specimens or in some subspecies these blotches may be stretched toward the sides so much that they look like crossbands, and in fact, on most snakes of the species crossbands do appear on the rear portion of the snake's body. A light stripe running from the eye to a point behind the mouth is another characteristic of the species. The absolute distinguishing feature, since color and pattern are highly variable, is found in the head scales. The western rattlesnake is the only rattlesnake with more than two internasal scales in contact with each nostril.

Ranging over the greater portion of every state in the American West and on Santa Catalina Island off the California coast, the west-

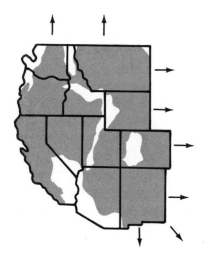

ern rattlesnake is found in a variety of habitats, avoiding only the desert, which it leaves to some of its generic relatives. In the five northern states of the American West it is the only species of rattlesnake. It is found also in British Columbia, Saskatchewan, and Alberta and appears throughout the northern half of Baja California and on the Mexican mainland. On the plains it is a snake of the grasslands; in the mountains, where it has been taken as high as 11,000 feet, it lives in the pine-oak forests, favoring rocky slopes and ledges and the rock-strewn beds of mountain streams. It eats rodents, birds, lizards, toads, even insects. Most of the subspecies have venom that is relatively high in toxicity. One study of bites by prairie rattlesnakes covering a seven-year period showed ten deaths out of 154 recorded bites. The young are six to twelve inches long.

It seems appropriate to end this book with the western rattlesnake. The snake symbolizes much of what is western about the West. It has seen and rattled at the mountain men, the fur trappers, the explorers, the Bunyanesque lumbermen, the cowboys, the farmers, the plainsmen and women plodding beside their wagons on the Oregon Trail. Today, in dwindling numbers, its habitats with accelerating pace being destroyed and the object of human predation, it still hangs on, seeking to avoid discovery, defiant when discovered. It may not last long, though its angry buzz is as much a part of the western scene as the screech of a bobcat or the howl of a coyote.

Cars run over it; bulldozers root it out; people kill it. Yet, in it remains something of nature and something of beauty.

APPENDIXES,
BIBLIOGRAPHY, INDEX

Appendix I

»»»»»

LIFE-SPANS OF SNAKES

The chart below lists the greatest *recorded* life-span up to January 1, 1973, for captive specimens of various snakes found in the American West. The sources of these records, all extending over a period of ten years or more, are coded in the fourth column below: CRH = Charles R. Hackenbrock; HPZ = Highland Park Zoo; JFC = Joseph F. Copp; MG = Mervin Giuntoli; NZP = National Zoological Park; PM = Provincial Museum, British Columbia; RHW = Robert H. Wilson; RMM = Richard M. Miller; SDZ = San Diego Zoo; SIZ = Staten Island Zoo; WHW = William H. Woodin, III.

	YEARS	MONTHS	SOURCE
BOAS (BOIDAE)			
Pacific rubber boa *(Charina bottae bottae)*	11	5	MG
Coastal rosy boa *(Lichanura trivirgata roseofusca)*	18	7	PM
COLUBRIDS (COLUBRIDAE)			
California glossy snake *(Arizona elegans occidentalis)*	10	1	SDZ
Trans-Pecos rat snake *(Elaphe subocularis)*	13	10	SIZ
*California kingsnake (striped) *(Lampropeltis getulus californiae)*	18	3	NZP
* California kingsnake (banded) *(Lampropeltis getulus californiae)*	18	3	NZP
* Yuma kingsnake *(Lampropeltis getulus yumensis)*	20	3	WHW
* Arizona mountain kingsnake *(Lampropeltis pyromelana pyromelana)*	12	7	HPZ
* Sierra mountain kingsnake *(Lampropeltis zonata multicincta)*	15	4	HPZ
Coast mountain kingsnake *(Lampropeltis zonata multifasciata)*	13	6	SDZ
Red racer *(Masticophis flagellum piceus)*	12	2	SDZ
Sonora gopher snake *(Pituophis melanoleucus affinis)*	13	4	SDZ
San Diego gopher snake *(Pituophis melanoleucus annectens)*	20	6	SDZ
San Diego gopher snake (albino) *(Pituophis melanoleucus annectens)*	17	7	SDZ
Pacific gopher snake *(Pituophis melanoleucus catenifer)*	11	0	SDZ
*Great Basin gopher snake *(Pituophis melanoleucus deserticola)*	16	8	RHW

*Snake still alive as of January 1, 1973.

239

	Years	Months	Source
COLUBRIDS (COLUBRIDAE) *continued*			
*Bullsnake *(Pituophis melanoleucus sayi)*	21	7	RMM
Western long-nosed snake *(Rhinocheilus lecontei lecontei)*	18	3	SDZ
*Texas long-nosed snake *(Rhinocheilus lecontei tessellatus)*	13	7	SIZ
*Desert patch-nosed snake *(Salvadora hexalepis hexalepis)*	12	6	SDZ
RATTLESNAKES (CROTALIDAE)			
Western diamondback rattlesnake *(Crotalus atrox)*	24	4	SDZ
Colorado Desert sidewinder *(Crotalus cerastes laterorepens)*	16	8	JFC
*Banded rock rattlesnake *(Crotalus lepidus klauberi)*	20	6	WHW
Mottled rock rattlesnake *(Crotalus lepidus lepidus)*	17	10	SIZ
Southwestern speckled rattlesnake *(Crotalus mitchellii pyrrhus)*	11	9	SDZ
Red diamond rattlesnake *(Crotalus ruber ruber)*	14	6	SDZ
Red diamond × southern Pacific rattlesnake (hybrid) *(Crotalus ruber ruber × Crotalus viridis helleri)*	13	3	SDZ
*Tiger rattlesnake *(Crotalus tigris)*	15	4	SIZ
Southern Pacific rattlesnake *(Crotalus viridis helleri)*	19	5	SDZ
*Great Basin rattlesnake *(Crotalus viridis lutosus)*	15	3	RHW
Prairie rattlesnake *(Crotalus viridis viridis)*	19	3	SDZ
*Arizona ridge-nosed rattlesnake *(Crotalus willardi willardi)*	18	6	CRH

*Snake still alive as of January 1, 1973.

Appendix II

» » » » »

GUIDE TO THE SNAKES
OF THE AMERICAN WEST

In the main text, we have assigned each snake to its family, genus, and species, mentioning subspecies only in cases of particular interest. Many readers, however, may wish more detailed information and for this reason we have developed the following guide, which lists and differentiates all the subspecies of the snakes described in the text.

In the guide, important articles or books are listed immediately under the descriptions of the snakes these writings deal with. In most instances we have used the same taxonomy as the authors of the given materials; however, on the basis of recent taxonomic conclusions, we have used different classifications from those in three articles, by James R. Dixon, George C. Gorman, and Wilmer W. Tanner, respectively.

The reader will find it useful to refer to the photographs and range maps while using this appendix. He would also be well advised to familiarize himself with the diagrams that explain the terms used in the scientific descriptions of snakes—terms such as labial, subcaudal, ventral, etc.

While referring to the photographs in this book, the student can be confident in the knowledge that they depict not only every species of snake in the American West but the correct subspecies when only one subspecies is found. For example, only one subspecies of the red-bellied snake *(Storer-*

ia occipitomaculata) is found in the American West. That subspecies, the Black Hills red-bellied snake *(S. o. pathasapae)* is the one depicted in this book.

Finally, the reader should note that subspecies often have common names entirely different from the common name of the species. For example, the "Panamint rattlesnake" *(Crotalus mitchellii stephensi)* is a subspecies of the "speckled rattlesnake" *(Crotalus mitchellii)*.

In providing this guide to the identifying characteristics of each subspecies, we have established a system which takes the reader through the

> **FAMILY**
> GENUS
> SPECIES (OR SUBSPECIES WHEN SOLE REPRESENTATIVE IN AREA)
> subspecies.

This is not a "key," as that term is ordinarily used. In each description the diagnostic characteristics are stated in terms of:

> *Size* if size is a differentiating characteristic
> *General appearance*
> *Color pattern*
> *Scale details* from head to tail and top to bottom
> *Geographical range* in the American West only, even though many
>> ranges extend out of the area

Unless otherwise noted, the general appearance and color pattern of each subspecies resemble those of the species. Differences are reflected in scale details and range. In the identification of individual snakes, the combination of characteristics is of prime importance rather than the order in which they are presented.

SLENDER BLIND SNAKES (LEPTOTYPHLOPIDAE)
> Small snakes (to 16 inches), slender and wormlike in appearance; head blunt; eyes vestigial, represented by black spots below ocular scales; scales smooth, uniform in size around body; tail extremely short, terminated by a nonvenomous spine. (Klauber, 1940B.)

NEW MEXICO BLIND SNAKE *(Leptotyphlops dulcis dissecta)*
> Median 7 dorsal scale rows brown; 3 scales on top of head between oculars; 3 scales bordering upper lip between rostral and ocular; southeastern Arizona and southern New Mexico.

WESTERN BLIND SNAKE *(Leptotyphlops humilis)*
> Only a single scale on top of head between oculars; 2 scales bordering upper lip between rostral and ocular.

Southwestern blind snake *(Leptotyphlops humilis humilis)*

> More than 6 heavily pigmented dorsal scale rows; fourth middorsal scale undivided; fifth middorsal scale little, if any, wider than sixth; 12 scales around tail; southern California exclusive of the Colorado Desert, southern Nevada, and south-central Arizona.

Desert blind snake *(Leptotyphlops humilis cahuilae)*

> Only 5 lightly pigmented dorsal scale rows; fourth middorsal scale undivided; fifth middorsal scale little, if any, wider than sixth; 12 scales around tail; Colorado Desert of southeastern California and southwestern Arizona.

Utah blind snake *(Leptotyphlops humilis utahensis)*

> Median 7 dorsal scale rows light brown; fourth middorsal scale often longitudinally divided; fifth middorsal scale much wider than sixth; 12 scales around tail; southeastern Nevada and extreme southwestern Utah.

Trans-Pecos blind snake *(Leptotyphlops humilis segrega)*

> Median 7 scale rows brown; ten scales around tail; southeastern Arizona and southwestern New Mexico.

BOAS (BOIDAE)

Heavy-bodied snakes; eyes small, pupils vertically elliptical; elongate chin shields absent; scales small, smooth; ventral scutes much narrower than in following families; spurs usually present on each side of anal plate, particularly prominent in males; anal plate and subcaudal scutes undivided; tail short and blunt in American West species.

Rosy Boa *(Lichanura trivirgata)*

Small scales on top of head between supraoculars. (Klauber, 1931; Gorman, 1965.)

Mexican rosy boa *(Lichanura trivirgata trivirgata)*

> Longitudinal stripes distinct, chocolate-brown on cream or beige background; ventral surface cream, sparsely flecked with black; Organ Pipe Cactus National Monument, Arizona.

Desert rosy boa *(Lichanura trivirgata gracia)*

> Longitudinal stripes distinct, rose, orange, or tan with even but finely serrated borders on gray or beige background; ventral surface flecked with brown; southeastern California and southwestern Arizona.

Coastal rosy boa *(Lichanura trivirgata roseofusca)*

> Longitudinal stripes, when evident, pink, rust, or drab with un-

even, wavy borders on gray background; ventral surface heavily flecked with black; southwestern California.

RUBBER BOA *(Charina bottae)*
  Uniform pinkish to brown above, occasionally with a few dark flecks low on sides; yellowish below; a large plate on top of head between suproaculars. (Klauber, 1943.)
  Pacific rubber boa *(Charina bottae bottae)*
    Parietal usually divided; dorsal scale rows 45 or more at midbody; the Coast Range and the Sierra Nevada of California, north through western Oregon and western Washington.
  Southern rubber boa *(Charina bottae umbratica)*
    Parietal usually undivided; posterior edge of frontal only slightly convex; dorsal scale rows 44 or fewer at midbody; ventrals fewer than 192; San Jacinto and San Bernardino mountains of southern California.
  Rocky Mountain rubber boa *(Charina bottae utahensis)*
    Parietal usually undivided; posterior edge of frontal sharply angular or semicircular; dorsal scale rows 44 or fewer at midbody; ventrals more than 191; northeastern California, eastern Oregon, eastern Washington, Idaho, western Montana, northwestern Wyoming, northern and central Utah, and northern Nevada.

COLUBRID SNAKES (COLUBRIDAE)

  In American West species, if color pattern consists of red bands bordered by yellow, red does not cross belly; 1 or 2 pairs of elongate chin shields present; dorsal scales smooth or keeled; ventral scutes wide; subcaudal scutes divided, except in long-nosed snake *(Rhinocheilus lecontei);* tip of tail pointed.

RINGNECK SNAKE *(Diadophis punctatus)*
  Dorsal surface olive, bluish, or blackish, usually with a yellow to orange-red neck ring; ventral surface yellow-orange to red, usually spotted with black, the red becoming brightest beneath tail; loreal scale present; preocular scales 2 or 3 on each side; dorsal scales smooth, usually in 15 rows at midbody (occasionally 13 or 17). (Blanchard, 1942; Croulet, 1965.)
  Regal ringneck snake *(Diadophis punctatus regalis)*
    Neck ring up to 4 scales wide, often absent: Dorsal extension of ventral color varies from a few spots on first dorsal scale row to nearly covering second row; subcaudal scutes 53 to 79 pairs; ventral scutes plus subcaudals 270 or more; western New Mexico, Arizona

exclusive of the southwestern quarter, eastern Nevada, western Utah, and extreme southeastern Idaho.

Prairie ringneck snake *(Diadophis punctatus arnyi)*

Neck ring 1 to 2 scales wide, sometimes interrupted; ventral color usually not extending up to first dorsal scale row; subcaudals 30–57; ventrals plus subcaudals less than 270; eastern New Mexico and southeastern Colorado.

San Bernardino ringneck snake *(Diadophis punctatus modestus)*

Neck ring ½ to 2 scales wide; ventral color not extending above first dorsal scale row, sometimes not reaching dorsals; belly densely spotted with black; dorsal scale rows usually 17–15 counted on neck and at posterior end of body; subcaudals 55–71; ventrals plus subcaudals fewer than 270; southwestern California in Los Angeles, Orange, northern San Diego, and western San Bernardino Counties; also on Santa Catalina Island.

Monterey ringneck snake *(Diadophis punctatus vandenburghi)*

Neck ring 1½ to 2 scales wide, sometimes interrupted; first dorsal scale row flecked with black; ventral color extending onto 1½ to 2 dorsal scale rows; belly sparsely spotted; dorsals usually 17–15; ventrals plus subcaudals fewer than 270; southwestern California from Ventura County to Santa Cruz County.

Northwestern ringneck snake *(Diadophis punctatus occidentalis)*

Neck ring 1½ to 3 scales wide; first 2 dorsal scale rows flecked with black; ventral color extending onto 1½ to 2 dorsal scale rows; belly sparsely spotted; dorsals usually 15–15; ventrals plus subcaudals fewer than 270; northwestern California, western Oregon, southern Washington, and western Idaho.

Coral-bellied ringneck snake *(Diadophis punctatus pulchellus)*

Neck ring 1½ to 3 scales wide; first 2 dorsal scale rows not flecked with black; ventral color extending onto 1½ to 2 dorsal scale rows; belly spots sparse or absent; dorsals usually 15–15; ventrals plus subcaudals fewer than 270; western slope of the Sierra Nevada of California.

Pacific ringneck snake *(Diadophis punctatus amabilis)*

Neck ring 1 to 1½ scales wide, sometimes interrupted; ventral color extending onto ½ to 1½ dorsal scale rows; belly densely spotted; dorsals usually 15–15; ventrals plus subcaudals fewer than 270; the San Francisco Bay region, and the foothills in the San Joaquin and Sacramento valleys of California.

San Diego ringneck snake *(Diadophis punctatus similis)*

Ventral color extending onto ⅓ to ⅔ of first dorsal scale row; belly moderately spotted; dorsals usually 15–13; ventrals plus sub-caudals fewer than 270; extreme southwestern California in San Diego, Riverside, and southwestern San Bernardino counties.

SHARP-TAILED SNAKE *(Contia tenuis)*

A small, stout species (to 18 inches); tail short and cone-shaped, term-inated by a non-venomous spine; dorsal surface reddish brown to gray, often with a faint yellowish or reddish line on each side; a heavy black mark extending across anterior part of each ventral scute; preocular single on each side; scales smooth; anal plate divided; Sierra Nevada and central coast of California, north into western Oregon and western Washington. (Stickel, 1951.)

WESTERN HOGNOSE SNAKE *(Heterodon nasicus)*

A heavy-bodied, blotched snake with rostral greatly enlarged, up-turned, and keeled above; dorsal scales keeled; anal plate divided. (Edgren, 1952.)

Plains hognose snake *(Heterodon nasicus nasicus)*

Middorsal body blotches usually more than 35 in males, more than 40 in females; 9 to 28 small scales on top of head behind rostral; loreals usually 2 or more on each side; eastern Montana, eastern Wyoming, eastern Colorado, and most of New Mexico.

Dusty hognose snake *(Heterodon nasicus gloydi)*

Middorsal body blotches usually fewer than 32 in males, fewer than 37 in females; 9 to 28 small scales on top of head behind rostral; loreals usually 2 or more on each side; extreme southeastern New Mexico.

Mexican hognose snake *(Heterodon nasicus kennerlyi)*

Middorsal body blotches usually fewer than 32 in males, fewer than 37 in females; 2 to 6 small scales on top of head behind rostral; loreal usually single on each side; southwestern New Mexico and southeastern Arizona.

LEAF-NOSED SNAKES *(Phyllorhynchus)*

Small, stout snakes (to 20 inches), with short tails; color pattern consist-ing of blotches; rostral extremely enlarged, with free edges, extending back on top of head between internasals; pupil vertically elliptical; anal plate undivided. (Klauber, 1940C.)

SADDLED LEAF-NOSED SNAKE *(Phyllorhynchus browni)*

Middorsal body blotches (excluding tail spots) fewer than 17.

Pima leaf-nosed snake *(Phyllorhynchus browni browni)*
> Body blotches considerably wider middorsally than interspaces; ventral scutes 166 or fewer in males, 179 or fewer in females; southeastern Pinal County and eastern Pima County in southern Arizona.

Maricopa leaf-nosed snake *(Phyllorhynchus browni lucidus)*
> Body blotches slightly, if any, wider (often considerably narrower) middorsally than interspaces; ventral scutes 167 or more in males, 180 or more in females; northeastern Maricopa County to western Pima County in southern Arizona.

SPOTTED LEAF-NOSED SNAKE *(Phyllorhynchus decurtatus)*
> Middorsal body blotches (excluding tail spots) 17 or more.

Clouded leaf-nosed snake *(Phyllorhynchus decurtatus nubilus)*
> Middorsal body blotches 42–60, usually equal to or wider than interspaces; ventrals 167 or fewer in males, 178 or fewer in females; eastern Pima County, Arizona.

Western leaf-nosed snake *(Phyllorhynchus decurtatus perkinsi)*
> Middorsal body blotches 24–48, usually narrower than interspaces; ventrals 168 or more in males, 179 or more in females; southeastern California, southern Nevada, and western Arizona.

GREEN SNAKES *(Opheodrys)*
> Slender snakes, with dorsal surface uniform green at all ages; ventral surface yellowish to white; anterior temporal scale single on each side; dorsal scale rows 15 or 17 at midbody. (Grobman, 1941.)

WESTERN SMOOTH GREEN SNAKE *(Opheodrys vernalis blanchardi)*
> Dorsal scales smooth, in 15 rows at midbody; New Mexico, Colorado, eastern Utah, extreme southeastern Idaho, southern and eastern Wyoming, and extreme northeastern Montana.

ROUGH GREEN SNAKE *(Opheodrys aestivus)*
> Dorsal scales keeled, in 17 rows at midbody; Colfax County in northeastern New Mexico.

RACER *(Coluber constrictor)*
> Adults uniform brown or olive above; juveniles blotched above; pale to bright yellow below; anterior temporal scales usually 2 or 3 on each side; scales smooth, in 15 to 17 rows at midbody, and 15 rows at posterior end of body. (Auffenberg, 1955.)

Eastern yellow-bellied racer *(Coluber constrictor flaviventris)*
    Upper labials usually 7 on each side; subcaudal scutes usually fewer than 85 pairs; northeastern quarter of New Mexico, eastern Colorado, eastern Wyoming, and eastern Montana.

Western yellow-bellied racer *(Coluber constrictor mormon)*
    Upper labials usually 8 on each side; subcaudal scutes more than 85 pairs; California exclusive of the southeastern portion and the San Joaquin Valley, Oregon, eastern Washington, southern Idaho, southwestern Montana, western Wyoming, most of Utah, and northern Nevada; also on Santa Cruz Island.

WHIPSNAKES *(Masticophis)*
    Slender snakes, with color pattern variable; loreal scale present; scales smooth, in 15 to 17 rows at midbody, and only 11 to 13 rows at posterior end of body.

COACHWHIP *(Masticophis flagellum)*
    A large species (to 102 inches) lacking distinct longitudinal lateral stripes; dorsal scale rows 17 at midbody. (Wilson, 1970.)
    Adults distinguished as follows:

Western coachwhip *(Masticophis flagellum testaceus)*
    Tan to pinkish red above, with narrow dark crossbands on neck; a double row of dark spots below; eastern Colorado and eastern New Mexico.

Lined whipsnake *(Masticophis flagellum lineatulus)*
    Tan to light gray above; each dorsal scale on anterior of body bearing a central longitudinal dark streak; salmon pink on posterior of belly; extreme southwestern New Mexico and southeastern Arizona.

Red racer or western black racer *(Masticophis flagellum piceus)*
    Two color phases: Red phase pink to red above, with wide crossbands of variable intensities; black phase completely black above, salmon pink to red on posterior of belly; southern Arizona, extreme southwestern Utah, southern and western Nevada, and southern California exclusive of the San Joaquin Valley.

Sonora coachwhip *(Masticophis flagellum cingulum)*
    Color pattern highly variable, ranging from a series of wide reddish brown crossbands separated by narrow, paired light crossbands to uniform reddish brown or completely black above; southeastern Arizona.

Baja California whipsnake *(Masticophis flagellum fuliginosus)*

   In American West, dark grayish brown above, with narrow pale
   lines arising on neck and extending variable distances posteriorly
   along sides; variable amounts of cream color below; extreme
   southern San Diego County, California.

San Joaquin whipsnake *(Masticophis flagellum ruddocki)*

   Light yellow to olive above, with crossbands usually lacking, or
   sometimes represented faintly on neck; San Joaquin and Sacramento valleys of central California.

STRIPED RACER *(Masticophis lateralis)*

   A distinct yellow or orange longitudinal stripe on each side continuing
   to or onto tail; dorsal scale rows 17 at midbody. (Riemer, 1954.)

California striped racer *(Masticophis lateralis lateralis)*

   Dorsolateral stripes cream, 2 half-scale rows wide; underside of
   head and neck usually conspicuously marked with black spots;
   anterior surface of belly with pale yellow to pale orange background; California exclusive of the San Francisco Bay region, the
   San Joaquin and Sacramento valleys, and the deserts.

Alameda striped racer *(Masticophis lateralis euryxanthus)*

   Dorsolateral stripes orange, 1 and 2 half-scale rows wide anteriorly;
   underside of head and neck nearly lacking black spots; anterior
   surface of belly orange-rufous; San Francisco Bay region.

SONORA WHIPSNAKE *(Masticophis bilineatus)*

   2 or 3 distinct light longitudinal stripes on each side not continuing
   posteriorly to tail; dorsal scale rows 17 at midbody. (Hensley, 1950.)

Sonora whipsnake *(Masticophis bilineatus bilineatus)*

   Dorsolateral light stripe 2 half-scale rows wide, usually arising on
   fourth scale posterior to last upper labial; southeastern Arizona
   and extreme southwestern New Mexico.

Ajo Mountain whipsnake *(Masticophis bilineatus lineolatus)*

   Dorsolateral light stripe 2 quarter-scale rows wide, usually arising
   on eighth scale posterior to last upper labial; Ajo Mountains in
   Organ Pipe Cactus National Monument, Arizona.

DESERT STRIPED WHIPSNAKE *(Masticophis taeniatus taeniatus)*

   A distinct white or cream longitudinal stripe on each side, divided by a
   black line along middle of fourth dorsal scale row; additional dark
   lines extending along middles of first, second, and third dorsal scale
   rows; dorsal scale rows 15 at midbody; southern and western New
   Mexico, northern Arizona, western Colorado, Utah exclusive of the

central and northeastern portions, Nevada, California east of the Sierra Nevada, southern Idaho, Oregon exclusive of the western and northeastern portions, and south-central Washington (Gloyd and Conant, 1934.)

PATCH-NOSED SNAKES *(Salvadora)*

Slender snakes with striped color pattern (stripes sometimes obscure); rostral enlarged, protruding and curving back over snout; dorsal scales smooth; anal plate divided.

MOUNTAIN PATCH-NOSED SNAKE *(Salvadora grahamiae grahamiae)*

Rostral rounded in dorsal profile; upper labials 8 on each side, second and third contacting loreal; posterior pair of chin shields in contact at midline or separated by only 1 small scale; New Mexico exclusive of the eastern and northern portions, and southeastern Arizona. (Hartweg, 1940.)

WESTERN PATCH-NOSED SNAKE *(Salvadora hexalepis)*

Rostral flat in dorsal profile; upper labials 9 on each side, third or fourth contacting loreal; posterior pair of chin shields separated by 2 or 3 small scales. (Bogert, 1945.)

Desert patch-nosed snake *(Salvadora hexalepis hexalepis)*

Top of head gray; middorsal stripe 3 scales wide; 1 upper labial reaching eye; loreal divided; southwestern Arizona and extreme southeastern California.

Big Bend patch-nosed snake *(Salvadora hexalepis deserticola)*

Two upper labials reaching eye; loreal single; southwestern New Mexico and southeastern Arizona.

Coast patch-nosed snake *(Salvadora hexalepis virgultea)*

Top of head brown; middorsal stripe 1 and 2 half-scales wide; 1 upper labial reaching eye; loreal divided; southwestern California.

Mojave patch-nosed snake *(Salvadora hexalepis mojavensis)*

Color pattern faint or consisting of narrow crossbars obscuring middorsal stripe; none of upper labials reaching eye; southeastern California, western and southern Nevada, southern Utah, and northwestern Arizona.

RAT SNAKES *(Elaphe)*

Slender snakes; dorsal scales weakly keeled, in 25 or more rows at midbody; anal plate divided. (Dowling, 1952.)

GREAT PLAINS RAT SNAKE *(Elaphe guttata emoryi)*

Gray to brown blotches on light gray background; 2 dark stripes on neck, converging to a point between eyes; longitudinal light and dark stripes on underside of tail; subocular scales absent; eastern New Mexico, southeastern and western Colorado, and eastern Utah.

GREEN RAT SNAKE *(Elaphe triaspis intermedia)*

Adults green to gray above, lacking a distinct color pattern; juveniles conspicuously blotched; underside of tail unmarked; subocular scales absent; mountains of extreme southeastern Arizona. (Dowling, 1960.)

TRANS-PECOS RAT SNAKE *(Elaphe subocularis)*

Dark H-shaped blotches on yellowish background, H's often giving way to separate stripes toward head; a row of small subocular scales between upper labials and eye; southern New Mexico. (Dowling, 1957.)

GOPHER SNAKE *(Pituophis melanoleucus)*

A large species (to 100 inches) with blotched color pattern; prefrontal plates usually 4; dorsal scales keeled, in 27 or more rows at midbody; anal plate single. (Klauber, 1947; Smith and Kennedy, 1951.)

Bullsnake *(Pituophis melanoleucus sayi)*

Snout sharp; rostral narrow, width less than height, elevated conspicuously above adjacent scales; eastern New Mexico, eastern Colorado, eastern and northern Wyoming, and Montana.

Sonora gopher snake *(Pituophis melanoleucus affinis)*

Snout blunt; rostral wide, width usually more than height, flush with or only slightly elevated above adjacent scales; anterior dorsal blotches brown, separated from each other and from adjacent lateral series; background color of sides cream or buff; dorsal scale rows usually more than 29 at midbody; western New Mexico, Arizona south of the Grand Canyon, and extreme southeastern California.

Great Basin gopher snake *(Pituophis melanoleucus deserticola)*

Snout blunt; anterior dorsal blotches black, connected with each other and adjacent lateral series; background color of sides cream or buff; dorsal scale rows usually more than 29 at midbody; extreme northwestern New Mexico, Arizona north of the Grand Canyon, western Colorado, Utah, southwestern Wyoming, Idaho, eastern Washington, eastern Oregon, Nevada, and eastern California.

Pacific gopher snake *(Pituophis melanoleucus catenifer)*

Snout blunt; anterior dorsal blotches usually brown, or, if black, separated from each other and adjacent lateral series; background color of sides suffused with gray; occasional striped specimens occur in the southern Sacramento Valley, and in the San Francisco and Monterey bay regions; dorsal scale rows usually more than 29 at midbody; western California south to Santa Barbara County and western Oregon.

San Diego gopher snake *(Pituophis melanoleucus annectens)*
Snout blunt; anterior dorsal blotches black, irregularly connected with each other and adjacent lateral series; background color of sides suffused with gray; dorsal scale rows usually more than 29 at midbody; southwestern California, north to and including most of Santa Barbara County; also on Santa Catalina Island.

Santa Cruz Island gopher snake *(Pituophis melanoleucus pumilus)*
Snout blunt; anterior dorsal blotches usually black, irregularly connected with each other and adjacent lateral series; black streaking absent from scales in interspaces between anterior dorsal blotches; dorsal scale rows usually 29 or less at midbody; Santa Cruz Island, California.

GLOSSY SNAKE *(Arizona elegans)*
A blotched snake, with underside of tail unmarked; prefrontal plates 2; dorsal scales smooth, in 27 to 31 rows at midbody; anal plate single. (Klauber, 1946; Fleet and Dixon, 1971.)

Texas glossy snake *(Arizona elegans elegans)*
Body blotches greater than interspaces in longitudinal extent middorsally, usually 13 or 14 scale rows wide across back; dorsal scale rows usually 29 to 31 at midbody; eastern New Mexico and eastern Colorado.

Painted Desert glossy snake *(Arizona elegans philipi)*
Body blotches greater than interspaces in longitudinal extent middorsally, usually 11 scale rows wide across back; dark markings usually present on lateral edges of ventrals; dorsal scale rows usually 27 or fewer at midbody; New Mexico exclusive of the eastern and north-central portions, southeastern and northeastern Arizona, and extreme southern Utah.

Arizona glossy snake *(Arizona elegans noctivaga)*
Body blotches equal to or greater than interspaces in longitudinal extent middorsally, usually 11 scale rows wide across back; dark markings absent from lateral edges of ventrals; dorsal scale rows usually 27 or fewer at midbody; southern and western Arizona exclusive of the extreme southeastern and southwestern corners.

California glossy snake *(Arizona elegans occidentalis)*
Body blotches less than, equal to, or greater than interspaces in

longitudinal extent middorsally, usually 9 scale rows wide across back; dark markings usually present on lateral edges of ventrals; occasional striped specimens occur in the zone of intermediacy between this subspecies and *A. e. eburnata* in eastern San Diego County; preocular usually single on each side; dorsal scale rows usually 27 or fewer at midbody; western California north to the San Francisco Bay region exclusive of the coast north of Los Angeles County.

Desert glossy snake *(Arizona elegans eburnata)*

Body blotches less than interspaces in longitudinal extent middorsally, usually only 7 scale rows wide across back; dark markings absent from lateral edges of ventrals; preocular usually single on each side; dorsal scale rows usually 27 or fewer at midbody; southeastern California, southern Nevada, extreme southwestern Utah, and extreme northwestern and southwestern Arizona.

Mojave glossy snake *(Arizona elegans candida)*

Body blotches less than interspaces in longitudinal extent middorsally, usually 9 scale rows wide across back; dark markings absent from lateral edges of ventrals; preoculars usually 2 on each side; dorsal scale rows usually 27 or fewer at midbody; western Mojave Desert in southern California.

KINGSNAKES *(Lampropeltis)*

Color pattern usually consisting of crossbands; red, when present, bordered by black; belly with dark markings; pupil round; loreal single on each side; dorsal scales smooth, in 17 to 27 rows at midbody; anal plate single. (Blanchard, 1921.)

COMMON KINGSNAKE *(Lampropeltis getulus)*

Usually brown to black, with white to yellow rings, the light rings tending to widen on lowermost scale rows; occasionally striped, speckled, or uniformly dark; red absent from color pattern. (Klauber, 1939B. Zweifel and Norris, 1955.)

Sonora kingsnake *(Lampropeltis getulus splendida)*

Scales on sides of body bearing light spots; New Mexico exclusive of the northwestern half, and extreme southeastern Arizona.

Western black kingsnake *(Lampropeltis getulus nigritus)*

Dorsal surface usually dark brown or black, with light rings extremely faint or absent; Santa Cruz and eastern Pima counties in southern Arizona.

Yuma kingsnake *(Lampropeltis getulus yumensis)*

Color pattern consisting of light rings on a dark background, with dark pigment at bases of light scales; southern Arizona exclusive of the southeastern corner, and extreme southeastern California.

California kingsnake *(Lampropeltis getulus californiae)*

Color pattern usually consisting of yellow to white rings on a brown to black background, lacking dark pigment at bases of light scales; some specimens in southwestern California have longitudinal stripes, and some in the San Joaquin Valley of California have light crossbands uniting low on the sides to form stripes; northwestern Arizona, southern Utah, southern and western Nevada, southwestern Oregon, and California exclusive of the extreme northeastern and southeastern corners; also on Santa Catalina Island.

MILK SNAKE *(Lampropeltis triangulum)*

Red, orange, or reddish brown rings or blotches edged with black and separated by white or yellow; white rings tending to widen on lowermost scale rows. (Tanner and Loomis, 1957.)

Central Plains milk snake *(Lampropeltis triangulum gentilis)*

Snout black or black with white mottling; red rings on body usually more than 23, occasionally interrupted middorsally by black; eastern Colorado.

Pale milk snake *(Lampropeltis triangulum multistrata)*

Snout orange, with black flecking; orange rings on body usually more than 23; eastern Wyoming and Montana exclusive of the western third.

Utah milk snake *(Lampropeltis triangulum taylori)*

Snout black or white with black on median margins of internasals and prefrontals; red rings on body usually more than 23, often interrupted middorsally by black; western Colorado, Utah, and northern Arizona.

New Mexico milk snake *(Lampropeltis triangulum celaenops)*

Snout black or black with white mottling; red rings on body usually 23 or fewer; New Mexico.

SONORA MOUNTAIN KINGSNAKE *(Lampropeltis pyromelana)*

Snout usually white or cream colored, sometimes black flecked with white; black, white, and red rings, the red bordered by black on both sides, the white not widening on lowermost scale rows, and the black becoming narrow or disappearing on the sides. (Tanner, 1953.)

Arizona mountain kingsnake *(Lampropeltis pyromelana pyromelana)*
Usually more than 43 white rings on body, fewer than half of which are complete across belly; lower labials 10 on each side; subcaudals minus white rings on body and tail, 17 or fewer; mountains of extreme southwestern New Mexico and southeastern and central Arizona.

Huachuca mountain kingsnake *(Lampropeltis pyromelana woodini)*
Usually fewer than 43 white rings on body, fewer than half of which are complete across belly; lower labials 10 on each side; subcaudals minus white rings on body and tail, 17 or more; the Huachuca Mountains of southern Arizona.

Utah mountain kingsnake *(Lampropeltis pyromelana infralabialis)*
Half or more of white rings on body complete across belly; lower labials 9 on each side; north-central Arizona, central and southwestern Utah, and east-central Nevada.

CALIFORNIA MOUNTAIN KINGSNAKE *(Lampropeltis zonata)*
Snout usually uniform black, sometimes with red markings; black, white, and, usually, red rings; the red, when present, bordered by black, and the white not widening on lowermost scale rows. (Zweifel, 1952.)

Saint Helena mountain kingsnake *(Lampropeltis zonata zonata)*
Snout without red markings; posterior margin of first white ring behind last upper labial; red usually continuous across back; the North Coast Range of California.

Sierra mountain kingsnake *(Lampropeltis zonata multicincta)*
Snout without red markings; posterior margin of first white ring behind last upper labial; red usually not continuous across back, sometimes entirely lacking in Yosemite National Park specimens; the Sierra Nevada of California.

Coast mountain kingsnake *(Lampropeltis zonata multifasciata)*
Snout with red markings; posterior margin of first white ring in front of, on, or behind last upper labial; red usually continuous across back; the South Coast Range of California.

San Bernardino mountain kingsnake *(Lampropeltis zonata parvirubra)*
Snout without red markings; posterior margin of first white ring in front of or on last upper labial; triads* 37 or more on body; the San Gabriel, San Bernardino, and San Jacinto mountains of southern California.

San Diego mountain kingsnake *(Lampropeltis zonata pulchra)*
Snout without red markings; posterior margin of first white ring in

*A triad is any black ring, split or not split by red, and bordered on each side by white or yellow.

front of or on last upper labial; triads* 36 or fewer on body; the Santa Monica Mountains, the Santa Ana Mountains, and the mountains of San Diego County, California.

LONG-NOSED SNAKE *(Rhinocheilus lecontei)*
Color pattern composed of black saddles on a light background, usually with pink to red within the light interspaces; light flecking on sides in black saddles, and black flecking on sides in light interspaces create the impression of a speckled snake; snout pointed; anal plate single; subcaudal scutes single. (Klauber, 1941; Shannon and Humphrey, 1963.)

Western long-nosed snake *(Rhinocheilus lecontei lecontei)*
Snout blunter than in Texas long-nosed snake, lacking upward tilt toward tip; rostral raised only slightly or not at all above nasals and internasals; southern and western Arizona, southern and western Utah, southwestern Idaho, Nevada, and California north to Mendocino and Lassen counties exclusive of the Sierra Nevada and the coast north of Orange County.

Texas long-nosed snake *(Rhinocheilus lecontei tessellatus)*
Snout sharper than in western long-nosed snake, with a distinct upward tilt toward tip; rostral raised appreciably above nasals and internasals; New Mexico exclusive of the northwestern third.

WATER SNAKES *(Natrix)*
Heavy-bodied snakes, usually blotched or crossbanded; scales heavily keeled, in 21 or more rows at midbody; anal plate usually divided.

BLOTCHED WATER SNAKE *(Natrix erythrogaster transversa)*
Middorsal blotches alternating with lateral series; belly yellow to pale orange, often faintly spotted; extreme southeastern New Mexico. (Conant, 1949.)

NORTHERN WATER SNAKE *(Natrix sipedon sipedon)*
Usually crossbanded, at least anteriorly, the bands greater than the interspaces in longitudinal extent; belly usually conspicuously and irregularly marked with black to reddish crescent-shaped blotches; eastern Colorado. (Conant, 1963.)

BLACK HILLS RED-BELLIED SNAKE *(Storeria occipitomaculata pahasapae)*
A small snake (to 16 inches), with belly red; top of head gray to black, usually darker than body; neck with or without small light spots; body grayish tan to dark gray above, sometimes with faint longitudinal light

---

*A triad is any black ring, split or not split by red, and bordered on each side by white or yellow.

lines; loreal scale absent; dorsal scales heavily keeled, in 15 rows at midbody; anal plate divided; the Black Hills of northeastern Wyoming. (Smith, 1963.)

GARTER SNAKES *(Thamnophis)*

Color pattern usually striped, sometimes spotted or checkered with one or all of stripes lacking; ventral scutes lacking transverse black bars; rostral unmodified; upper labials usually 7 or more on each side; lower labials 8 or more on each side; scales keeled, in 17 to 23 rows at midbody; anal plate usually single.

NARROW-HEADED GARTER SNAKE *(Thamnophis rufipunctatus)*

Head noticably elongate; olive to brown above, with distinct dark brown spots; dorsal and lateral stripes lacking, or represented only by traces on neck; upper labials 8 on each side; dorsal scale rows 21 at midbody; anal plate sometimes divided; southwestern New Mexico and central and east-central Arizona. (Thompson, 1957.)

COMMON GARTER SNAKE *(Thamnophis sirtalis)*

Dorsal and lateral stripes usually well defined, the lateral stripes usually on second and third scale rows anteriorly; red blotches usually present on sides between stripes; upper labials usually 7 on each side; lower labials usually 10 on each side; dorsal scale rows 19 at midbody. (Fox, 1951B; Webb, 1966.)

Red-sided garter snake *(Thamnophis sirtalis parietalis)*

Top of head usually olive; middorsal stripe comparatively wide, occupying 1 and 2 half-scale rows; sides between stripes black or brown with black blotches, with red marks extending up to mid-dorsal stripe; red often invading lateral stripes; sides of belly with black spots; eastern Colorado, eastern and northern Wyoming, and Montana.

Rio Grande garter snake *(Thamnophis sirtalis dorsalis)*

Top of head usually olive; middorsal stripe wide; sides between stripes olive with black blotches, the upper series fusing to form a black border on each side of middorsal stripe; red marks on sides extending up to middorsal stripe; sides of belly with black spots; upper Rio Grande Valley of south-central Colorado and New Mexico.

Valley garter snake *(Thamnophis sirtalis fitchi)*

Top of head black; middorsal stripe wide; sides between stripes black, with red marks largely confined to lower half of area; red usually not invading lateral stripes; belly usually unmarked;

north-central Utah, northwestern Wyoming, western Montana, Idaho, central and eastern Washington, Oregon exclusive of the northwestern portion, west-central Nevada, and California east of the Coast Range and south to the southern end of the San Joaquin Valley.

Puget Sound red-sided garter snake *(Thamnophis sirtalis pickeringii)*

Top of head dark; middorsal stripe confined to middorsal scale row; lateral stripes sometimes obscure; sides black with reduced red marks, the dark pigment extending down onto heavily marked belly; western Washington.

Red-spotted garter snake *(Thamnophis sirtalis concinnus)*

Top of head red; middorsal stripe wide; lateral stripes sometimes obscure; sides black with reduced red marks, the dark pigment extending down onto heavily marked belly; extreme southwestern Washington and northwestern Oregon.

San Francisco garter snake *(Thamnophis sirtalis tetrataenia)*

Top of head red; middorsal stripe wide; sides with a continuous longitudinal red stripe bordered above and below by black stripes; red invading lower lateral stripes; belly greenish blue; the San Francisco Peninsula of California.

California red-sided garter snake *(Thamnophis sirtalis infernalis)*

Top of head red; middorsal stripe wide; lateral stripes often merging with belly color; sides black with red marks; sides of belly sometimes with small black spots; coastal California from Humboldt County to northern San Diego County.

WESTERN TERRESTRIAL GARTER SNAKE *(Thamnophis elegans)*

Dorsal and lateral stripes usually well defined, the lateral stripes on second and third scale rows anteriorly; internasals usually wider than long, not pointed anteriorly; upper labials usually 8 on each side, sixth and seventh enlarged and often higher than long; lower labials usually 10 on each side; dorsal scale rows usually 19 or 21 at midbody. (Fox, 1951A; Rossman, 1963B.)

Mountain garter snake *(Thamnophis elegans elegans)*

Middorsal stripe wide, occupying 1 and 2 half-scale rows to nearly 3 scale rows; sides between stripes black with light (not red or orange) flecking; belly usually unmarked; sometimes lightly spotted; preocular single on each side; the San Bernardino Mountains of southern California, the Sierra Nevada, northern California exclusive of the Sacramento Valley and the coast, and western Oregon.

Coast garter snake *(Thamnophis elegans terrestris)*
   Middorsal stripe wide; sides and belly with red or orange flecking; coastal California south to Santa Barbara County and extreme southwestern Oregon.

Wandering garter snake *(Thamnophis elegans vagrans)*
   Middorsal stripe narrow, faint, and irregular; sides brown with dark spots of variable size; New Mexico, northeastern Arizona, central and western Colorado, Utah, Wyoming, Montana, Idaho, Washington, eastern Oregon, Nevada, and east-central California.

Klamath garter snake *(Thamnophis elegans biscutatus)*
   Middorsal stripe wide; sides between stripes black with light flecking; belly often marked with black or dark gray; preoculars 2 on one or both sides; extreme northeastern California and south-central Oregon.

WESTERN AQUATIC GARTER SNAKE *(Thamnophis couchii)*
Usually spotted or blotched, with stripes often absent; lateral stripes, when present, on second and third scale rows anteriorly; internasals usually narrower than long and pointed anteriorly; upper labials usually 8 on each side, sixth and seventh not enlarged; dorsal scale rows usually 19 or 21 at midbody. (Fox, 1951A; Rossman, 1963B.)

Sierra garter snake *(Thamnophis couchii couchii)*
   Middorsal stripe narrow and faint; sides with blotches arranged in checkered pattern; lower labials usually 11 on each side; the Sierra Nevada of California and west-central Nevada.

Oregon garter snake *(Thamnophis couchii hydrophila)*
   Middorsal stripe narrow and faint; sides with blotches arranged in checkered pattern; lower labials usually 10 on each side; northwestern California and southwestern Oregon.

Aquatic garter snake *(Thamnophis couchii aquaticus)*
   Middorsal stripe usually wide and prominent; sides dark olive to black; belly suffused with salmon; sixth and seventh upper labials longer than high; from the north shore of San Francisco Bay to Trinity County, California.

Santa Cruz garter snake *(Thamnophis couchii atratus)*
   Middorsal stripe usually wide and prominent; sides dark olive to black; belly suffused with orange; sixth and seventh upper labials usually higher than long; coastal California from the south shore of San Francisco Bay to San Luis Obispo County.

Giant garter snake *(Thamnophis couchii gigas)*
   Middorsal stripe faint; sides with small spots arranged in checkered pattern; the San Joaquin Valley of California.

Two-striped garter snake *(Thamnophis couchii hammondii)*
  Middorsal stripe absent or represented only by a trace on neck; lower sides above lateral stripes with small spots; western California north to Monterey Bay; also on Santa Catalina Island.

NORTHWESTERN GARTER SNAKE *(Thamnophis ordinoides)*
  Stripes present or absent, the middorsal stripe, if present, yellow, orange, or red, the lateral stripes, if present, on second and third scale rows anteriorly; belly often with red blotches, sometimes marked with black; upper labials usually 7 on each side; lower labials usually 8 or 9 on each side; dorsal scale rows usually 17 at midbody; extreme northwestern California, western Oregon, and western Washington. (Fox, 1948.)

WESTERN BLACK-NECKED GARTER SNAKE *(Thamnophis cyrtopsis cyrtopsis)*
  Neck with paired black blotches, each separated from corner of mouth by a white crescent; stripes conspicuous, the lateral stripes on second and third scale rows anteriorly; sides olive brown with 2 alternating rows of black spots; upper labials usually 8 on each side; dorsal scale rows usually 19 at midbody; New Mexico, extreme southern Colorado, southeastern Utah, and eastern Arizona. (Webb, 1966.)

MEXICAN GARTER SNAKE *(Thamnophis eques megalops)*
  Neck with paired black blotches, each separated from corner of mouth by a light crescent; stripes conspicuous, the lateral stripes on third and fourth scale rows anteriorly; sides olive to brown with 2 alternating rows of distinct or indistinct black spots, the scales often with central light streaks forming longitudinal light lines on body; upper labials usually 8 on each side; dorsal scale rows 19 or 21 at midbody; extreme western New Mexico and southeastern and central Arizona. (Smith, 1951.)

CHECKERED GARTER SNAKE *(Thamnophis marcianus marcianus)*
  Neck with paired black blotches, each separated from corner of mouth by a light crescent; stripes conspicuous, the lateral stripes usually confined to third scale row anteriorly; sides light brown or olive with 2 rows of black blotches arranged in a checkered pattern; upper labials usually 8 on each side; dorsal scale rows usually 21 at midbody; eastern, central, and southern New Mexico, southern Arizona, and extreme southeastern California. (Rossman, 1971.)

WESTERN PLAINS GARTER SNAKE *(Thamnophis radix haydenii)*
  Stripes conspicuous, the lateral stripes on third and fourth scale rows anteriorly; sides gray, olive, or brown, with 2 alternating rows of black

blotches; upper labials usually 7 on each side; dorsal scale rows usually 19 at midbody; northeastern New Mexico, eastern Colorado, eastern Wyoming, and eastern Montana. (Smith, 1949.)

ORANGE-STRIPED RIBBON SNAKE *(Thamnophis proximus diabolicus)*
A slender snake with a long tail (¼ to ⅓ of total length); stripes conspicuous, the middorsal stripe orange, the lateral stripes on third and fourth scale rows anteriorly; sides between stripes uniform olive gray; upper labials pale and unmarked, usually 8 on each side; dorsal scale rows usually 19 at midbody; eastern New Mexico and extreme southeastern Colorado. (Rossman, 1963A.)

LINED SNAKE *(Tropidoclonion lineatum)*
A small, stout species (to 21 inches); conspicuously striped, the stripes bordered by black spots on an olive-gray background; belly with two rows of midventral black spots; loreal present; upper labials usually fewer than 7 on each side; lower labials fewer than 8 on each side; dorsal scales keeled, usually 19 at midbody; anal plate single. (Ramsey, 1953; Smith, 1965.)

Northern lined snake *(Tropidoclonion lineatum lineatum)*
Upper labials usually 5 or 6 on each side; dorsal scale rows usually 17 at posterior end of body; eastern Colorado.

New Mexico lined snake *(Tropidoclonion lineatum mertensi)*
Upper labials never 5, usually 6 on each side; dorsal scale rows usually 15 at posterior end of body; eastern New Mexico.

GROUND SNAKES *(Sonora)*
Small snakes (to 19 inches), with variable color patterns ranging from crossbanded or striped to uniform; rostral unmodified; loreal scale present; scales smooth, in 13 to 15 rows at midbody; anal plate divided; subcaudals fewer than 65 pairs. (Stickel, 1943.)

WESTERN GROUND SNAKE *(Sonora semiannulata)*
Dorsal scale rows usually 14 at posterior end of body; subcaudals usually 53 or more pairs in males, 45 or more pairs in females.

Santa Rita ground snake *(Sonora semiannulata semiannulata)*
Crossbanded, the bands not crossing belly; subcaudals 52 or fewer in males, probably 44 or fewer in females; ventrals minus subcaudals usually more than 109 in males, probably more than 127 in females; the Santa Rita Mountains of southern Arizona.

Great Basin ground snake *(Sonora semiannulata isozona)*
Crossbanded, striped, or uniform; if banded, few or none of bands cross belly; if striped, the stripe merges gradually with color of

sides; subcaudals 53 or more in males, 45 or more in females; ventrals minus subcaudals 98 or more in males, 116 or more in females; extreme southwestern New Mexico, southern and western Arizona, extreme southwestern Utah, southeastern California exclusive of the extreme southeastern corner, southern and western Nevada, southeastern Oregon, and southwestern Idaho.

Trans-Pecos ground snake *(Sonora semiannulata blanchardi)*
Crossbanded to uniform; subcaudals 53 or more in males, 45 or fewer in females; ventrals minus subcaudals 97 or fewer in males, 115 or fewer in females; south-central New Mexico.

Grand Canyon ground snake *(Sonora semiannulata gloydi)*
Crossbanded, with most of bands crossing belly; ventrals minus subcaudals 98 or more in males, 116 or more in females; the Grand Canyon of Arizona.

Vermilion-lined ground snake *(Sonora semiannulata linearis)*
Striped, the stripe with sharp edges giving way abruptly to color of sides; southeastern California.

GREAT PLAINS GROUND SNAKE *(Sonora episcopa episcopa)*
Color pattern extremely variable, ranging from crossbanded or striped to uniform, with various combinations often occurring at same locality; dorsal scale rows usually 15 at posterior end of body in American West; subcaudals 52 or fewer in males, 42 or fewer in females; eastern New Mexico, and extreme southeastern Colorado.

SHOVEL-NOSED SNAKES *(Chionactis)*
Small, crossbanded snakes (to 17 inches); red bands, if present, not crossing belly; snout shovel-shaped; rostral not separating internasals, not reaching prefrontals on top of head; lower jaw countersunk; loreal present; scales smooth, usually in 15 rows at midbody; anal plate divided. (Klauber, 1951.)

ORGAN PIPE SHOVEL-NOSED SNAKE *(Chionactis palarostris organica)*
Snout convex above; dark bands on body usually less than 21; body bands plus unmarked anterior band positions on belly usually fewer than 23; Organ Pipe Cactus National Monument, Arizona.

WESTERN SHOVEL-NOSED SNAKE *(Chionactis occipitalis)*
Snout flat above; dark bands on body usually 21 or more; body bands plus unmarked anterior band positions on belly usually 23 or more.

Mojave shovel-nosed snake *(Chionactis occipitalis occipitalis)*
Bands brown; light interspaces between primary bands lacking

orange saddles or dark secondary bands; body bands plus unmarked anterior band positions on belly usually 45 or more; the
Mojave Desert of California, extreme southern Nevada, and west-
central Arizona.

Colorado Desert shovel-nosed snake *(Chionactis occipitalis annulata)*
Bands usually black; light interspaces between primary bands
usually with orange saddles, lacking dark secondary bands; body
bands plus unmarked anterior band positions on belly usually
fewer than 45; extreme southeastern California and southwestern
Arizona.

Tucson shovel-nosed snake *(Chionactis occipitalis klauberi)*
Bands usually black; light interspaces between primary bands with
distinct secondary bands; ventrals usually fewer than 152 in males,
fewer than 160 in females; south-central Arizona.

Nevada shovel-nosed snake *(Chionactis occipitalis talpina)*
Bands brown; light interspaces between primary bands with indistinct secondary bands; ventrals usually 152 or more in males,
fewer than 160 in females; the Death Valley region of California
and southwestern Nevada.

BANDED SAND SNAKE *(Chilomeniscus cinctus)*
A small, stout snake (to only 10 inches); color pattern consisting of black
crossbands on a pale yellow to reddish orange background, with orange
sometimes in saddles not crossing belly; snout shovel-shaped; rostral
separating internasals, reaching prefrontals on top of head; lower jaw
deeply countersunk; loreal absent; scales smooth, in 13 rows at midbody; central and southwestern Arizona. (Banta and Leviton, 1963.)

HOOK-NOSED SNAKES *(Gyalopion)*
Small, stout species (to 14 inches); rostral enlarged, upturned, not
keeled above; scales smooth, usually in 17 rows at midbody. (Smith and
Taylor, 1941.)

MEXICAN WEST COAST HOOK-NOSED SNAKE *(Gyalopion quadrangularis)*
Color pattern composed of black saddles on a yellowish background,
with a longitudinal reddish band on each side; loreal scale present in
American West; anal plate single; Santa Cruz County in extreme southern Arizona. (Hardy and McDiarmid, 1969.)

WESTERN HOOK-NOSED SNAKE *(Gyalopion canum)*
Color pattern composed of brown crossbands edged with black on a
grayish brown to yellowish gray background; loreal scale absent; anal

plate divided; central and southern New Mexico and southeastern Arizona.

BLACK-HEADED SNAKES *(Tantilla)*

Small, slender snakes (to 18 inches); head with black or dark brown cap; body uniform tan to brown above; belly salmon to coral red without dark spotting, the red not reaching the dorsal scales; usually with a white collar followed by black band or row of black dots; loreal absent; scales smooth, in 15 rows at midbody.

YAQUI BLACK-HEADED SNAKE *(Tantilla yaquia)*

Black cap extending 2 to 3 scales behind parietals, not pointed posteriorly, extending laterally to or below corner of mouth; light coloration of upper labials extending upward to lower postocular and anterior temporal scales, producing a large white area behind each eye; collar pronounced; ventral scutes fewer than 160; ventrals plus subcaudal pairs fewer than 225; vicinity of Bisbee in southeastern Arizona. (McDiarmid, 1968.)

WESTERN BLACK-HEADED SNAKE *(Tantilla planiceps)*

Black cap extending 0 to 3 scale rows behind parietals, usually not pointed behind; cap color occasionally extending below corner of mouth; collar usually present, sometimes bordered by black dots; anal plate divided. (Tanner, 1966.)

Mexican black-headed snake *(Tantilla planiceps atriceps)*

Black cap usually extending fewer than 2 scales behind parietals, not reaching corner of mouth; collar rarely present; ventral scutes in males 135–151, in females 145–160; ventrals plus subcaudal pairs usually fewer than 220, averaging 207; Arizona and southern New Mexico.

Utah black-headed snake *(Tantilla planiceps utahensis)*

Black cap usually extending fewer than 2 scales behind parietals, not reaching corner of mouth; collar rarely present; ventral scutes in males 153–165, in females 162–174; ventrals plus subcaudal pairs more than 220, averaging 225; lower Sierra Nevada of California, southern Nevada, northwestern Arizona, southern Utah, and western Colorado.

California black-headed snake *(Tantilla planiceps eiseni)*

Black cap extending 1½ to 2½ scales behind parietals and laterally to or below corner of mouth; collar usually present; ventral scutes in males 163–175, in females 167–185; ventrals plus subcaudal pairs fewer than 245; southwestern California north to Fresno County.

Desert black-headed snake *(Tantilla planiceps transmontana)*

Black cap extending 1½ to 2¼ scales posterior to parietals; collar usually present; ventral scutes in males 175–185, in females 187–198; ventrals plus subcaudal pairs more than 245; transmontane San Diego and Riverside counties, California.

PLAINS BLACK-HEADED SNAKE *(Tantilla nigriceps nigriceps)*

Black or gray-brown cap usually pointed posteriorly, extending 3 to 5 scale rows behind parietals; collar lacking; anal plate single; New Mexico and southeastern Arizona. (Smith, 1941.)

HUACHUCA BLACK-HEADED SNAKE *(Tantilla wilcoxi wilcoxi)*

Black cap not reaching posterior tips of parietals, extending laterally to corner of mouth; collar pronounced, crossing tips of parietals, bordered behind by a black band; anal plate divided; Huachuca Mountains of southeastern Arizona. (Smith, 1942.)

VINE SNAKE *(Oxybelis aeneus)*

An extremely slender snake, vinelike in shape and color; head long; snout sharp; tail more than half of body length; head marked with a black eyestripe; anal plate divided; extreme south-central Arizona in the Pajarito Mountains. (Keiser, 1967.)

LYRE SNAKE *(Trimorphodon biscutatus)*

A slender, blotched species; head enlarged; neck narrow; pupil vertical; lyre-shaped mark on top of head; loreal scales present; scales smooth, in 24 or fewer rows at midbody. (Gehlbach, 1971.)

Sonora lyre snake *(Trimorphodon biscutatus lambda)*

Primary blotches averaging 26 on body, 13 on tail; lyre-shaped mark on head pronounced; anal plate divided; southwestern Utah, southern Nevada, southeastern California, and western and southern Arizona.

California lyre snake *(Trimorphodon biscutatus vandenburghi)*

Primary blotches averaging 37 on body, 15 to 18 on tail; blotches roughly hexagonal in shape, split by a pale crossbar; lyre-shaped mark on head pronounced; anal plate single; southern California.

Texas lyre snake *(Trimorphodon biscutatus vilkinsonii)*

Primary blotches averaging 20 on body, 11 on tail; lyre-shaped mark on head faint or lacking; extreme southern New Mexico.

NIGHT SNAKE *(Hypsiglena torquata)*

A small snake (to 18 inches), usually with a pair of large dark-brown blotches on neck; side of head behind eye marked with a black or dark brown bar contrasting with whitish upper labials; belly unmarked;

pupil vertical; scales smooth, in 19 or 21 rows at midbody; anal plate divided. (Tanner, 1946; Dixon, 1965.)

Spotted night snake *(Hypsiglena torquata ochrorhyncha)*
>Two spots or a narrow band on neck; upper labials 8 on each side; loreal single on each side; scale rows 21 at midbody; Arizona, extreme south-central Utah, and western New Mexico.

Texas night snake *(Hypsiglena torquata janii)*
>Three large spots on neck, the median spot elongated, in contact with parietals; upper labials 8 on each side; loreal single on each side; scale rows 21 at midbody; New Mexico exclusive of the western and northern portions, and southeastern Colorado.

Mesa Verde night snake *(Hypsiglena torquata loreala)*
>Upper labials 8 on each side; loreals paired on each side; scale rows 21 at midbody; eastern Utah, extreme northeastern Arizona, extreme northwestern New Mexico, and extreme southwestern and west-central Colorado.

Desert night snake *(Hypsiglena torquata deserticola)*
>Three large spots on the neck, the median spot greatly expanded posteriorly; upper labials 8 on each side; loreal single on each side; scale rows 21 at midbody; south-central Washington, eastern Oregon exclusive of the northeastern corner, southern Idaho, western Utah, extreme northwestern Arizona, and southeastern California.

California night snake *(Hypsiglena torquata nuchalata)*
>Upper labials 7 on each side; loreal single on each side; scale rows 19 at midbody; foothills surrounding the Great Valley of central California.

San Diego night snake *(Hypsiglena torquata klauberi)*
>Three large spots on neck, the median spot not in contact with parietals; upper labials 8 on each side; loreal single on each side; scale rows 21 at midbody; California north to San Luis Opispo County; also on Santa Cruz Island.

CORAL SNAKES (ELAPIDAE)
>Dangerously venomous snakes with short, permanently erect venom-conducting fangs at the front of the upper jaws; see following species account for color pattern of only American West representative; scale characteristics similar to those of the Colubridae.

ARIZONA CORAL SNAKE *(Micruroides euryxanthus euryxanthus)*
>A small snake (to 20 inches), with alternating rings of red and black separated by narrower rings of white or yellow, the markings encircling

body but becoming pale on belly; light band at back of head extending across the tips of parietals; loreal absent; scales smooth, in 15 rows at midbody; anal plate divided; southwestern New Mexico and southern and central Arizona. (Roze, 1967.)

PIT VIPERS (CROTALIDAE)

Dangerously venomous snakes with long, folding venom-conducting fangs at the front of the upper jaws; broad-headed and stout bodied with slender neck; in representatives in American West, tail terminated by rattles (inaudible prebutton or button in juveniles); loreal pit evident between eye and nostril; scales keeled; single rows of subcaudals. (Klauber, 1972.)

DESERT OR SOUTHWESTERN MASSASAUGA *(Sistrurus catenatus edwardsii)*

Dark brown normal complement of 9 enlarged plates on top of head including a frontal and 2 contacting, symmetrical parietals; elongate head markings extending onto neck; southeastern Colorado, eastern and southern New Mexico, and extreme southeastern Arizona.

RATTLESNAKES *(Crotalus)*

Scales on top of head varying in size anteriorly; more than 1 scale in frontal area; parietals, if enlarged, are neither in contact nor symmetrical.

WESTERN DIAMONDBACK RATTLESNAKE *(Crotalus atrox)*

To over 7 feet in length; dark flecking conspicuous in body blotches; alternating black and white rings of equal width on tail; prenasals not separated from rostral by small scales; supraoculars unbroken; first lower labials usually not divided transversely; usually 25 scale rows at midbody; southeastern California, extreme southern Nevada, southern Arizona, and New Mexico exclusive of west-central and northern portions.

RED DIAMOND RATTLESNAKE *(Crotalus ruber ruber)*

Dark flecking in body blotches is inconspicuous or absent; tail marked with prominent black and white rings; usually there are 29 scale rows; first lower labials usually divided transversely; restricted to west of the San Bernardino Mountains in southern California.

ROCK RATTLESNAKE *(Crotalus lepidus)*

Light background with widely spaced dark bands either black or dark brown.

Mottled rock rattlesnake *(Crotalus lepidus lepidus)*

Well-defined postocular stripe; occipital blotches separated; extreme southeastern New Mexico.

Banded rock rattlesnake *(Crotalus lepidus klauberi)*
>Postocular stripe usually absent; occipital blotches are fused; southeastern Arizona and southwestern New Mexico.

SPECKLED RATTLESNAKE *(Crotalus mitchellii)*
>Heavily speckled; tail banded with light and dark rings contrasting with color pattern on posterior region of body; small scales between supraoculars; prenasals usually separated from rostral by granular scales or supraoculars pitted, creased, or with rough outer edges.

Southwestern speckled rattlesnake *(Crotalus mitchellii pyrrhus)*
>Indistinct pattern; normally there is a row of scales between the rostral and prenasal scales; western Arizona, extreme southern Nevada, extreme southwestern Utah, and southern California.

Panamint rattlesnake *(Crotalus mitchellii stephensi)*
>Band pattern distinct; rostral and prenasal scales are in contact; southern Nevada and adjacent California, not reaching California coastal areas.

SIDEWINDER *(Crotalus cerastes)*
>Small (to 30 inches); outer edges of the supraoculars extended into raised and flexible hornlike processes distinctly pointed at the tip.

Mojave Desert sidewinder *(Crotalus cerastes cerastes)*
>First segment of rattle is brown in adults; normally there are 21 rows of scales; southeastern California to within 100 miles of the Mexican border and not reaching the coastal areas, southwestern Utah, southern Nevada, and west-central Arizona.

Sonora sidewinder *(Crotalus cerastes cercobombus)*
>First segment of rattle is black in adults; midbody scale rows are normally 21; ventrals in the males 141 or fewer, in females 145 or fewer; south-central Arizona.

Colorado Desert sidewinder *(Crotalus cerastes laterorepens)*
>First segment of rattle is black in the adults; midbody scale rows normally 23; ventrals in males more than 141, in females more than 145; extreme southeastern California and adjacent extreme southwestern Arizona.

BLACK-TAILED RATTLESNAKE *(Crotalus molossus molossus)*
>Snout sometimes black; tail usually black but occasionally faintly ringed; 8 or fewer large flat scales in frontal and prefrontal areas; frontals and prefrontals usually divided by a suture; anterior frontal scales

larger than posterior ones; ventral scales not fewer than 180; usually not fewer than 15 supralabials; Arizona exclusive of extreme western and northern regions, and southwestern half of New Mexico exclusive of extreme northwest corner.

TIGER RATTLESNAKE *(Crotalus tigris)*
Relatively small head and large rattles; banded color pattern composed of dark flecks; bands are closely spaced; tail banded with light and dark ring not contrasting with posterior body coloration; rostral and prenasals in contact; south-central Arizona.

WESTERN RATTLESNAKE *(Crotalus viridis)*
Blotched; more than two internasals in contact with the rostral scale.

Prairie rattlesnake *(Crotalus viridis viridis)*
Ground color green or occasionally brown; well-defined brown dorsal patches; light postocular stripe 1 or 1½ scales wide; extreme east-central Idaho, most of Montana, New Mexico, Wyoming exclusive of extreme western region, and eastern Colorado.

Grand Canyon rattlesnake *(Crotalus viridis abyssus)*
Ground color vermilion to salmon; body blotches usually faint; restricted in Arizona to the Grand Canyon.

Arizona black rattlesnake *(Crotalus viridis cerberus)*
Ground color olive to black, with dark dorsal patches wider than their interspaces; secondary series of lateral blotches evident; at the rostral there are usually one or more scales between the first supralabial and the prenasal; extreme west-central New Mexico, and from the Grand Canyon area in Arizona southeast, exclusive of U.S.-Mexico border region.

Midget faded rattlesnake *(Crotalus viridis concolor)*
Rarely larger than 2 feet; ground color cream-yellow; blotching faint or absent; eastern Utah, western Colorado, and extreme southwestern Wyoming.

Southern Pacific rattlesnake *(Crotalus viridis helleri)*
Final dark ring on tail approximately twice as wide as the others and poorly defined; young with yellow toward end of tail; coastal southern California; also on Santa Catalina Island.

Northern Pacific rattlesnake *(Crotalus viridis oreganus)*
Dark rings on tail are equal in width; young with yellow towards end of tail; north of range of *C. v. helleri*, from San Luis Obispo Bay north through western and northern Oregon, in Washington east of the Cascade Mountains and in west-central Idaho.

Great Basin rattlesnake *(Crotalus viridis lutosus)*
> Ground color light, buff to drab; blotches approximately equal in width as the interspaces; southern Idaho exclusive of extreme eastern region, western Utah exclusive of southern portion, Nevada, extreme northeastern California, and southeastern Oregon.

Hopi rattlesnake *(Crotalus viridis nuntius)*
> Rarely more than 24 inches long; color pink, red, or red-brown; well-defined dorsal blotches; extreme south-central Utah, extreme southwestern Colorado, extreme northwestern New Mexico, and northeastern Arizona.

MOJAVE RATTLESNAKE *(Crotalus scutulatus scutulatus)*

Well-defined dorsal pattern; alternating light and dark rings on tail, with dark rings narrower than the light ones; prefrontal and frontal scales are divided; scales between supraoculars not more than 2; supraoculars bordered inwardly and posteriorly by crescent-shaped scale; southern Nevada, extreme southwestern Utah, extreme southwestern New Mexico, southwestern portion of Arizona, and in California west of the Arizona and Nevada ranges exclusive of coastal California and the extreme southeastern corner of California.

TWIN-SPOTTED RATTLESNAKE *(Crotalus pricei pricei)*

Small snakes to 26 inches; two rows of dark spots on either side of mid-dorsal line; southeastern Arizona.

RIDGE-NOSED RATTLESNAKE *(Crotalus willardi)*

Not longer than two feet; reddish dorsum, marked with white crossbars that are edged with dark brown or black, merging with the color on the flanks.

Arizona ridge-nosed rattlesnake *(Crotalus willardi willardi)*
> Vertical white lines on rostral and mental scales; Santa Rita and Huachuca mountains of southeastern Arizona.

Chihuahua ridge-nosed rattlesnake *(Crotalus willardi silus)*
> No vertical white line on rostral and mental scales; restricted to the Animas Mountains of extreme southwestern New Mexico.

BIBLIOGRAPHY

» » » » »

GENERAL REFERENCE WORKS

BUCHERL, WOLFGANG, and BUCKLEY, ELEANOR E., eds. 1971. *Venomous Animals and Their Venoms.* Venomous Vertebrates, vol. 2. New York: Academic Press.

CARR, ARCHIE. 1963. *The Reptiles.* New York: Time-Life Books.

COCHRAN, DORIS M., and GOIN, COLEMAN J. 1970. *The New Field Book of Reptiles and Amphibians.* New York: G. P. Putnam's Sons.

CONANT, ROGER. 1958. *A Field Guide to Reptiles and Amphibians of the United States and Canada East of the 100th Meridian.* Boston: Houghton Mifflin Co.

DITMARS, RAYMOND L. 1946. *The Reptiles of North America.* Garden City, New York: Doubleday & Co., Inc.

GANS, CARL, and PARSONS, THOMAS S., eds. 1969– . *Biology of the Reptilia.* 3 vols., 7 vols forthcoming. New York: Academic Press, Inc.

GOIN, COLEMAN J., and GOIN, OLIVE B. 1971. *Introduction to Herpetology,* 2nd ed. San Francisco: W. H. Freeman and Co.

KEISER, EDMUND DAVIS, JR. 1967. *A Monographic Study of the Neotropical Vine Snake,* Oxybelis aeneus *(Wagler).* Ph.D. dissertation, Louisiana State University and Agricultural and Mechanical College.

KLAUBER, LAURENCE M. 1972. *Rattlesnakes: Their Habits, Life Histories, and Influence on Mankind.* 2 vols., 2nd ed. Berkeley: University of California Press.

MINTON, SHERMAN A., JR., and MINTON, MADGE RUTHERFORD. 1969. *Venomous Reptiles.* New York: Charles Scribner's Sons.

OLIVER, JAMES A. 1955. *The Natural History of North American Amphibians and Reptiles.* New York: Van Nostrand Reinhold Co.

———. 1959. *Snakes in Fact and Fiction.* New York: Macmillan.

SCHMIDT, KARL P. 1953. *A Check List of North American Amphibians and Reptiles.* 6th ed. New York: American Society of Ichthyologists and Herpetologists.

STEBBINS, ROBERT C. 1966. *A Field Guide to Western Reptiles and Amphibians.* Boston: Houghton Mifflin Co.

WICKLER, WOLFGANG. 1968. *Mimicry in Plants and Animals.* Translated from the German by R. D. Martin. New York: McGraw-Hill Book Co., World University Library.

WRIGHT, ALBERT H., and WRIGHT, ANNA A. 1957. *Handbook of Snakes of the United States and Canada,* 2 vols. Ithaca, New York: Cornell University Press, Comstock Publishing Associates.

SELECTED ARTICLES

AUFFENBERG, WALTER. 1955. "A Reconsideration of the Racer, *Coluber constrictor,* in Eastern United States." *Tulane Studies in Zoology* 2: 87–155.

BAKER, ROBERT J., BULL, JAMES J., and MENGDEN, GREG A. 1971. "Chromosomes of *Elaphe subocularis* (Reptilia: Serpentes), with the Description of an in vivo Technique for Preparation of Snake Chromosomes." *Experientia* 27 (10) [fasc.]: 1228–9.

BAKER, ROBERT J., MENGDEN, GREG A., and BULL, JAMES J. 1972. "Karyotypic Studies of Thirty-eight Species of North American Snakes.'' *Copeia* 1972 (2): 257–65.

BANTA, BENJAMIN H., and LEVITON, ALAN E. 1963. "Remarks on the Colubrid Genus *Chilomeniscus* (Serpentes: Colubridae)." *Proceedings of the California Academy of Sciences,* 4th ser., 31: 309–27.

BARRET, ROBERT, MADERSON, P. A. F., and MESZLER, RICHARD M. 1970. "The Pit Organs of Snakes." In *Biology of the Reptilia,* 2. Carl Gans and Thomas S. Parsons, eds. New York: Academic Press: 217–314.

BLANCHARD, FRANK N. 1921. "A Revision of the King Snakes: Genus *Lampropeltis.*" *United States National Museum Bulletin* 114: 1–260.

BLANCHARD, FRANK N. 1942. "The Ring-neck Snakes, Genus *Diadophis.*" *Bulletin of the Chicago Academy of Sciences* 7: 1–144.

BOGART, CHARLES M. 1933. "Notes on the Snake Dance of the Hopi Indians." *Copeia* 1933 (4): 219–21.

———. 1945. "Two Additional Races of the Patch-nosed Snake, *Salvadora hexalepis.*" *American Museum Novitates* 1285: 1–14.

BOGERT, CHARLES M., and ROTH, VINCENT D. 1966. "Ritualistic Combat of Male Gopher Snakes, *Pituophis melanoleucus affinis* (Reptilia, Colubridae)." *American Museum Novitates* 2245 (May 19): 1–27.

BRAGG, ARTHUR N. 1960. "Is *Heterodon* Venomous?" *Herpetologica* 16 (2): 121–3.

BRISBIN, I. LEHR, JR. 1968. "Evidence for the Use of Postanal Musk as an Alarm Device in the King Snake, *Lampropeltis getulus.*" *Herpetologica* 24 (2): 169–70.

BRODIE, EDMUND D., JR., Nussbaum, Ronald A., and Storm, Robert M. 1969. "An Egg-laying Aggregation of Five Species of Oregon Reptiles." *Herpetologica* 25 (3): 223–7.

BURGHARDT, GORDON M. 1967. "Chemical-Cue Preferences of Inexperienced Snakes: Comparative Aspects." *Science* 157 (3789): 718–21.

BURY, R. BRUCE, GRESS, FRANKLIN, and GORMAN, GEORGE C. 1970. "Karyotypic Survey of Some Colubrid Snakes from Western North America." *Herpetologica* 26 (4): 461–6.

CARPENTER, CHARLES C. 1952. "Comparative Ecology of the Common Garter Snake *(Thamnophis s. sirtalis)*, the Ribbon Snake *(Thamnophis s. sauritus)*, and Butler's Garter Snake *(Thamnophis butleri)* in Mixed Populations." *Ecological Monographs* 22 (4): 235–58.

COHEN, ALLEN C., and MYRES, BRIAN C. 1970. "A Function of the Horns (Supraocular Scales) in the Sidewinder Rattlesnake, *Crotalus cerastes,* with Comments on Other Horned Snakes." *Copeia* 1970 (3): 574–5.

CONANT, ROGER. 1949. "Two New Races of *Natrix erythrogaster.*" *Copeia* 1949 (1): 1–15.

———. 1963. "Evidence for the Specific Status of the Water Snake *Natrix fasciata.*" *American Museum Novitates* 2122: 1–38.

COOK, FRANCIS R. 1964. "Communal Egg Laying in the Smooth Green Snake." *Herpetologica* 20 (3): 206.

COOK, SHERBURNE F., JR. 1960. "On the Occurrence and Life History of *Contia tenuis.*" *Herpetologica* 16 (3): 163–73.

COWLES, RAYMOND B. 1938. "Unusual Defense Postures Assumed by Rattlesnakes." *Copeia* 1938 (1): 13–16.

CRIDDLE, STUART. 1937. "Snakes from an Ant Hill." *Copeia* 1937 (2): 142.

CROULET, C. H. 1965. "Evidence of Conspecificity of the Western Ringneck Snakes (Genus *Diaophis*)." *Herpetologica* 21: 80.

DEGENHARDT, WILLIAM G., and DEGENHARDT, PAULA B. 1965. "The Host-Parasite Relationship Between Elaphe subocularis (Reptilia: Colubridae) and Aponomma elaphensis (Acarina: Ixodidae)." *Southwestern Naturalist* 10 (3): 167–78.

DIXON, JAMES R. 1965. "A Taxonomic Reevaluation of the Night Snake *Hypsiglena ochrorhyncha* and Relatives." *Southwestern Naturalist* 10: 125–31.

DOWLING, HERNDON G. 1952. "A Taxonomic Study of the Ratsnakes, Genus *Elaphe* Fitzinger." IV: A check list of the American forms. *Occasional Papers of the Museum of Zoology,* University of Michigan, 541: 1–12.

——. 1957. "A Taxonomic Study of the Ratsnakes, Genus *Elaphe* Fitzinger." V: The rosalie section. *Occasional Papers of the Museum of Zoology,* University of Michigan, 583: 1–22.

——. 1960. "A Taxonomic Study of the Ratsnakes, Genus *Elaphe* Fitzinger." VII: The triaspis section. *Zoologica* 45: 53–80.

DUELLMAN, WILLIAM E. 1958. "A Monographic Study of the Colubrid Snake Genus *Leptoderia.*" *Bulletin of the American Museum of Natural History* 114 (Article 1): 1–152.

DUNDEE, HAROLD A., and MILLER, M. CLINTON, III. 1968. "Aggregative Behavior and Habitat Conditioning by the Prairie Ringneck Snake, *Diadophis punctatus arnyi. Tulane Studies in Zoology and Botany* 15 (2): 41–58.

EBERLE, W. GARY. 1972. "Comparative Chromosomal Morphology of the New World Natricine Snake Genera *Natrix* and *Regina.*" *Herpetologica* 28 (2): 98–105.

EDGREN, RICHARD A. 1952. "A Synopsis of the Snakes of the Genus *Heterodon,* with the Diagnosis of a New Race of *Heterodon nasicus* Baird and Girard." *Natural History Miscellanea* 112: 1–4.

FICKEN, ROBERT W., MATTHIAE, PAUL E., and HORWICH, ROBERT. 1971. "Eye Marks in Vertebrates: Aids to Vision." *Science* 173 (4000): 936–8.

FITCH, HENRY S. 1949. "Study of Snake Populations in Central California." *American Midland Naturalist* 41 (3): 513–79.

——. 1963. "Natural History of the Racer *Coluber constrictor.*" *University of Kansas Museum of Natural History Publication* 15 (8): 351–468.

FLEET, ROBERT R., and DIXON, JAMES R. 1971. "Geographic Variation Within the Long-tailed Group of the Glossy Snake, *Arizona elegans* Kennicott." *Herpetologica* 27 (3): 295–302.

FOX, WADE. 1948. "The Relationships of the Garter Snake *Thamnophis ordinoides.*" *Copeia* 1948 (2): 113–20.

———. 1951A. "Relationships Among the Garter Snakes of the *Thamnophis elegans* Complex." *University of California Publications in Zoology* 50: 485–530.

———. 1951B. "The Status of the Gartersnake, *Thamnophis sirtalis tetrataenia*." *Copeia* 1951 (4): 257–67.

GEBHARDT, LOUIS P., STANTON, G. JOHN, and ST. JEOR, STEPHEN DE. 1966. "Transmission of WEE Virus to Snakes by Infected *Culex tarsalis* Mosquitoes." *Proceedings of the Society for Experimental Biology and Medicine* 123: 233–5.

GEHLBACH, FREDERICK R. 1970. "Death-feigning and Erratic Behaviour in Leptotyphlopid, Colubrid, and Elapid Snakes." *Herpetologica* 26 (1): 24–34.

———. 1971. "Lyre Snakes of the *Trimorphodon biscutatus* Complex: A Taxonomic Resume." *Herpetologica* 27 (2): 200–11.

GEHLBACH, FREDERICK R., WATKINS, JULIAN F., II, and KROLL, JAMES C. 1971. "Pheromone Trail-following Studies of Typhlopid, Leptotyphlopid, and Colubrid Snakes." *Behaviour* 40 (parts 3–4): 282–94.

GENNARO, JOSEPH F., JR., LEOPOLD, ROBERT S., and MERRIAM, THORNTON W. 1961. "Observations on the Actual Quality of Venom Introduced by Several Species of Crotalid Snakes in Their Bite." *Anatomical Record* 139 (2): 303 (Abstract).

GLASS, JAMES K. 1972. "Feeding Behavior of the Western Shovel-nosed Snake, *Chionactis occipitalis klauberi,* with Special Reference to Scorpions." *Southwestern Naturalist* 16 (3 & 4): 445–7.

GLOYD, HOWARD K., and CONANT, ROGER. 1934. "The Taxonomic Status, Range, and Natural History of Schott's Racer." *Occasional Papers of the Museum of Zoology,* University of Michigan, 287: 1–17.

GOODMAN, JOHN D. 1953. "Further Evidence of the Venomous Nature of the Saliva of *Hypsiglena ochrorhyncha.*" *Herpetologica* 9 (part 4): 174–6.

GORMAN, GEORGE C. 1965. "The Distribution of *Lichanura trivirgata* and the Status of the Species." *Herpetologica* 21: 283–7.

GRINNELL, JOSEPH, and GRINNELL, HILDA WOOD. 1907. "Reptiles of Los Angeles County, California." *Throop Institute Bulletin,* no. 35 (science series no. 1): 1–64.

GROBMAN, ARNOLD B. 1941. "A Contribution to the Knowledge of Variation in *Opheodrys vernalis* (Harlan), with the Description of a New Subspecies." *Miscellaneous Publications, Museum of Zoology,* University of Michigan, 50: 1–38.

HARDY, LAURENCE M., and McDIARMID, ROY W. 1969. "The Amphibians and Reptiles of Sinaloa, Mexico." *University of Kansas Publications,* Museum of Natural History, 18: 39–252.

HARTLINE, PETER H., and CAMPBELL, HOWARD W. 1969. "Auditory and Vibratory Responses in the Midbrains of Snakes." *Science* 163 (3872): 1221–3.

HARTLINE, PETER H. 1971. "Physiological Basis for Detection of Sound and Vibration in Snakes." *Journal of Experimental Biology* 54 (2): 349–71.

HARTWEG, NORMAN. 1940. "Description of *Salvadora intermedia,* New Species, with Remarks on the *Grahamiae* Group." *Copeia* 1940 (3): 256–9.

HENSLEY, M. MAX. 1950. "Results of a Herpetological Reconnaissance in Extreme Southwestern Arizona and Adjacent Sonora, with a Description of New Subspecies of the Sonoran Whipsnake: *Masticophis bilineatus.*" *Transactions of the Kansas Academy of Science* 53 (2): 270–88.

HIBBARD, CLAUDE W. 1964. "A Brooding Colony of the Blind Snake, *Leptotyphlops dulcis dissecta* Cope." *Copeia* 1964 (1): 222.

HIRTH, HAROLD F. 1966. "Weight Changes and Mortality of Three Species of Snakes During Hibernation." *Herpetologica* 22 (1): 8–12.

HULSE, ARTHUR C. 1971. "Fluorescence in *Leptotyphlops Humilis* (Serpentes: Leptotyphlopidae)." *Southwestern Naturalist* 16 (1): 123–4.

KAPUS, EDWARD J. 1964. "Anatomical Evidence for *Heterodon* Being Poisonous." *Herpetologica* 20 (2): 137–8.

KAUFFELD, C. F. 1948. "Notes on a Hook-nosed Snake from Texas." *Copeia* 1948 (4): 301.

KLAUBER, LAURENCE M. 1931. "A New Subspecies of the California Boa, with Notes on the Genus *Lichanura.*" *Transactions of the San Diego Society of Natural History* 6: 305–18.

———. 1932. "A Herpetological Review of the Hopi Snake Dance." *Bulletins of the Zoological Society of San Diego* 9: 1–93.

———. 1936. "The California King Snake, A Case of Pattern Dimorphism." *Herpetologica* 1 (1): 18–27.

———. 1939A. "Studies of Reptile Life in the Arid Southwest." *Bulletins of the Zoological Society of San Diego* 14: 1–100.

———. 1939B. "A Further Study of Pattern Dimorphism in the California King Snake." *Bulletins of the Zoological Society of San Diego* 15: 1–23.

———. 1940A. "The Lyre Snakes (Genus *Trimorphodon*) of the United States." *Transactions of the San Diego Society of Natural History* 9 (19): 163–94.

———. 1940B. "The Worm Snakes of the Genus *Leptotyphlops* in the United States and Northern Mexico." *Transactions of the San Diego Society of Natural History* 9: 87–162.

———. 1940C. "Two New Subspecies of *Phyllorhynchus,* the Leaf-nosed Snake, with Notes on the Genus." *Transactions of the San Diego Society of Natural History* 9: 195–214.

———. 1941. "The Long-nosed Snakes of the Genus *Rhinocheilus.*" *Transactions of the San Diego Society of Natural History* 9: 289–332.

———. 1943. "The Subspecies of the Rubber Snake, *Charina.*" *Transactions of the San Diego Society of Natural History* 10: 83–90.

———. 1946. "The Glossy Snake, *Arizona,* with Descriptions of New Subspecies." *Transactions of the San Diego Society of Natural History* 17: 311–98.

———. 1947. "Classification and Ranges of the Gopher Snakes of the Genus *Pituophis* in the Western United States." *Bulletins of the Zoological Society of San Diego* 22: 1–81.

———. 1951. "The Shovel-nosed Snake, *Chionactis,* with Descriptions of Two New Subspecies." *Transactions of the San Diego Society of Natural History* 11 (9): 141–204.

KROLL, JAMES C. 1971. "Combat Behavior in Male Great Plains Ground Snakes *(Sonora episcopa episcopa)*." *Texas Journal of Science* 23 (2): 300.

KURFESS, JOHN F. 1967. "Mating, Gestation, and Growth Rate in *Lichanura r. roseofusca.*" *Copeia* 1967 (2): 477–9.

LEVITON, ALAN E., and TANNER, WILMER W. 1960. "The Generic Allocation of *Hypsiglena slevini* Tanner (Serpentes: Colubridae)." *Occasional Papers of the California Academy of Sciences* 27: 1–7.

LEVITON, ALAN E., and ANDERSON, STEVEN C. 1970. "Review of the Snakes of the Genus *Lytorhynchus.*" *Proceedings of the California Academy of Sciences* (4th series) 37 (7): 249–74.

LICHT, LAWRENCE E., and LOW, BOBBI. 1968. "Cardiac Response of Snakes after Ingestion of Toad Parotoid Venom." *Copeia* 1968 (3): 547–51.

LIST, JAMES CARL. 1966. "Comparative Osteology of the Snake Families Typhlopidae and Leptotyphlopidae." *Illinois Biological Monographs* 36: 1–112.

MCALISTER, WAYNE H. 1963. "Evidence of Mild Toxicity in the Saliva of the Hognose Snake *(Heterodon).*" *Herpetologica* 19 (2): 132–7.

MCDIARMID, ROY W. 1968. "Variation, Distribution and Systemic Status of the Black-headed Snake *Tantilla yaquia* Smith." *Bulletin of the Southern California Academy of Sciences* 67: 159–77.

MCCOY, CLARENCE J., JR., 1964. "The Snake *Tantilla yaquia* in Arizona: An Addition to the Fauna of the United States." *Copeia* 1964 (1): 216–17.

MCCOY, CLARENCE J., JR., and GEHLBACH, FREDERICK R. 1967. "Cloacal Hemorrhage and the Defense Display of the Colubrid Snake *Rhinocheilus lecontei.*" *Texas Journal of Science* 19 (4): 349–52.

MARTIN, WM. F., and HUEY, R. B. 1971. "The Function of the Epiglottis in Sound Production (Hissing) of *Pituophis melanoleucus.*" *Copeia* 1971 (4): 752–4.

MEEKS, ROBERT L. 1968. "The Accumulation of [36]Cl Ring-Labeled DDT in a Freshwater Marsh." *Journal of Wildlife Management* 32 (2): 376–98.

MILSTEAD, WILLIAM W., MECHAM, JOHN S., and McCLINTOCK, HASKELL. 1950. "The Amphibians and Reptiles of the Stockton Plateau in Northern Terrell County, Texas." *Texas Journal of Science* 2 (4): 543–62.

MURDAUGH, H. V., JR., and JACKSON, JOSEPH E. 1962. "Heart Rate and Blood Lactic Acid Concentration During Experimental Diving of Water Snakes." *American Journal of Physiology* 202 (6): 1163–5.

MYERS, CHARLES W. 1965. "Biology of the Ringneck Snake, *Diadophis punctatus,* in Florida." *Bulletin of the Florida State Museum, Biological Sciences* 10 (2): 43–90.

NORRIS, KENNETH S., and KAVANAU, J. LEE. 1966. "The Burrowing of the Western Shovel-nosed Snake, *Chionactis occipitalis* Hallowell, and the Undersand Environment" *Copeia* 1966 (4): 650–64.

ORTENBURGER, ARTHUR I. 1928. "The Whip Snakes and Racers: Genera *Masticophis* and *Coluber.*" *Memoirs, University of Michigan Museum* 1: 1–247.

PARRISH, HENRY M. 1957. "Mortality from Snakebites, United States, 1950–54." *Public Health Reports* 72 (11): 1027–30.

RAMSEY, L. W. 1953. "The Lined Snake, *Tropidoclonion lineatum* (Hallowell)." *Herpetologica* 9: 7–24.

RIEMER, WILLIAM J. 1954. "A New Subspecies of the Snake *Masticophis lateralis* from California." *Copeia* 1954 (1): 45–8.

ROSSMAN, DOUGLAS ATHON. 1963A. "The Colubrid Snake Genus *Thamnophis:* A Revision of the Sauritus Group." *Bulletin of the Florida State Museum, Biological Sciences* 7: 99–178.

——. 1963B. "Relationships of the *Elegans* Complex of the Garter Snakes, Genus *Thamnophis.*" *Year Book of the American Philosophical Society* 1963: 347–8.

——. 1971. "Systematics of the Neotropical Populations of *Thamnophis marcianus* (Serpentes: Colubridae)." *Occasional Papars of the Museum of Zoology,* Louisiana State University, 41: 1–13.

ROZE, JÁNIS A. 1967. "A Check List of the New World Venomous Coral Snakes (Elapidae), with Descriptions of New Forms." *American Museum Novitates* 2287: 1–60.

RUSSELL, FINDLAY E. 1961. "Folklore Remedies Suggested for Tiger Snake Bite." *Western Medicine* 2 (3): 101–3, 122–3.

SEISS, C. FEW. 1890. "The Garter Snake." *Scientific American* 63: 105.

SHANNON, FREDERICK A., and HUMPHREY FRANCIS L. 1963. "Analysis of Color Pattern Polymorphism in the Snake, *Rhinocheilus lecontei.*" *Herpetologica* 19 (3): 153–60.

SHAW, CHARLES E. 1951. "Male Combat in American Culubrid Snakes with Remarks on Combat in Other Colubrid and Elapid Snakes." *Herpetologica* 7 (part 4): 149–68.

SMITH, ALBERT G. 1949. "The Subspecies of the Plains Garter Snake, *Thamnophis radix.*" *Bulletin of the Chicago Academy of Sciences* 8: 285–300.

SMITH, HOBART M. 1941. "Synonymy of *Tantilla nigriceps fumiceps* Cope." *Copeia* 1941 (2): 112.

———. 1942. "A Resume of Mexican Snakes of the Genus *Tantilla.*" *Zoologica* 27: 33–42.

———. 1951. "The Identity of the Ophidian Name *Coluber eques* Reuss." *Copeia* 1951 (2): 138–40.

———. 1957. "Curious Feeding Habit of a Blind Snake, *Leptotyphlops.*" *Herpetologica* 13 (part 2): 102.

———. 1963. "The Identity of the Black Hills Population of *Storeria occipitomaculata,* the Red-bellied Snake." *Herpetologica* 19: 17–21.

———. 1965. "Two New Colubrid Snakes from the United States and Mexico." *Journal of the Ohio Herpetological Society* 5: 1–4.

SMITH, HOBART M., and KENNEDY, J. P. 1951. "*Pituophis melanoleucus* Ruthveni in Eastern Texas and Its Bearing on the Status of *P. catenifer.*" *Herpetologica* 7 (3): 93–6.

SMITH, HOBART M., and TAYLOR, EDWARD H. 1941. "A Review of the Snakes of the Genus *Ficimia.*" *Journal of the Washington Academy of Sciences* 31: 356–68.

SMITH, HOBART M., and WHITE, FRED N. 1955. "Adrenal Enlargement and Its Significance in the Hognose Snakes *(Heterodon).*" *Herpetologica* 11 (2): 137–44.

STICKEL, WILLIAM H. 1938. "The Snakes of the Genus *Sonora* in the United States and Lower California." *Copeia* 1938 (4): 182–90.

———. 1943. "The Mexican Snakes of the Genera *Sonora* and *Chionactis* with Notes on the Status of Other Colubrid Genera." *Proceedings of the Biological Society of Washington* 56: 109-27.

———. 1951. "Distinctions Between the Snake Genera *Contia* and *Eirenis.*" *Herpetologica* 7 (3): 125–31.

TANNER, WILMER W. 1946. "A Taxonomic Study of the Genus *Hypsiglena.*" *Great Basin Naturalist* 5: 25–92.

———. 1953. "A Study of Taxonomy and Phylogeny of *Lampropeltis pyromelana* Cope." *Great Basin Naturalist* 13: 47–66.

———. 1966. "A Re-evaluation of the Genus *Tantilla* in the Southwestern United States and Northwestern Mexico." *Herpetologica* 22: 134–52.

TANNER, WILMER W., and LOOMIS, RICHARD B. 1957. "A Taxonomic and Distributional Study of the Western Subspecies of the Milk Snake,

Lampropeltis doliata." *Transactions of the Kansas Academy of Science* 50: 12–42.

TAYLOR, EDWARD H. 1931. "Notes on Two Specimens of the Rare Snake *Ficimia cana* and the Description of a New Species of *Ficimia* from Texas." *Copeia* 1931 (1): 4–7.

THOMPSON, FRED G. 1957. "A New Mexican Gartersnake (Genus *Thamnophis*) with Notes on Related Forms." *Occasional Papers of the Museum of Zoology,* University of Michigan, 584: 1–10.

WATKINS, JULIAN F., II, GEHLBACH, FREDERICK R., and BALDRIDGE, ROBERT S. 1967. "Ability of the Blind Snake, *Leptotyphlops dulcis,* to Follow Pheromone Trails of Army Ants." *Southwestern Naturalist* 12 (4): 455–62.

WATKINS, JULIAN F., II, GEHLBACH, FREDERICK R., and KROLL, JAMES C. 1969. "Attractant-Repellent Secretions of Blind Snakes *(Leptotyphlops dulcis)* and Their Army Ant Prey *(Neivamyrmex nigrescens)*." *Ecology* 50 (6): 1098–1102.

WEBB, ROBERT G. 1966. "Resurrected Names for Mexican Populations of the Black-necked Garter Snakes, *Thamnophis cyrtopsis* (Kennicott)." *Tulane Studies in Zoology* 13: 55–70.

WILSON, LARRY DAVID. 1970. "The Coachwhip Snake, *Masticophis flagellum* (Shaw): Taxonomy and Distribution." *Tulane Studies in Zoology and Botany* 16: 31–99.

ZWEIFEL, RICHARD G. 1952. "Pattern Variation and Evolution of the Mountain Kingsnake, *Lampropeltis zonata.*" *Copeia* 1952 (3): 152–168.

——. 1954. "Adaptation to Feeding in the Snake *Contia tenuis.*" *Copeia* 1954 (4): 299–300.

ZWEIFEL, RICHARD G., and NORRIS, KENNETH S. 1955. "Contribution to the Herpetology of Sonora, Mexico: Descriptions of New Subspecies of Snakes *(Micruroides euryxanthus* and *Lampropeltis getulus)* and Miscellaneous Collecting Notes." *American Midland Naturalist* 54: 230–49.

INDEX

rear-fanged colubrids, 162–73, 181; harmless to man, 162–3, 166, 169; *see also* black-headed snake; lyre snake; night snake; vine snake

rectilinear locomotion, 16 *and illus.*, 17

red-bellied snake *(Storeria occipito-maculata)*, 132–3, 241–2; Black Hills *(S. o. pahasapae)*, 133, 242, 256–7; hibernation, 81, 82

regurgitation, 23, 92

release of captive snakes, 29, 30

relictual populations, 122, 133, 173

reproduction, 23–6; *see also* birth; courtship behavior; eggs; gestation; mating; sperm storage

reptiles, 10

Rhinocheilus lecontei, see long-nosed snake; *R. l. lecontei, see* long-nosed snake, western; *R. l. tessellatus, see* long-nosed snake, Texas

ribbon snake *(Thamnophis)*: eastern *(T. sauritus)*, 140–1; Pecos, or orange-striped *(T. proximus diabolicus)*, 148, 261; western *(T. proximus)*, 148–9

ribs, 15, 16

ringneck snake *(Diadophis punctatus)*, 5, 59, 60, 64–7, 244–6; coral-bellied *(D. p. pulchellus)*, 245; defensive behavior, 64–5; feeding habits and prey, 63, 67; habitats, 63, 66; Monterey *(D. p. vandenburghi)*, 245; northwestern *(D. p. occidentalis)*, 66, 245; ophiophagous, 46, 63, 67; Pacific *(D. p. amabilis)*, 66, 245; prairie *(D. p. arnyi)*, 245; regal *(D. p. regalis)*, 244–5; reproduction, 67, San Bernardino *(D. p. modestus)*, 66, 245; San Diego *(D. p. similis)*, 245–6; sizes of, 65, 66

rodent control: destruction of snakes by, 6; role of snakes in, 4, 99, 108, 113, 124, 214

rostral scale, *illus. 12*; enlarged, function of, 96, 98; in leaf-nosed snake, 73, 96; in patch-nosed

snake, 95, 96, 98

rosy boa *(Lichanura trivirgata)*, 22, 51, 54–8, 243–4; albinism in, 54; anal spur of, 54, 57; coastal *(L. t. roseofusca)*, 54, 55, 239, 243–4; defensive behavior, 56; desert *(L. t. gracia)*, 54, 55, 243; dual constriction by, 56–7, 103; feeding habits and prey, 56–7; habitat, 55; live birth, 57–8; locomotion, 56, 57; Mexican *(L. t. trivirgata)*, 55, 243; as pet, 55; reproduction of, 57–8; size, 54

rubber boa *(Charina bottae)*, 51–4, 244; anal spur of, 52; burrowing behavior, 52, 55; defensive behavior, 51; feeding habits and prey, 53; habitat, 53–4; live birth, 54; Pacific *(C. b. bottae)*, 239, 244; Rocky Mountain *(C. b. utahensis)*, 244; southern *(C. b. umbratica)*, temperature tolerance, 51, 52–3; tree-climbing ability, 52, 53; two-headedness simulated, 51

salivary gland, 181

Salvadora, see patch-nosed snake; *S. lemniscata*, 98; *S. grahamiae, see* patch-nosed snake, mountain; *S. g. grahamiae*, 97, 250; *S. g. lineata, see* patch-nosed snake, Texas; *S. hexalepis, see* patch-nosed snake, western; *S. h. deserticola, see* patch-nosed snake, Big Bend; *S. h. hexalepis, see* patch-nosed snake, desert; *S. h. mojavensis, see* patch-nosed snake, Mojave; *S. h. virgultea, see* patch-nosed snake, coast

San Diego Zoo, 27, 49, 51, 101, 110, 117, 120–1, 188, 196, 221, 230

sand snake, banded *(Chilomeniscus cinctus)*, 158–60, 196, 263

sand swimmers, 151–61; prey of, 151; *see also* ground snake; hook-nosed snake; sand snake, banded;

shovel-nosed snake

"sand viper," 69

scales, 11–12; cases of sexual dimorphism in, 95, 131, 137; as classfication criteria, 60, 217; identification of, *illus. 12–13*; patterns, snakes versus lizards, 11; size differences, 42; *see also* parietal scales; rostral scale; ventral scales

"schoolboy's snake," 149; *see also* lined snake

scutes, *see* ventral scales

sea snakes (Hydrophiidae), 190

Seminatrix, 60

sensory organs and perception, 10, 18–22; *see also* ears; eyes; hearing; heat-sensing ability; Jacobson's organ; nose; pit organ; smell, sense of; taste, sense of; tongue; touch, sense of; vision

Serpentes, suborder, 10

serpentine movement, 16 *and illus.*, 17; in swimming, 18

sex organs, 24; loss of left oviduct, 48, 164

sexual dimorphism: in common garter snake, 137; in common water snake, 131; in western ground snake, 152; in western patch-nosed snake, 95

sharp-tailed snake *(Contia tenuis)*, 59, 60–4, 137, 246; classification, 59–60; egg aggregations, 63–4; feeding habits and prey, 62–3; gregariousness, 62; habitats, 61–2, 66; size of, 60; tail spine, 60; temperature tolerance, 61

shedding, 13–14; by captive snakes, 35

shovel-nosed snake *(Chionactis)*, 11, 60, 75, 154–8, 159, 262–3; Colorado Desert *(C. occipitalis annulata)*, 158, 263; mimicry of coral snake by, 154, 191, 193; Mojave *(C. occipitalis occipitalis)*, 158, 262–3; Nevada *(C. occipitalis talpina)*,

BLIND SNAKE
SOUTHWESTERN BLIND SNAKE
(Leptotyphlops humilis humilis)

1

RUBBER BOA
PACIFIC RUBBER BOA
(Charina bottae bottae)

2

ROSY BOA
DESERT ROSY BOA
(Lichanura trivirgata gracia)

3

SHARP-TAILED SNAKE
(Contia tenuis)

4

295

RINGNECK SNAKE
SAN DIEGO RINGNECK SNAKE
(Diadophis punctatus similis)

5

WESTERN HOGNOSE SNAKE
PLAINS HOGNOSE SNAKE
(Heterodon nasicus nasicus)

6

296

SADDLED LEAF-NOSED SNAKE
PIMA LEAF-NOSED SNAKE
(Phyllorhynchus browni browni)
7

SPOTTED LEAF-NOSED SNAKE
WESTERN LEAF-NOSED SNAKE
(Phyllorhynchus decurtatus perkinsi)
8

SMOOTH GREEN SNAKE
WESTERN SMOOTH GREEN SNAKE
(Opheodrys vernalis blanchardi)
9

ROUGH GREEN SNAKE
(Opheodrys aestivus)
10

298

RACER
WESTERN YELLOW-BELLIED RACER
(Coluber constrictor mormon)

11

COACHWHIP SNAKE
RED RACER
(Masticophis flagellum piceus)

12

STRIPED RACER
CALIFORNIA STRIPED RACER
(Masticophis lateralis lateralis)
13

SONORA WHIPSNAKE
(Masticophis bilineatus bilineatus)
14

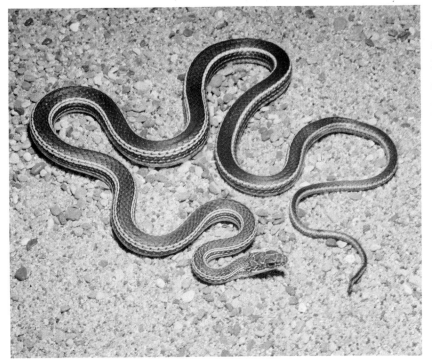

STRIPED WHIPSNAKE
DESERT STRIPED WHIPSNAKE
(Masticophis taeniatus taeniatus)

15

WESTERN PATCH-NOSED SNAKE
DESERT PATCH-NOSED SNAKE
(Salvadora hexalepis hexalepis)

16

MOUNTAIN PATCH-NOSED SNAKE
(Salvadora grahamiae grahamiae)

17

CORN SNAKE
GREAT PLAINS RAT SNAKE
(Elaphe guttata emoryi)

18

GREEN RAT SNAKE
(Elaphe triaspis intermedia)

19

TRANS-PECOS RAT SNAKE
(Elaphe subocularis)

20

GLOSSY SNAKE
ARIZONA GLOSSY SNAKE
(Arizona elegans noctivaga)
21

GOPHER SNAKE
BULL SNAKE
(Pituophis melanoleucus sayi)
22

COMMON KINGSNAKE
CALIFORNIA KINGSNAKE
(Lampropeltis getulus californiae)

23

CALIFORNIA MOUNTAIN
KINGSNAKE
SAN DIEGO MOUNTAIN KINGSNAKE
(Lampropeltis zonata pulchra)

24

SONORA MOUNTAIN KINGSNAKE
HUACHUCA MOUNTAIN
KINGSNAKE
(Lampropeltis pyromelana woodini)
25

MILK SNAKE
NEW MEXICAN MILK SNAKE
(Lampropeltis triangulum celaenops)
26

LONG-NOSED SNAKE
WESTERN LONG-NOSED SNAKE
(Rhinocheilus lecontei lecontei)
27

PLAIN-BELLIED WATER SNAKE
BLOTCHED WATER SNAKE
(Natrix erythrogaster transversa)
28

COMMON WATER SNAKE
NORTHERN WATER SNAKE
(Natrix sipedon sipedon)
29

RED-BELLIED SNAKE
BLACK HILLS RED-BELLIED SNAKE
(Storeria occipitomaculata pahasapae)
30

NARROW-HEADED GARTER SNAKE
(Thamnophis rufipunctatus)

31

COMMON GARTER SNAKE
SAN FRANCISCO GARTER SNAKE
(Thamnophis sirtalis tetrataenia)

32

WESTERN TERRESTRIAL
GARTER SNAKE
WANDERING GARTER SNAKE
(Thamnophis elegans vagrans)

33

WESTERN AQUATIC
GARTER SNAKE
SANTA CRUZ GARTER SNAKE
(Thamnophis couchii atratus)

34

NORTHWESTERN GARTER SNAKE
(Thamnophis ordinoides)

35

BLACK-NECKED GARTER SNAKE
WESTERN BLACK-NECKED
GARTER SNAKE
(Thamnophis cyrtopsis cyrtopsis)

36

MEXICAN GARTER SNAKE
(Thamnophis eques megalops)
37

CHECKERED GARTER SNAKE
(Thamnophis marcianus marcianus)
38

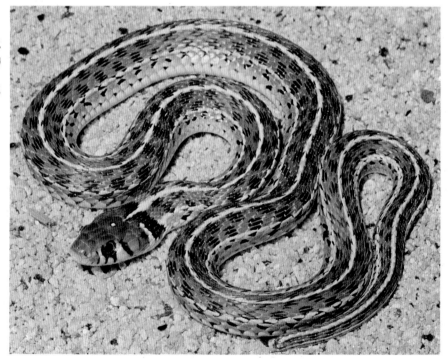

PLAINS GARTER SNAKE
WESTERN PLAINS GARTER SNAKE
(Thamnophis radix haydenii)

39

WESTERN RIBBON SNAKE
ORANGE-STRIPED RIBBON SNAKE
(Thamnophis proximus diabolicus)

40

LINED SNAKE
NORTHERN LINED SNAKE
(Tropidoclonion lineatum lineatum)

41

WESTERN GROUND SNAKE
GREAT BASIN GROUND SNAKE
(Sonora semiannulata isozona)

42

GROUND SNAKE
GREAT PLAINS GROUND SNAKE
(Sonora episcopa episcopa)

43

SONORA SHOVEL-NOSED SNAKE
ORGAN PIPE SHOVEL-NOSED
SNAKE
(Chionactis palarostris organica)

44

315

WESTERN SHOVEL-NOSED SNAKE
COLORADO DESERT
SHOVEL-NOSED SNAKE
(Chionactis occipitalis annulata)
45

BANDED SAND SNAKE
(Chilomeniscus cinctus)
46

WESTERN HOOK-NOSED SNAKE
(Gyalopion canum)

47

MEXICAN WEST COAST
HOOK-NOSED SNAKE
(Gyalopion quadrangularis)

48

PLAINS BLACK-HEADED SNAKE
(Tantilla nigriceps nigriceps)

49

WESTERN BLACK-HEADED SNAKE
CALIFORNIA BLACK-HEADED
SNAKE
(Tantilla planiceps eiseni)

50

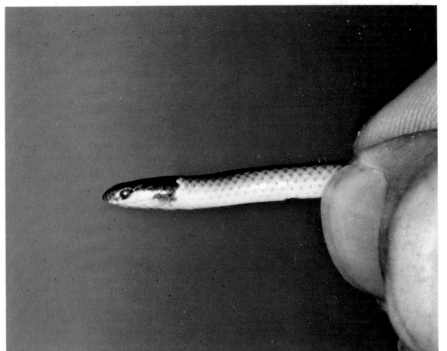

YAQUI BLACK-HEADED SNAKE
(Tantilla yaquia)

51

HUACHUCA BLACK-HEADED
SNAKE
ARIZONA BLACK-HEADED SNAKE
(Tantilla wilcoxi wilcoxi)

52

VINE SNAKE
MEXICAN VINE SNAKE
(Oxybelis aeneus auratus)
53

LYRE SNAKE
CALIFORNIA LYRE SNAKE
(Trimorphodon biscutatus
vandenburghi)
54

NIGHT SNAKE
SAN DIEGO NIGHT SNAKE
(Hypsiglena torquata klauberi)

55

CORAL SNAKE
ARIZONA CORAL SNAKE
*(Micruroides euryxanthus
euryxanthus)*

56

PIGMY RATTLESNAKE
SOUTHWESTERN MASSASAUGA
(Sistrurus catenatus edwardsii)

57

WESTERN DIAMONDBACK
RATTLESNAKE
(Crotalus atrox)

58

RED DIAMOND RATTLESNAKE
(Crotalus ruber ruber)

59

SPECKLED RATTLESNAKE
SOUTHWESTERN SPECKLED
RATTLESNAKE
(Crotalus mitchellii pyrrhus)

60

ROCK RATTLESNAKE
BANDED ROCK RATTLESNAKE
(Crotalus lepidus klauberi)

61

SIDEWINDER
COLORADO DESERT SIDEWINDER
(Crotalus cerastes laterorepens)

62

BLACK-TAILED RATTLESNAKE
NORTHERN BLACK-TAILED
RATTLESNAKE
(Crotalus molossus molossus)

63

TIGER RATTLESNAKE
(Crotalus tigris)

64

MOJAVE RATTLESNAKE
(Crotalus scutulatus scutulatus)
65

TWIN-SPOTTED RATTLESNAKE
(Crotalus pricei pricei)
66

RIDGE-NOSED RATTLESNAKE
ARIZONA RIDGE-NOSED
RATTLESNAKE
(Crotalus willardi willardi)
67

WESTERN RATTLESNAKE
HOPI RATTLESNAKE
(Crotalus viridis nuntius)
68

WESTERN RATTLESNAKE
GRAND CANYON RATTLESNAKE
(Crotalus viridis abyssus)

69

WESTERN RATTLESNAKE
NORTHERN PACIFIC
RATTLESNAKE
(Crotalus viridis oreganus)

70

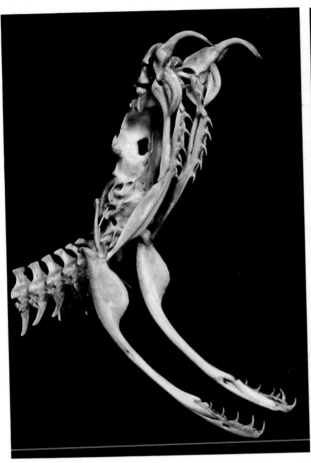

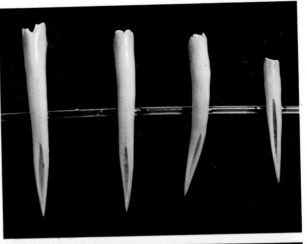

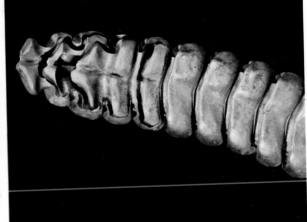

Above:
RATTLESNAKE SKULL

Top right:
RATTLESNAKE RESERVE FANG

Center right:
RATTLESNAKE RATTLE

Right:
TWO-HEADED CALIFORNIA KINGSNAKE

COMBAT DANCE
OF TWO RED DIAMOND RATTLESNAKES

During the vigorous combat dance (once thought to be a courtship dance) one snake is always the aggressor, although not always the victor. Initially, moving into the raised fighting position, both are nervously alert, with flicking tongues, and heads and necks slowly weaving. There is constant movement—sparring, entwining, pressing, maneuvering for an advantageous position—until, with a swift and powerful blow, one knocks the other to the ground.

Photo Credits

A Note About the Authors

The late Charles Shaw was born in San Diego in 1918. After graduating from San Diego State University he joined the San Diego Zoo, becoming Head Keeper and then Curator of Reptiles. At the time of his death in 1972, he was also Assistant Director of the zoo. Shaw received several awards for special breeding programs he initiated at the San Diego Zoo, including a successful attempt to breed the endangered Galápagos tortoise in captivity.

Sheldon Campbell, by profession a stockbroker but by enthusiastic avocation a herpetologist, was born in San Diego in 1919. Educated at San Diego State and Stanford University, he for a time taught college English before returning to San Diego and taking up his present occupation. Campbell is a trustee of the San Diego Zoo and is active in its direction.

A Note on the Type

The text of this book was set in a film version of the Linotype face called Baskerville. The face is a facsimile reproduction of types cast from molds made for John Baskerville (1706–75) from his designs. The punches for the revived Linotype Baskerville were cut under the supervision of the English printer George W. Jones. John Baskerville's original face was one of the forerunners of the type style known as "modern face" to printers—a "modern" of the period A.D. 1800.

The book was composed by University Graphics, Shrewsbury, New Jersey; printed and bound by The Book Press, Brattleboro, Vermont.

Typography and binding design by Earl Tidwell.